MW01039728

COMMUNICATION AND KNOWLEDGE

STUDIES IN RHETORIC/COMMUNICATION
Carroll C. Arnold, *Series Editor*

Richard B. Gregg
Symbolic Inducement and Knowing: A Study in the Foundations of Rhetoric

Communication and Knowledge:
AN INVESTIGATION IN
RHETORICAL EPISTEMOLOGY

By
Richard A. Cherwitz,
The University of Texas at Austin,
and
James W. Hikins,
Tulane University

N *University of South Carolina Press*

Published in Columbia, South Carolina, by the
University of South Carolina Press

First Edition

Manufactured in the United States of America

Library of Congress Cataloging-in-Publication Data

Cherwitz, Richard A., 1952–
    Communication and knowledge.

    (Studies in rhetoric/communication)
    Bibliography: p.
    Includes index
    1. Communication—Philosophy.   2. Knowledge, Theory
of.   3. Rhetoric.   4. Ontology.   I. Hikins, James W.,
1947–   . II. Title.   III. Series.
P90.C5175   1985   001.51   85–17763
ISBN 0–87249–465–9

Douglas W. Ehninger
(1913–1979)

*who, through the example of his
teaching and research, set a
standard of scholarly excellence
that we have endeavored to emulate.*

CONTENTS

FOREWORD

Communication and Knowledge is the second book issued in the Rhetoric/Communication Series published by The University of South Carolina Press. Richard B. Gregg's *Symbolic Inducement and Knowing* was the first. It is fortuitous that both books have epistemological thrusts. The Rhetoric/Communication Series will not be confined to works having that orientation.

Where Gregg's study of relations between symbolic behavior and knowing was predominantly a psychological and sociological investigation, Richard Cherwitz and James Hikins approach the topic philosophically. Their central claim is that coming to know something is inevitably, although not exclusively, rhetorical activity; hence their subtitle: "An Investigation in Rhetorical Epistemology."

It is widely held among twentieth-century epistemologists that knowledge arises in the functional relationship of a perceiving organism and a perceived universe. Cherwitz and Hikins accept this general notion, but they contend that the outcomes of relationships between perceiver and perceived are languaged, communicable descriptions of reality. These descriptions, or "epistemic judgments," they argue, are not of equal philosophical or even pragmatic worth. How such descriptions can be sorted out and their relative merits assessed philosophically is the problem that motivates Cherwitz and Hikins' inquiry.

Cherwitz and Hikins proceed in their investigation using a modified version of the philosophical position known historically as "direct realism." Direct realism is usually associated with the philosopher Thomas Reid and the "common sense" school of Scottish philosophy. A theory long in eclipse at the hands of representational theories and phenomenalism, realist theories are currently enjoying somewhat of a renaissance. Recent adherents to realist philosophical positions range from John Searle in philosophy to Stuart Katz and Gordon Frost in psychology. Cherwitz and Hikins articulate a variation of direct realism that was originally termed "perspective realism" by the late philosopher, Evander Bradley McGilvary. From this position the authors develop an explicit ontological and epistemological foundation for their theory, which they call "rhetorical perspectivism." They posit that humans are a part of the natural world, and we know by direct apprehension of that which we acquire through perception. The human perceptual and cognitive apparatus is, as it were,

Foreword

programmed to see the world directly, but part of this "seeing" involves recording and transmitting knowledge through language. According to Cherwitz and Hikins, it is the capacity of language to "embody" the various relationships that comprise the directly-perceived universe that permits emergence of meaning.

A distinctive feature of Cherwitz and Hikins' theory is the claim that derived meanings, though inherently linguistic, are directly tied to a real and knowable world. Reality exists independently of the perceiver yet is directly ascertainable. In consequence, say the authors, rhetorical activity is inerradicable from the formation of claims and judgments about what we take to be so.

Cherwitz and Hikins argue that on pragmatic grounds, if no other, it is dangerous to grant the status of *knowledge* to descriptions of reality unless those descriptions can withstand full, rational critique in a free marketplace of ideas. By "rational critique" the authors mean application of what John Dewey defined as philosophy: intelligence become conscious of its own nature and method. The authors recognize that many of their arguments are associated with "traditional epistemology" and are apt to be challenged by relativists, pragmatists, phenomenologists, and representatives of other schools of philosophical and rhetorical thought. This does not deter them, for their theory of rhetorical epistemology itself asserts that comprehensive argument and counterargument are essential if *knowledge* is to be attained on any subject. From their viewpoint, to engage them in argument is to validate much of what they claim.

Communication and Knowledge presents a systematic theory purporting to explain the interfacings of language, rhetoric, presumed reality, and coming to know. To meet the case this book offers, challengers will need to put forth their counter-affirmations with similar comprehensiveness.

To further understanding of rhetoric and communication through serious, systematic discussion is the primary objective of the Rhetoric/Communication Series. *Communication and Knowledge* pursues that goal and is likely to stimulate readers to think comprehensively about the epistemological functions of human communication.

Carroll C. Arnold
Editor, *Rhetoric/Communication*
University of South Carolina Press

ACKNOWLEDGMENTS

It would be impossible to express our full appreciation to all of those individuals who, in the past six years, have contributed to the conceptualization and writing of this book. We are certainly indebted to the University Research Institute and College of Communication of the University of Texas at Austin for their generous financial support of this project. In addition, the initial impetus for this research was made possible by a grant as part of the 1978 Speech Communication Association Karl R. Wallace Memorial Award.

We shall remain forever indebted to Carroll Arnold who saw the value of our project in its embryonic stage; through his encouragement and meticulous editing, our research was nurtured to its present form. No one could ask for a more diligent and supportive editor. We are also indebted to Roderick P. Hart, who reminded us of the importance of "thinking audience," to William Keith for assisting in preparing the index and serving as a sounding board for many of our ideas, and to Tonya Cline Cherwitz, who spent many hours proofreading various drafts of this text.

We would be remiss if we did not acknowledge, at least in general, the input provided by our colleagues and students. If we are accurate in our assessment of the fundamental connectedness of knowledge and communication, input from others cannot be overstated. It is our contention throughout this book that through rigorous argument we are better able to apprehend and know the world we live in.

INTRODUCTION

Human knowledge has preoccupied philosophers for centuries. Given the extensive literature in epistemology, and the accompanying technical vocabulary that sometimes seems virtually impenetrable to all but professional philosophers, one might justifiably ask: Why another treatise on the subject? Why one written from the perspective of communication studies?

The answers are varied and complex. With the decline of positivism in the second half of the twentieth century and the consequent emergence of significant doubt regarding what constitutes even "scientific proof," the questions, What can we depend on? and Do we or can we know anything? have become serious and troubling concerns for both laymen and scholars. Despite the geometrical, almost explosive growth of information—growth that has prompted some to argue that we have entered a new "information age"—we appear to have much that we can label "information" but little that we can agree deserves to be described as "knowledge." In short, communication abounds, but "truths" seem few and frail.

Increasing use of communication for persuasive, informative, and ceremonial purposes is symptomatic of the information explosion. Indeed, recognition of this fact has prompted the reemergence of the art of "rhetoric." Communication that persuades, informs, or celebrates, but fails to attain certainty, is the kind of communication that has been traditionally designated as rhetoric. Most of what we read, speak, write, and hear today falls into this category of relatively weak dependability. The problem of when this type of communication can be trusted increasingly troubles listeners, readers, speakers, historians, psychologists, ethicists, and even "hard" scientists. The problem serious and careful thinkers, both lay and scholarly, face is whether *knowledge* can ever be extracted from or provided through the growing mass of less-than-certain information and communication.

The importance of this observation can be gauged if one considers a small but significant part of the information explosion, computer technology. With sophisticated computer systems, including word processors, finding their way into the nooks and crannies of science, industry, education, and homes, it is all too tempting to treat the products of that technology as final, certain, and infallible. Where in other days one might spend leisure time reading books, magazines, and newspapers, most being

1

frankly opinionated sources, temptation now appears to be toward toying with a computer. For recreation one may put a conveniently available game cartridge into the computer and, after playing one's own version of "Star Wars," turn the machine to processing information. A fear of many commentators is that preoccupation with the new, impersonal technologies of information will displace such traditional cognitive and intellectual activities as *invention*.

As classically conceived and as discussed throughout the history of ideas, invention had to do with conscious choices of strategies after canvassing the available stock of alternatives. As rhetoric has been traditionally conceptualized, invention is the *creative* process by which a speaker or writer brings forth his or her stock of ideas, assesses them in terms of their veracity and potential usefulness in discourse, and then marshals them into cogent frameworks for delivery to an auditor or other audience. In short, invention was conceived of as a *thinking* activity. The information explosion in general and the technology attendant to it threaten to supplant such thinking. The new result may be to accept uncritically the options the technology of information presents to us—information chosen and prepared by others. Options come in the form of "software."

This twentieth-century tendency to replace one of the most basic human activities, thinking, with mechanistic simulations forms part of the rationale for reconsidering the concept, *knowledge*. The communication-information explosion is just that—a massive eruption of data collected and fully organized by others. But no matter how efficiently and elegantly produced and displayed, these data are not *our* knowledge. Our problems become: What of all available, technologically produced data shall we count as knowledge, for us? What do we or can we certify as true?

At no time in human history has decision making been as complex as now, or had such far-reaching potentials for impact on others. At the same time, the ways we can approach choices and the data available to us multiply. Increasing numbers of ideologies, paradigms, and methodologies are espoused and employed by individuals seeking knowledge on which to rest decisions. There has also come a proliferation of specializations, to the point where scholars and other experts seem to address ever smaller and more provincial audiences. Accompanying specialization, and perhaps in consequence of it, comes a tacit acceptance of "pluralism". Because of differing assumptions and methods of investigation, and the sheer increase of choices presented by the information explosion, there is a proclivity to view conclusions as self-contained. It is enough for many to proclaim consistency within their own private domains of inquiry and eschew or even renounce the importance of inspecting the consistency of

2

their conclusions and conclusions arrived at within other domains of inquiry. The old cliché that there is more than one way to look at the world becomes elevated to the status of an overall doctrine, serving to insulate particular intellectual enterprises from critical inspection from other points of view and modes of inquiry.

We also see a weakening of the concept of a marketplace of ideas, a marketplace within which individual enterprises of knowledge-seeking clash and where methods, conclusions, and the contents of various specialties are scrutinized by all who are interested or potentially affected.

Another accompaniment of the information explosion is the emergence of relativism, both epistemological and ethical. Because many of us are willing to grant autonomy to fields of specialization, and because such fields generate knowledge claims that are often inconsistent with if not contradictory to those arrived at by other paths of inquiry, we are put in the unhappy position of introducing such concepts as "field dependence," wherein assessment of knowledge claims is referred to so-called "experts" within a particular field. Consider some familiar claims: "The generals say we need a new missile system; generals know all about missile systems; therefore, we need a new missile system." "Scientists have determined that cocaine may have long-term health effects; scientists know all about the effects of substances on the body; therefore, I should not use cocaine." "The President and his advisers claim that we must intervene in Grenada. They have access to information and expertise; therefore, we ought to accept their public justifications for intervention."

Contrary to appearances, such deference to authority and presumed expertise reflects a peculiar sort of relativism. Knowledge is presumed to be based on information contained within a particular domain of inquiry; the "outsider" defers, not to information or claims themselves, but to the *ethos* of the "experts." Put another way, recognition of specialization leads to belief that knowledge is field dependent, and those outside a given "field" are inhibited from making reasoned judgments based on knowledge as such. Instead, commitments to claims about the way the world is are made relative to the perceived expertise that presumably exists within encapsulated academic or professional territories that *we* do not explore for ourselves. The consequences of such deference can be unhappy. We make the wrong decisions.

Perhaps it turns out as the result of fuller knowledge and reflection that the missile system was unnecessary and contributed little or nothing to security; the harms of using cocaine may turn out to have been exaggerated by the "experts"; or, intervening in Grenada may turn out to have been counterproductive. Probably the general or scientist or president will be

3

blamed in the end, perhaps even dismissed. But in point of fact, the mistakes to which we committed ourselves can be traced to the act of deferring itself—to our failure to inspect data and judgments for ourselves, in a critical way. We treated knowledge claims as inviolable parts of a remote domain, and we relieved ourselves *and the "experts"* from the burdens of defending judgments and evidence in the marketplace of ideas. The result, if not a relativism based on provincialism, is surrender of individual rights and abilities to judge the wisdom and appropriateness of deciding for ourselves on matters that vitally affect our lives.

At least to classical rhetoricians such as Aristotle and Cicero and to such modern philosophers of rhetoric as Chaim Perelman and Stephen Toulmin, prudential or wise decisions and the weighing of communicated knowledge claims are problems central to the study of rhetoric. That is the subject of this book, for it is by studying the nature of knowledge in relation to the nature of communication that we acquire the tools for finding and assessing information in any area of human thought where interchange of ideas is at issue. Embedded in the notions of knowledge and of communication are the most basic, if not field-invariant, criteria for evaluation of public ideas. None would suppose that an individual citizen can have the same technical levels of expertise as a general, or a scientist, or a president, but the wisdom of adopting courses of *action* based on technical expertise depends on considerations that even laypersons are equipped to raise in the face of data and recommendations furnished by "experts." In this book we shall contend that those considerations are founded in the nature of knowledge and the nature of communication.

We propose a philosophical account of communication in relation to knowledge. What can such an inquiry contribute that other modes of inquiry have not? In a sense, that question has already been answered. Whether we are psychologists, historians, or aestheticians, we pursue knowledge. At some point, therefore, we must broach the question of what constitutes knowledge. But to discuss that problem is to imply that knowledge is something shareable, that is, communicable. In other words, regardless of what special topics we deal with, we are concerned with *communicable* knowledge. This fact makes relevant to the scholar of human communication the philosophical questions: What is knowledge? How do we acquire it? What are the limits of knowledge? Without answers to these questions we cannot begin with any confidence a search for what is defensibly shareable within whatever domain of inquiry interests us or across domains.

It is for these reasons that we undertake here a philosophical investigation of communication and its place and functions in human acquisition

4

of knowledge. Believing that the relationship between communication and knowledge is symbiotic, we propose to explore that relationship in detail and to discern what epistemologically productive rhetoric is. All sharing of ideas involves rhetorical activity. In our view, understanding when and how that activity can become epistemologically productive is essential to understanding communication; indeed, to understanding all scholarship.

1

ON COMMUNICATING
AND KNOWING

As we began writing this chapter, a centuries old conflict between Israel and the Arab world raged. In Lebanon, Yasir Arafat's Palestine Liberation Organization army was surrounded by an Israeli invasion force. In the same part of the world a smoldering war between Iran and Iraq had reignited. Iranian forces were on the offensive, filled with the same Islamic fervor that a few months earlier emboldened the followers of the Ayatollah Khomeini to challenge the United States by seizing the American Embassy in Teheran and fifty-two of its staff. Half a world away, shock waves had just begun to subside after a short but bloody conflict between the British and the Argentines over the possession of a few barren, windswept islands known as the Falklands or Malvinas.

One of the authors of this text had recently quit smoking. The other never has smoked and probably never will. Some of our colleagues had recently been divorced, others were contemplating marriage, still others grappled with less momentous but nonetheless important dimensions of human relationships.

All of us, on a daily basis, spend a large part of our waking hours making decisions of a personal nature which engender greater or lesser consequences for the conduct of our lives. These human problems may range from issues of religious conversion to a decision about where to dine.

As we began this book it was being said that theoretical physics had been thrown into turmoil with the discovery of black holes and quasars—astronomical objects whose existence calls into question the most fundamental laws of the physical sciences. As one scientist described the plight of astronomers, the existence of black holes implies that matter may eventually become infinitely compressed, reducing what was once trillions of tons of matter into a point. The scientists' quandry was put clearly and simply. All of contemporary physics is three-dimensional: How can one have a physics of a point?

The literate world remains intrigued, often preoccupied, with our origins. A vigorous dispute between creationists and evolutionists illustrated this preoccupation as we began writing. On an individual basis, there continued a fascination with discovering family roots. Genealogists maintained a thriving business in America.

After its demise on expiration of the constitutionally prescribed ratification period, the Equal Rights Amendment to the Constitution had just been reintroduced in Congress. The President of the United States had signed into law an extension of the Voting Rights Act. In short, Americans continued to discharge responsibilities as social beings, struggling to determine what was just and unjust within the context of a humane society.

In Arecibo, Puerto Rico, the world's largest radio telescope was spending a portion of its time listening for signals from extraterrestrial civilizations. At that moment, somewhere beyond our solar system, the *Voyager* spacecraft carried with it a plaque and a phonographic disc with human messages to any extraterrestrial forms of intelligence that might find the craft in space.

There is a sense in which this book is about war and peace. It is also about decisions to smoke cigarettes, to get married or become divorced, to convert to Christianity, and where to go to dinner. It is about black holes and quasars, communicating with life on other worlds, and framing scientific explanations. The book also concerns itself with human rights and social responsibility. *For this book is about communication and knowing.* Inevitably, then, it is also about learning, thinking, deciding, and telling.

The diverse examples of human experience we have enumerated are bound together by two issues which are their progenitors. The first issue is concerned with the nature of *human communication*. What is communication? Why is some discourse understood and other discourse misunderstood? Why do some instances of discourse evoke persuasive outcomes while others achieve little impact? Within the context of our examples, why did seventeen years of talk between Britain and Argentina suddenly collapse into a nondiscursive form of conflict in which several thousand people lost their lives? Why and how has the American Cancer Society's campaign of talk regarding the risks of smoking altered patterns of human behavior? What role does talk among and between scientists play in their attempts to solve puzzles such as how to integrate black holes into a theoretical framework of thought about the universe? Equally important, what is the nature and effect of talk between the scientific community and the society of which it is a part? Has the argumentative talk between proponents of creation and proponents of evolution furthered understanding of the origin of human life? Why did the talk of Equal Rights Amendment advocates fail to result in constitutional change? And, will human talk allow us to discover, relate, and coexist peacefully with other forms of intelligence?

The second issue is concerned with the nature of *knowledge*. What is knowledge? How do we acquire knowledge? What are the scope and limitations of human knowledge? What are the differences between knowledge and belief, doubt and certainty, appearance and reality? Again within the context of our examples, how and when can we *know* that further negotiation is fruitless and that our only recourse is to armed conflict? How do we *know* an admonition to change behavior is justified by scientific or other evidence? What do we mean when we say that we *know* creationism is an accurate account of the origin of the world? How do we *know* the moral and social correctness of positions taken on legislation such as the Equal Rights Amendment and the Voting Rights Act? And, how will we *know* when the impulses recorded by our radio telescopes represent communication from intelligent life as opposed to mere background noise?

Questions about communication and about knowledge are inherently interrelated. This interrelatedness is revealed not only by commonsense appraisal of the examples just given but by the difficulties scholars have in separating such matters as content and form, discovery and propagation of knowledge, invention and disposition. The processes by which we discover the world we live in and the methods we employ to articulate that world are intertwined. This is reason to believe that *epistemology*—the study of the nature, grounds, criteria, and limits of human knowledge—and *rhetoric*—the study of human efforts to influence one another through communication—are kindred enterprises whose questions, answers, and methods of analysis require awareness of more than intradisciplinary study customarily reveals.

Consider this claim as it is borne out by our examples. In conflicts between nations, both knowledge and communication play vital and interrelated roles in determining whether disputes will degenerate into violence. Prevention of war requires nations to negotiate over issues in dispute, that is, to communicate; effective negotiation requires that the parties involved have accurate knowledge of the intentions, strengths, weaknesses, and dispositions of their adversaries. It is obvious that communication and knowledge in the execution of geopolitical affairs function symbiotically: knowledge of intent, strength, weakness, and disposition must eventually be determined through communication, and the very inception of communication, as well as its ultimate effectiveness, is a function of what the parties *know* of their adversaries.

9

In the conduct of daily life, the kindred nature of knowledge and communication is equally apparent. Decisions about smoking, marriage and divorce, and the like are not made in vacuums. Personal decisions are admixtures of communication and knowledge. We realize the dangers inherent in smoking because government and private industry, supported by a large and complex scientific infrastructure, have communicated the dangers to us. At the same time, we are confronted by a bevy of messages—often in competition with antismoking communication—encouraging us to consume more cigarettes because smoking is pleasurable, done by admired others, and so on. In the course of making a decision to smoke or not to smoke we may elicit from family, friends, and colleagues additional communication to defer or reinforce a final decision. And, of course, after the decision to quit smoking has been taken, the success or failure of the effort may be determined in large measure by the kinds of messages we receive from those around us. Within this communicative context a host of knowledge claims operate, and we evaluate: The Surgeon General's report; research sponsored by the American Cancer Society and other private research findings; our own and others' definitions of what is pleasurable. As in the case of international relations, it becomes impossible to conceive of knowledge apart from communication and vice versa.

Even in the most esoteric example we provided, theoretical physics, the relationship between communication and knowing is symbiotic, for it is virtually impossible to separate communication from the process by which scientists come to discover "facts." The very act of calling something "knowledge" is the product of discussion and debate among scientists. This is to say that any scientific community is an audience to be persuaded and dissuaded; members interact communicatively in the pursuit of knowledge, and decisions as to what constitutes knowledge result as much from processes of communication as from direct observation of "facts." Similar implications regarding the communication/knowledge interface are present in our other examples.

There is a long tradition of implicit and explicit comment on this interface. Discussions of relations between knowing and communicating can be found in rhetorical, literary, and philosophical works dating back to the classical period in Greece. The relationship between theories of discourse and theories of knowing has been a point of debate between rhetoricians and philosophers at least since the time of Gorgias and Plato. The questions, What may be said? and How does one know that what has been said is "true"? seem inseparable; they mark out, for example, the fundamental distinctions between Platonic and Sophistic rhetorical theory.

10

These distinctions are grounded in large measure in differing epistemological assumptions.

Platonism assumed the existence of truths that could be known absolutely and that, therefore, must be incorporated in all serious discourse. For Plato the ideal political speaker was one who spoke not merely well but truthfully. 1 The Sophistic tradition, on the other hand, assumed truth to be a function of the subjective nature of human beings, with the attendant implication that one need not and can not incorporate absolute truth in rhetorical discourse. 2 Such opposed philosophical assumptions unavoidably led to very different conceptions of the nature of rhetoric.

The relationship between rhetoric and philosophy (and especially epistemology) is evident in other historical periods. Particularly in the seventeenth and eighteenth centuries, rhetoric and philosophy continued to interact. Francis Bacon, 3 among others, commented on rhetorical matters within his philosophical corpus. And George Campbell, 4 as well as many of his contemporaries, discussed complex philosophical issues within the context of rhetorical theory.

In contemporary times the symbiosis between rhetoric and philosophy has become more directly noticed than ever before. Thinkers such as Wittgenstein, Searle, Toulmin, Johnstone, Perelman, Natanson, Kuhn, and many more have in their own ways made extensive comment on rhetorical issues as an integral part of their philosophizing. 5 Similarly, Richards, Weaver, Booth, Burke, and Ehninger have contributed to the understanding of philosophical questions through explorations in rhetorical theory. 6

Perhaps the most significant recent exploration of the interface between rhetoric and philosophy has occurred in sustained discussions of *rhetorical epistemology—the investigation of how through communication we come to know.* 7 With this development, there have emerged distinct and often competing views of how we come to know through communication. Some scholars have argued that there is no knowable reality independent of our perceptions, attitudes, beliefs, and values. It is argued that communication functions to define, create, shape, maintain, and transmit a reality distinctively constructed by humans. 8 This implies that reality itself is linguistic and intersubjective—a product of symbolic interaction. According to this view, even the most empirical of the sciences, which appear to involve measurement and discovery within a world independent of us, are to be explained not in terms of concepts such as measurement, observation, and the like but in terms of consensual agreement among scientists. Here, "audience," "persuasion," "shared meaning," "adherence," and "agreement" underscore the social—or as some have put it, the sociological—character of science. To use one of our earlier examples, advocates of this sociological analysis of science would claim that the discoveries made during the course of cancer research are not the undistorted consequences of observation. Instead, such "discoveries" are at best *representations* of reality, humanly conceived and rhetorically embellished. They are representations that have, for the moment, the status of scientific truth, and that may be employed in persuasive campaigns to dissuade individuals from smoking, sunbathing, polluting, and so on. However, so the argument goes, these scientific truths are transitory, subject to revision or replacement by subsequent rhetorical realities.

A competing view argues that reality, including perceptions, attitudes, beliefs, and values, exists wholly independent of us and is knowable. Rhetoric, according to these theorists, performs the dual functions of propagating and discovering truth. [9] On the one hand, rhetoric communicates what is discovered by the other arts and sciences. Considered alone, this view has generally led to relegating rhetoric to an inferior position, viewing the art as a handmaiden to other disciplines. More recently, rhetorical scholars have taken the view that communication functions as more than the vehicle for transmitting discoveries, that, in fact, communication has an important role in discovery. These theorists identify a major function of rhetorical communication as argument or *dialectic*, the process by which interpretations and accounts of reality are articulated, kept alive, critically appraised, and placed into perspectives. Rhetoric, therefore, is taken as an essential component of humankind's striving to attain knowledge, to *discover* the independent objects of reality. Like the sociological perspective, this view posits that rhetoric is central to knowing, even in empirical investigations typically the domain of science; however, the exact nature of rhetoric's centrality and its specific role in scientific knowing is much different according to proponents of this "objectivist" camp. Unlike the sociological position, the objectivist position contends that observations conducted during the course of cancer research are observations of data whose existence is not dependent on the observer nor on his or her attitudes, beliefs, and values. That is, the objects of scientific inquiry enjoy independent status. The task for rhetoric in the scientific method, so conceived, is to insure that the scientist's descriptions and measurements accurately reflect the independent objects of reality and conform to their various characteristics, interrelations, and processes. At the most basic level, rhetoric is seen as an integral part of the scientist's framing of statements which purport to reflect the way the world is. In addition, however, rhetoric functions in argument and analysis within the scientific community and society at large. There, rhetoric performs an important *dialectical* service; through discussion and debate scientists validate the conformity of theories and observations to the ever-impinging world which is the object of their inquiry.

We have referred to scientific research purposefully, for to do so illustrates how even subject matters that have characteristically been thought of as operating in relatively self-contained domains of inquiry are nonetheless conceivable in terms of the communication/knowledge symbiosis. It is easy to see how this symbiosis applies in other fields encompassed by the examples enumerated earlier in this chapter. The sociological perspective, for example, would characterize disputes among nations in terms of the social realities that each nation creates in, of, and for itself. From this view, when Argentina claims that a group of islands in the South Atlantic rightfully belongs to her, a host of arguments are raised in support of that position. The consensual agreement exhibited in intense pride and fervor of the Argentine citizenry is viewed as predominantly the result of linguistic interaction characterized by such events as naming the islands the *Malvinas* and labeling Britain a colonial power. What is viewed as important from the vantage point of the scholar taking the sociological stance is not whether "in fact" the islands belong to Argentina or whether "in fact" the British exercise neocolonialist tendencies. Such questions are vacuous, given the sociologically relative nature of the communication/knowledge relationship. What is important in the sociological view is how the positions of the two sides—or of several sides in a broader dispute—come to fruition on the basis of symbolic interaction of the participants.

Those taking the objectivist position would agree that matters of consensus and linguistic interaction are important, but they would view communication among the parties as having referents beyond the rhetorical community. These referents, it would be said, are composed of discrete facts locatable *in the world* and existing independently of the things said about them. Who discovered and settled on the islands first, Argentines or Britons? What is the relevance of the geographic location of the islands? Do British actions constitute colonialism? Was the British position intractable during the seventeen years of negotiations that preceded the short war in May–June 1982? It is argued by objectivists that answers to such questions have a status independent of human consensus, one that must be determined through investigation, including rhetorical analysis.

The two positions that we have just outlined do not exhaust the array of stances taken by contemporary rhetoricians. Each of the two camps contains within it more specific positions.10 Our purpose here is merely to highlight the basic differences of opinion that permeate the literature on rhetorical epistemology. Broadly speaking, debate is between intersubjectivist and objectivist. 11 Our immediate point is that no matter which side of the issue one embraces, and regardless of one's specific interests and expertise, the interface between communication (rhetoric) and knowing is uniformly present.

In this book we propose to argue for a particular position regarding the communication/knowledge relationship. It is our purpose to develop a rhetorical epistemology in a systematic, fully articulated form. The need for a systematic, fully articulated rhetorical epistemology arises in part from such intuitive and historical considerations as we have already discussed, but at least two additional rationales support our endeavor. First, the relationship between communication and knowing has traditionally been commented upon as a subsidiary part of exploring allegedly broader issues. We have philosophical comment on rhetoric and rhetorical comment on philosophy; however, there has been little effort to bridge systematically the concerns of philosophy and rhetoric or to explore fully and directly the interface between communication and knowing.

The consequences of this state of affairs are several. To begin with, there ensues a tendency toward intellectual provincialism, wherein "experts" in one "field" find themselves compelled to rebuff attempts by "experts" in other "fields" to treat issues as matters of shared concern. Such scholastic territoriality inhibits understanding across disciplinary boundaries, and scholarly discourse can degenerate into harangue that is counterproductive to the search for truth and understanding. We believe that much of the misunderstanding between philosophers and rhetoricians has its roots in the heated debates between the Platonists and Sophists, still best exemplified in the Platonic dialogues. Accordingly, a major aim of this book is to encourage interdisciplinary focus in order to provide a technical explication of the relationship between communication and knowing that has relevance to scholarship of many kinds and to everyday living.

An additional consequence of the lack of systematic scholarly attention to the communication/knowledge interface is the tendency of particular groups of scholars to overlook much valuable work that has been accomplished by other groups. For example, rhetorical scholars are frequently inattentive to developments in philosophical epistemology. This is manifested in imprecision in defining seminal concepts in rhetorical epistemology, such as "knowledge," "reality," "belief" (terms treated systematically in philosophical literature), and in the absence from rhetorical scholarship of the rigor in analysis and argument that is characteristic of philosophical method. Similar parochialism can be found among philosophers. Due to a long historical estrangement between philosophers and rhetoricians, valuable scholarship by contemporary rhetoricians has escaped notice by the

14

philosophical community. Such developments include the extensive work by rhetorical scholars on speech acts, theory of argument, and the rhetoric of science—all topics of both rhetorical and philosophical importance.

The second rationale for developing a fully articulated rhetorical epistemology stems from recognition that scholarly appraisal of human problems may assist—and at times has assisted—in their amelioration. The vital issues mentioned earlier in this chapter are of such magnitude and complexity that all potential solutions—including those that might emerge from a technical appraisal of the relationship between communication and knowledge—demand consideration. We therefore appeal to readers not trained in one of the academic disciplines relevant to our discussion to bear with the early chapters of our text which provide a technical groundwork for our rhetorical epistemology. Such forbearance, we believe, will pay dividends in later portions of the book where application to more pragmatic issues occurs.

Among the first tasks necessary in developing a coherent rhetorical epistemology is to explain what one means by the term "knowledge." Any exploration of the function of communication in knowing presupposes a clear and distinct conception of "knowledge." This issue we address in Chapter 2, where we develop distinctions among the concepts belief, knowledge, dogma, opinion, and certainty. Such distinctions afford linguistic precision to our use of these often equivocal terms. We will also show why this clarification is important in practical affairs. At the close of Chapter 2, we offer the specific definition of knowledge that we shall use throughout the remainder of our book.

Chapter 3 provides a conceptualization of "rhetoric." Working from past formulations of the concept, we undertake to synthesize a conception of rhetoric that is consistent with contemporary understanding of rhetoric as an object of systematic study. The resulting formulation is predicated upon what we believe are the common denominators of past treatments of the subject.

Chapter 4 explores the interface between knowledge and rhetoric, the interface that permits the development of rhetorical epistemology. We seek to answer the question: What is the most basic common feature connecting communication and knowledge? Chapter 4 is predominantly an exercise in theory building, focusing on the nature of language and meaning.

Chapter 5 expands the discussion begun in Chapter 4 and identifies those characteristics of discourse which, when present, allow rhetoric to be taken as "epistemic," that is, as "a way of knowing." The characteristics of epistemic discourse are ordered hierarchically, beginning with elementary language functions and concluding with what we call the "perspective" feature of rhetoric.

Chapter 6 endeavors to make explicit a number of epistemological concepts whose importance to human knowledge lies in their uniquely *rhetorical* character. Further, we discuss what we take to be the most basic ontological issues in *relational theory*—issues that form the foundations of perspective and the view we call "rhetorical perspectivism."

Our final chapter addresses the implications and applications of our theory for a variety of human concerns. Our hope is that our conclusions will make conspicuous both the interdisciplinary nature of rhetorical epistemology and its applicability to problems of contemporary experience.

Our goal is to bring together in a spirit of interdisciplinarity the discoveries of a number of fields, especially rhetoric and philosophy. Our undertaking is to build a theory of rhetorical epistemology that incorporates whatever subject matters and enterprises are inseparable from communicative functions. The test of the theory developed in the pages that follow will be its ability to explain, on a theoretical level, all that is encountered in communicative, ideational experience.

NOTES

1. See, for example, Plato's *Phaedrus* and *Republic*. A good annotated source is Plato, *The Collected Dialogues of Plato,* Edith Hamilton and Huntington Cairns, eds. (Princeton, N.J.: Princeton University Press, 1961).

2. Foremost among the Sophistic thinkers whose epistemological skepticism led eventually to subjectivism are Protagoras and Gorgias. Protagoras has been interpreted as claiming that "the perceptions of individuals are equally true," even when they contradict. This appears to be a corollary of his doctrine that "man is the measure of all things, of the things that are, that they are, and of the things that are not, that they are not." For Protagoras, any proposition could be opposed by its contradictory (the doctrine of *dissoi logoi*). Gorgias propounded an even more radical thesis. In his argument in *On Not Being* or *On Nature*, Gorgias argued that nothing exists; if anything exists, it is incomprehensible; and if anything is comprehensible, it is incommunicable. See Ralph M. McInerny, *A History of Western Philosophy*, Vol. 1 (Chicago: Henry Regnery, 1963), pp. 98–104. See also, James J. Murphy, ed., *A Synoptic History of Classical Rhetoric* (New York: Random House, 1972), pp. 7–10.

3. The most significant ideas by Bacon concerning rhetoric appear in his *Advancement of Learning*, 1605. An excellent collection is John M. Robertson, ed., *The Philosophical Works of Francis Bacon* (London: George Routledge and Sons, 1905).

4. See George Campbell, *The Philosophy of Rhetoric*, Lloyd Bitzer, ed. (Carbondale: Southern Illinois University Press, 1963).

16

5. Works by these scholars which impinge most directly upon rhetoric include Ludwig Wittgenstein, *Philosophical Investigations* (New York: Macmillan, 1953) and *On Certainty* (New York: Harper & Row, 1969); John R. Searle, *Speech Acts: An Essay in the Philosophy of Language* (London: Cambridge University Press, 1969); Stephen Toulmin, *The Uses of Argument* (Cambridge: Cambridge University Press, 1958); Maurice Natanson and Henry W. Johnstone, Jr., eds., *Philosophy, Rhetoric, and Argumentation* (University Park: Pennsylvania State University Press, 1965); Ch. Perelman and L. Olbrechts-Tyteca, *The New Rhetoric: A Treatise on Argumentation*, trans. John Wilkinson and Purcell Weaver (Notre Dame: University of Notre Dame Press, 1969); and Thomas S. Kuhn, *The Structure of Scientific Revolutions*, 2nd ed. (Chicago: University of Chicago Press, 1970).

6. Rhetoricians who have made contributions to the philosophical literature include I. A. Richards, *The Philosophy of Rhetoric* (London: Oxford University Press, 1936); Richard Weaver, *The Ethics of Rhetoric* (Chicago: Henry Regnery, 1953); Wayne C. Booth, *Modern Dogma and the Rhetoric of Assent* (Chicago: University of Chicago Press, 1974); Kenneth Burke, *A Rhetoric of Motives* (Berkeley: University of California Press, 1950); and Douglas W. Ehninger, "On Systems of Rhetoric," *Philosophy and Rhetoric*, 1 (1968), 131–44.

7. The initial impetus for this view came in Robert L. Scott, "On Viewing Rhetoric as Epistemic," *Central States Speech Journal*, 18 (1967), 9–17. Additional works on this topic are cited throughout and appear in the bibliography.

8. The most representative expression of this formulation appears in Barry Brummett, "Some Implications of 'Process' or 'Intersubjectivity': Postmodern Rhetoric," *Philosophy and Rhetoric*, 9 (1976), 21–51.

9. See, for example, Richard A. Cherwitz and James W. Hikins, "Toward A Rhetorical Epistemology," *Southern Speech Communication Journal*, 47 (1982), 135–62.

10. Some of these additional positions appear in Thomas B. Farrell, "Knowledge, Consensus, and Rhetorical Theory," *Quarterly Journal of Speech*, 62 (1976), 1–14; Walter M. Carleton, "What Is Rhetorical Knowledge? A Reply to Farrell—and More," *Quarterly Journal of Speech*, 64 (1978), 313–28; and Celeste Condit Railsback, "Beyond Rhetorical Relativism: A Structural-Material Model of Truth and Objective Reality," *Quarterly Journal of Speech*, 69 (1983), 351–63.

11. See, for example, Brummett; Earl Croasmun and Richard A. Cherwitz, "Beyond Rhetorical Relativism," *Quarterly Journal of Speech*, 68 (1982), 1–16; C. Jack Orr, "How Shall We Say: 'Reality Is Socially Constructed Through Communication'?" *Central States Speech Journal*, 29 (1978), 263–74; and Barry Brummett, "On To Rhetorical Relativism," *Quarterly Journal of Speech*, 68 (1982), 425–437.

17

KNOWLEDGE

Since the dawn of western philosophy in the seventh century, B.C., questions of what we know and how we know what we know have been of central importance in the search for truth. In more than two millennia of philosophical investigation, numerous theories of knowledge have been proposed and debated. The variety of these theories is easily accounted for: each philosophical school has been required by the nature of the philosophical enterprise to explain and justify the epistemological grounds on which it rested. Additionally, as the stock of knowledge has increased, new theories of knowledge have been required to accommodate new arrays of information. Hence, all theories of knowledge have evolved out of a common requirement: the need for criteria by which to choose among competing ways of viewing the world. In the absence of such criteria, a thinker would have no warrant for preferring one belief or claim over another.

This *raison d'etre* of epistemology pervades all areas of human activity. For theorist and practitioner, epistemological concerns are relevant. Without an acceptable epistemological basis for our beliefs, how could we justify attempts to persuade or dissuade others about anything? On questions involving health, welfare, happiness, and even the most mundane matters, we presume that some answers are superior to others—that some alternatives will, in fact, result in the most desirable ends. Consequently, any thoughtful person must be prepared to answer the questions: How do you know? and How do you know that you know?

This consideration alone should be sufficient to demonstrate that epistemological issues are not merely abstract considerations to be sequestered in some remote domain of philosophy. Epistemological questions are of seminal importance to the conduct of our everyday lives. Regrettably, however, most of us make what we consider "intelligent" judgments in the execution of daily routines without ever stopping to consider the foundations of the *knowledge claims* upon which our choices are based.

Before we can deal with questions about how we know and how we know that we know, we must define what we mean by the term "knowledge." In defining knowledge, we make the following assumptions. First, we assume that matters of epistemology (how knowledge is acquired) are conceptually and logically *prior* to matters of ontology (what exists). Any veridical human system of ontological claims presupposes a defensible epistemology. An object must exist before it can be known; however, an understanding of what should be granted the status of knowledge ought to precede consideration of any specific statement about what exists. To advance claims about what exists is necessarily to make a series of knowledge-claims. One cannot assess rival statements about reality without first determining the criteria for judging the truth-value of epistemic judgments. We believe we cannot say that we know something about the world unless we have determined what it means to "know." To say what we mean by "knowing" does not, we believe, involve us in making assertions about what is. Hence, we ask readers not to attach any of the traditional philosophical baggage represented by such terms as "objectivity," "absolutism," "positivistic," or the like in following the development of our analysis of the concept "knowledge." What we seek are the qualifications to be met by anything to which we would assign the status of "knowledge" rather than of, say, "opinion." In what follows we wish especially to avoid statements about the nature of the particular "furnishings" or "objects" that may or may not exist as part of "reality."

While we shall avoid developing a full-blown ontological theory antecedent to a theory of rhetorical epistemology, we do make the assumption that a reality exists independently of individuals. This assumption is not arbitrary. It is presumed in the use, if not always in the theory, of communication. In the acts of persuading, informing, praising, or blaming, all communicators take as given that they are persuading, informing, or offering evaluations to an audience that exists and thinks independently of the communicator. To assume that no reality exists independent of oneself is to render any communication otiose. Some may argue that audiences are no more than constructed collections of attitudes, beliefs, values, and expectations, but the origins of those constructs are located in particular *others*. Any person who argues that our assumption regarding the independence of reality is mistaken must embrace the ensuing solipsism. Implicit in his or her suggestion that it is mistaken to assume that reality exists apart from us is recognition of other people who can and perhaps do think independently of the critic. Put another way, notions such as "mistaken," "incorrect," "deluded," and the like assume the existence of something independent of the claims made with those terms. Regardless of how we theorize, our actions (physical and intellectual) betray the fact that we do assume the existence of some sort of independent reality. This is not an assumption *ad hoc*; it is *ad omnia*. Not even the most committed subjectivist nor the most thoroughgoing idealist would test the thesis that reality is *purely* a mental construct by venturing into the path of an oncoming locomotive on the assumption that mind could alter the unpleasant consequences of the ensuing collision. It is true that we can and do exercise the will to determine certain events—such as the decision whether or not to commit suicide by leaping from a cliff—but it is equally true that most events in human experience cannot be wished away. Once one has jumped from the cliff, no amount of willing can prevent the outcome of the fall. As one contemporary philosopher was fond of pointing out, "even the solipsist continues to have social moments when he tries to convince others of the correctness of his views, and would probably become as mad in behavior as he is in theory if the social denizens of his world were persistently to deny that they and he are what he and they seem to them and to him to be.[1]

Finally, we assume that a definition of knowledge is useful and productive only if it affords linguistic and conceptual clarification of the ways in which epistemic judgments and their terminology are employed. A definition of knowledge can be valuable even if there are no items within human cognition that correspond to the definition. An analogy will illustrate. The word "God" is meaningful and useful, linguistically and conceptually. It is meaningful not because we all agree that God exists, nor because there is an immediate referent to which we can apply the term. Instead, the term is valuable, among other reasons, because it limits and makes more precise the meaning of our expression. For example, when a rhetorical critic observes that a speaker has uttered a "God term," the critic's remark is both useful and enlightening because it permits one to distinguish a quality inhering in one part of the speech from qualities inhering in other terms. Similarly, a definition of "knowledge," whether or not it refers to something humanly attainable, allows us to distinguish between knowledge and related concepts that are represented by such terms as "opinion," "belief," "perception," "feeling," and "emotion."

What knowledge is and how it is attained are issues that can be raised and answered separately. Methodological problems inherent in the question, "How does one apprehend God?" do not make impossible the definition of God as delineated in Judeo-Christian theology; similarly, problems inherent in the question "How does one attain knowledge?" do not deny a definition of knowledge, whether the definition is the one presented in this book or some other. Thus, a clear definition of the term "knowledge" enables one to separate *definitional* from *methodological* issues. In addition, explaining each of the definitional constituents of the concept of knowledge will show why these topics yield both useful and essential insight into any non-trivial formulation of the assertion that through communication we come to know—that "rhetoric is epistemic."[2]

DEFINITION OF KNOWLEDGE

For a number of decades, philosophers have debated what constitutes the criteria of knowledge.[3] Although a wide variety of answers to the

20

question, "What is knowledge?" have been offered, the debate has tended to focus on three notions that are frequently mentioned as requisite to knowledge: (1) truth, (2) belief, and (3) justification. Thus, for example, Panayot Butchvarov equates knowledge with "true belief based on sufficient evidence."4 A number of other contemporary philosophers concur in holding that truth, belief, and justification are three constituents of knowledge; such writers include Ayer, Chisholm, and Lehrer. 5

Truth, belief, and justification as criteria for knowledge have been subjected to extensive critical analysis by philosophers, most notably by Gettier. 6 Such criticism has raised issues concerning the tripartite criteria of knowledge that proponents must address, but in our judgment, the attack has been largely unsuccessful in demonstrating that truth, belief, and justification are erroneous as definitional components of knowledge. Lehrer, for one, has responded to Gettier's critique and has managed to preserve the three criteria largely intact. 7 Thus, while it would be imprudent to suggest that the traditional philosophical formulation of knowledge is uncontroversial and should be accepted uncritically, recent efforts in its defense put the burden again on the shoulders of the tradition's detractors. We hold, therefore, that for any statement that purports to describe the way the world is to qualify as "knowledge," the proposition that the statement advances must be true, its utterer must believe it to be true, and it must be supported by justification or evidence sufficient to establish it as true. In what follows we shall examine each of these three components of knowledge, commenting at appropriate points on the controversies concerning each criterion. It is not our purpose, however, to treat the philosophical debates extensively. We seek only to give readers a sense that defining knowledge as justified true belief is, at the least, a *plausible* position to take in dealing with epistemological issues.

In justifying our deference to the traditional philosophical position, we shall not simply appeal to authority. We seek to provide grounds upon which our view can be held with consistency. When we postulate truth, belief, and justification as criteria of knowledge, we do not do so for the purpose of proving any larger claims about rhetoric, epistemology, or their interrelationship. Instead our postulates will be offered to illustrate the *consistency* and *possibility* of the rhetorical epistemology we advocate. We do contend that the criteria of truth, belief, and justification provide a foundation both consistent with and supportive of the theory of rhetorical epistemology we shall present. It is a fundamental implication of that theory that its own continued discussion and review is a *sine qua non* of its defensibility as knowledge.

TRUTH

We take it to be axiomatic that propositions of genuine knowledge must be true. This requirement is plausible because to claim that knowledge need not be knowledge of something true entails a contradiction. As Quinton puts it, "If I admit that p is false, I must admit that I did not know it and no one else did, although I may have thought and said so."8 Logically, to say "I know that X" is to say that "I know that X is true." To suggest that X could be both true and not true (false), at the same time and under the same conditions, would be to violate a fundamental "law of thought."9 Moreover, in ordinary language we use the word "knowledge" to designate those opinions we strongly believe are true.

Some, however, may point to cases in everyday language where this principle seems to be violated. For example, in response to the statement, "Nixon was a bad President," one might receive the reply, "Well your statement is both true and false." By such a reply one's interlocutor is probably not suggesting that Nixon was both a good president and a bad president *at the same time and under the same conditions*, that is, in the same way(s). Instead he or she is likely to be referring to different aspects of Nixon's presidency. Pressed to explain the statement further, this interlocutor might indicate that what he or she meant was that in foreign policy Nixon demonstrated good or noble qualities, whereas in domestic policy Nixon failed to measure up to those political standards we appraise as good.

What appears to be a contradiction of the criterion of truth is in fact analyzable into two separate epistemic judgments, each of which is either true or false, but not both. Nevertheless, there is still a sense in which one might speak of knowing what is false. Take as an example the declaration, "I know the Titanic is unsinkable." Prior to the ship's sinking on April 14, 1912, numerous individuals could and did hold this knowledge claim. Yet we now know that the claim was false. Are we to say that prior to April 14, 1912, individuals *knew* what was false? Of course not. They *believed* a statement to be true when it was in fact false. To use Plato's language, the statement that the "Titanic is unsinkable" is an example of *doxa* or opinion, and not a case of *episteme* or knowledge.10

Of course, we are not suggesting that one cannot have knowledge *about* or *of* falsehood. We only suggest that one cannot have knowledge that *is false*. The position that one can only have knowledge of what is true may be questioned for other reasons, however. If, as we suggest, truth is one of the independent criteria of knowledge, there remains the question: How can one ever *know* that something is the case? It has been argued that "if knowledge entails truth, we can never attain knowledge or, at any rate never know that we have done so."11 From this vantage point, most of our beliefs can never be assessed if the vast majority of contemporary philosophical, scientific, and rhetorical theories are correct in denying that we are ever directly confronted by external reality. After all, so the argument goes, there are few things that present themselves to us in such a fashion that we can make judgments about their intrinsic existence and nature; simply put, we are not in direct contact with reality. In place of any view to the contrary, theorists who hold this position are either representationalists, in believing that some medium(s) stands between us and the reality existing beyond us (such as photons which bounce off objects and then impinge upon the retina of the eye and start a complex chain of events between the object and the eventual perception of its color), or they are subjectivists. The latter are likely to hold that reality is a *creation* of individuals. We shall have a good deal more to say about each of these positions later.

Occasionally some theorists seem to argue that there are items of experience that, philosophical conundrums aside, are revealed to us directly, namely, matters of scientific, that is, empirical inquiry. "The earth is round," "Water freezes at 32° under conditions of standard temperature and pressure," "Two hydrogen atoms combine with one atom of oxygen to form water" are all examples of statements that some hold refer to reality as it directly confronts us. This contention is part and parcel of a familiar distinction that has enjoyed wide currency since Aristotle. We are referring to those theories that hold there is a fundamental *qualitative* difference between scientific matters that are amenable to empirical investigation (apodictic questions) and questions in moral, political, and religious realms for which there is no apparent empirical evidence upon which to base a knowledge claim (contingent questions).12 This distinction has been underscored in recent times by philosophical positivism and has been exacerbated by the growth of modern science.13

The objection that we cannot assess the truth or falsity of claims directly can be resolved without resorting either to an epistemology based on representationalism (and consequently the ensuing skepticism that our representation of the world may be very much different from the way the world really is) or to a separation of the world into empirical and nonempirical constituents.

It can be held, for example, that reality itself is *active* (a term not to be confused or equated with the term "empirical"); that is, reality impinges directly upon our cognitive and affective lives. If this is so, the alleged distinction between scientific/apodictic questions and probable/contingent

23

ones is amenable to resolution. It is not that there exists a qualitative difference between two types of knowledge such that scientific matters are somehow wholly distinct from contingent ones; it is the case that we have chosen to group all aspects of reality where impingement has allowed appraisal (whether empirical or otherwise) into the category of "scientific truths." In other words, once we have determined that a particular reality has impinged to a sufficient degree, or once we have developed the capability to assess impingement, the reality we are dealing with becomes a question of scientific interest. This has occurred most often in the past two centuries as a result of refinements in observational techniques: new scientific instruments and devices have refined ability to perceive the impingement process.

History illustrates our point. In classical times and for centuries later, physics was conceived of as a subdiscipline of speculative philosophy. Questions about what we now call physics fell into the category of what we now label "contingent." The reason for this was that the cues of reality (reality impingement) were both unidentified and unidentifiable. The tools of contemporary physics were yet to be conceived. Lucretius' *De Rerum Natura*, an early exposition of the theory of atomism,14 could be labeled a treatise on a contingent matter. This was reasonable because Lucretius and his contemporaries were unable to view atoms directly; moreover, to use familiar positivistic language, they were unable to suggest how one might, even theoretically, observe atoms. In the twentieth century, we have the scientific apparatus with which to observe atomic effects, if not atoms themselves. In short, physicists can now directly view the cues of reality that are relevant to the structure of nuclear physics; they can *see* reality's impingement. Hence, atomic physics has been excised from the body of contingent subjects properly the domain of speculative philosophy and has been transferred to the class of scientifically explainable topics.

All of this is to say that while there are differences between contingent and scientific issues, these distinctions are not epistemologically qualitative. We rightly glorify science due to its success in isolating, making perspicuous, and communicating elements of reality. Its subject matter has metamorphosed from the obscurity of contingency to the clearer status of that which can be empirically observed—where our ability to scrutinize the objects of reality has direct, practical application. This is, however, a result rather than a cause of scientific inquiry itself.

Of course, one could retort that the questions we now label contingent—questions that seem unanswerable like, Is justice the right of the stronger? or Is there a God?—are of a nature wholly different from the

24

question, Are there atoms? The last question has, we might say, a conceivable answerability; the former ones do not; but so to reply begs the question. The reply is clearly the result of atomic-age hindsight. The reply is possible because of familiarity with an answer, not because of the nature of the question. If one imagines oneself living in the middle of the first century B.C., one can realize that, to Lucretius' auditors, atoms were as speculative from an empiricist's standpoint as God, angels, and values are today.

The point of our argument here is to cast doubt upon the long-held contingent-apodictic distinction. We are not adopting a position in the camps of either "positivists" or "empiricists." The theory of rhetorical epistemology we will develop is not a wholesale endorsement of these or of similar theoretical frameworks.

In reference to our beginning point, namely that *truth* is a criterion of knowledge, we are getting ahead of ourselves. Later we shall take up the notion of apprehension of truth as a humanly possible experience. For the present it is sufficient to have established that one's capacity to assess directly the impingement of something is not itself a reliable measure of that thing's truth or falsity.

In summary, the notion of an active reality that impinges on us clarifies the concept of truth as a first criterion of knowledge. Because of the logical and conceptual consequences of its absence, truth must be taken as a necessary constituent of knowledge. Regardless of the viability of our metaphysical claim that reality is active, it is clear that an essential criterion of knowledge is that it be true, and this is the important theoretical point being made here. Whether there *is* a reality that can be known—indeed, even if it should be the case that the objects of reality can never be known—we can still conceive of the conditions that would have to be fulfilled for such knowledge to exist. One of those conditions is that any knowledge we *could* possess must be true. Whatever other levels or kinds of epistemic assessments we might make or recognize, including such assessments as "opinion," "belief," "conviction," such designations and such contents must be clearly differentiated from what we are willing to admit into the category of knowledge. While other levels of epistemic assessment (opinion, belief, conviction) need not meet the truth criterion, knowledge must consist of propositions/statements that are true; the other levels of assessment need not meet the truth criterion to exist.

BELIEF

A second condition that must obtain if we are to have genuine knowledge is belief. That is, to say that one has knowledge of any truth, X, X

25

must not only be the case, but in addition one must *believe* that X is the case. As Butchvarov notes, "Whatever one really knows one also believes; for a statement of the form 'x knows that p but does not believe that p' seems to be, if not incoherent, puzzling without any redeeming informativeness . . ."15 Butchvarov's contention is easily elucidated. Take as an example, the statement uttered by Jones, "I know that it is raining outside." If we were to respond to Jones' utterance by asking whether he *believed* it is raining outside, he would likely be puzzled and reply, "What a curious question! Not only do I believe it is raining outside, as I said, I know it is raining outside." We, like Jones, would never seriously contend that we knew it to be raining and yet did not believe it. Of course, there are cases in which one might reply, "I do not believe it, I *know* it." In cases like these, one is attempting to underscore that the state of affairs being reported goes beyond and is stronger than mere belief. The distinction between belief and knowledge turns on certain criteria *additional to* those assigned to belief. Two such additional criteria are the concept of "truth," already discussed, and the concept of "sufficiency of evidence," to be discussed later. Nonbelief can never be attendant to knowledge except in that it must be absent if there is knowledge.

There are, however, cases in the world of discourse where individuals make statements like "I know our house has been destroyed by fire and we have lost all our possessions, but I cannot believe it happened." Such instances do not establish that belief is not a criterion of knowledge. First, such a person may be using the term "belief" metaphorically or allegorically to indicate that what he or she really knows is so shocking or devastating that it defies human understanding and hence falls outside human knowledge. Or, such a statement may simply be a misreporting of a real, cognitive state of affairs. The unfortunate person who has lost his or her treasures in a fire really knows and does believe what has occurred, but for psychological reasons (such as the vain hope that by withholding assent from a state of affairs, an unpleasant situation will "go away") the person cannot yet bear to articulate that belief.

A final kind of apparent knowledge without belief is illustrated by the statement "I know X but do not believe it." This can be a prelude to a search for evidence of X. Consider a father who, wanting a son, is told by a nurse that his wife has given birth to their eighth daughter. The father might be incredulous at the prospects of having no son and of having eight daughters. His response could be to demand that the physician reconfirm physiologically the reported sex of his new infant. In this situation, we could ask whether the father actually felt he really *knew* he had become the parent of another daughter. There can be little doubt that the physician knew the gender of the infant immediately; but the father did not possess the same sort of knowledge until additional evidence in the form of confirmation rendered knowledge—and hence belief—possible.

There seem good reasons, then, to claim that without belief, one cannot be said to know, that belief is a logically and psychologically necessary component of knowledge.

JUSTIFICATION

Besides X being true and one's believing it to be so, a third constituent of knowledge is necessary, namely, justification. At first blush, the requirement of justification seems unproblematic. We do not, for example, call it knowledge when a novice at the racetrack predicts that Spectacular Bid will triumph, and then after his prediction comes true, makes the statement, "I knew he would win." We should say this individual made a lucky guess. On the other hand, we might take seriously the claim "I know Spectacular Bid will win" if it were uttered by an experienced gambler whose prognostication is justified by certain evidence, 16 such as statistical data from other races, knowledge of the horse's performance in recent training sprints, track conditions and their implications, the skill of the jockey, and the strength of the competition. If, in this second case, the prediction that Spectacular Bid will win comes to fruition, we might say that the sage of the racetrack did, in fact, *know* that the event would occur. Nevertheless, in the real world, predictions by race enthusiasts, regardless of how expert, often fail. For this reason, many of us might reconsider the assertion that even the gambler's prediction was in fact knowledge, reserving the label "knowledge" for claims supported by additional or better evidence.

Imagine a statement in the morning newspaper reminding you that at 2:05 P.M. a total eclipse of the sun will begin. Upon inquiring of the editor how he or she knew such an event would occur, the editor might refer you to an astronomer at the Naval Observatory in Washington, D.C. Pressing the issue further, you could call the astronomer and ask how he or she knew an eclipse would take place. The astronomer's response might take the form of a lengthy exposition on astrophysics, including historical evidence from the time of the ancient Babylonians to the present day. Moreover, the astronomer's lecture might conclude with the confident assertion that not only could the time and duration of the eclipse this afternoon be predicted but, in addition, it is possible to predict with accuracy eclipses for ages to come. Faced by the preponderance of evidence presented, the record of past successes in predicting eclipses, the obvious competence and professionalism of the astronomer, and the quality and quantity of the astronomer's equipment, you would be justified in concluding that the expert possessed genuine knowledge relevant to astronomical phenomena.

The novice gambler issued a dubious claim "I knew"; the experienced gambler also claimed to know but doubts remained justified; yet there could be no doubt in any rational person's mind that the astronomer did, in a far different sense, *know* what was claimed. If we compare these examples, the striking feature allowing us to conclude that the astronomer really knew is the overwhelming *sufficiency*, both qualitative and quantitative, of the evidence supporting the knowledge claim.

If the experienced gambler had a corresponding amount of evidence, including the tools to evaluate such evidence, he or she would be able to predict the winners of horse races with the same accuracy and consistency as the astronomer predicts eclipses. Even the novice gambler could achieve the same success if equipped with enough sophisticated devices and information, even though the gambler may have never visited the track. The upshot is that our judgment that any of these three prognosticators has knowledge is to an important degree a judgment of whether sufficient evidence lies behind the forecast. So it is with any knowledge claim.

Earlier, we noted that the definition of knowledge as justified true belief has not been without its detractors. Indeed, it is the notion of justification that has borne the brunt of criticism. The objections that have gained the widest currency in philosophical and other circles are those launched by Edmund Gettier and his followers. Gettier attempted to demonstrate the shortcomings of the justification criterion by formulating counterexamples that purportedly show one can be justified in believing a knowledge claim when, in fact, the knowledge claim is, or may be, false.17 For example, suppose one is confronted with five doors, behind one of which there is a prize of great value. Suppose further that the prize is behind door number 4. After receiving several hints, let us say that a contestant, Bernie, comes to believe that the prize is behind *either* door 2 or door 4 on the basis of the justified belief that it is behind door 2. We may surmise that something in common between door 2 and door 4 results in this belief. Now Bernie is not only justified in believing that the prize is behind either door 2 or door 4, it is true that the prize *is* behind door 2 or door 4. Yet it is obvious that Bernie does not *know* the prize is behind either door 2 or door 4. Shall we conclude, on the basis of such an example, that the criteria of truth, belief, and justification are defective as a whole? Or should we reject specifically the criterion of justification because of examples such as the one illustrated? We suggest not, for several reasons.

First, one must question the employment of the term "justification" in the Gettier examples. To begin with, in ordinary language, when we make an utterance like, "Jones is justified in believing that Mary went to the store," we generally mean something like, "Jones has *sufficient evidence to prove* that Mary went to the store." If it turns out that Mary is sleeping upstairs and did not go to the store, we do not generally claim that Jones was justified in believing Mary went to the store, but rather that Jones was mistaken and his justification itself was in some way defective.

Hence, we suggest that there are at least two senses in which one may use the term "justified." In its weaker sense, it may mean that one has some reason to believe that something is the case, even though the reason(s) may not be relevant to the truth of the knowledge claim in question. In this weaker sense of the term "justified," Jones might have been justified in believing Mary was at the store because her purse was nowhere in sight and neither was she. Yet in a stronger sense of the term "justified," Jones' conclusion that Mary had gone to the store is certainly not based on a sense of justification anything like an astronomer's evidence for prediction of an eclipse. If we return to some of our examples, our point will be clear. Our novice predicted that Spectacular Bid would win a race. Spectacular Bid won the race, and the novice proclaimed, "I knew that horse would win." If we asked for the justification on which the novice based his knowledge, he might reply, "I had a strong intuition." ESP aside, our response to the claim of intuition would in all likelihood be something like, "You were just lucky. Your intuition had no relevance to Spectacular Bid's success."

The key word in the above hypothetical exchange is *relevance*. Gettier's objections to the justification criterion really boil down to the assertion that some justifications for knowledge claims are not relevant to the truth of such claims, thus the criterion of justification is defective. But this is the case only if the weak sense of justification is intended when it is claimed that knowledge is justified true belief.

There is a second problem with Gettier-type objections to the tripartite definition of knowledge in general and justification in particular. This may be illustrated by the cases of the sage of the racetrack or the quizz show contestant trying to determine behind which door the prize lies. The sage based his or her knowledge claim that a horse would win on evidence we would all agree was relevant in the sense just mentioned. Yet most of us would not elevate the *claim* of the sage to the status of knowledge because the science (if it is a science) of predicting winners of horse races is at this point in the history of the sport too inexact. Here, the problem is not that there is no justification for knowledge, but that sufficiency of justification is lacking. For this reason, when we claim that knowledge consists in justified true belief, we must add the stipulation that we mean "justified" in the very strong sense, namely, that the justification is *sufficient* as well as *relevant* to establish the truth of any knowledge claim.

Combining the concepts of sufficiency and relevance, one would expect to find no genuine counterexamples to a fully justified true belief. Hence, we may use the phrase "persistent justification" to distinguish the formulation of "justification"as we use the term.

It may be very difficult to determine, in any given case, just what constitutes persistent justification; nonetheless, there are instances of knowledge we can point to where the justification is so obviously sufficient that to deny it would be only to quibble. The astronomer's predictions of eclipses of the sun are such cases. Who would deny that the astronomer's justification is both relevant and sufficient, that it is so persistent as to establish the truth of the knowledge claims offered?

To summarize our discussion of objections to justification as a criterion of truth, we reassert that in the formulation of knowledge-as-justified-true-belief, the "persistent justification" referred to must be both relevant to the truth of the knowledge claim and sufficient to establish its truth. [18] The questions of what degree of evidence is required, how sufficiency is to be determined, and by whom are *methodological* questions, and we will consider them later. For the present, our claim is that to be taken seriously, a claim of "I know" must entail truth of the assertion, belief in it, and sufficient evidence for its justification.

The importance of these three criteria of knowledge is not merely philosophical. Application of these criteria has enormous practical and even ethical implications. As Lloyd Bitzer has reminded us, "The exigencies of our time are dangerous almost beyond the power of imagination to conceive: war, famine, threat of accidental destruction by instruments of technology, ruin of an irreplaceable environment—these and other exigencies threaten to destroy individuals and societies." [19] These exigencies are of great consequence; we therefore need to be particularly careful in our choices of actions to meet them. Hence, it is incumbent upon everyone to be cautious about elevating propositions to the status of *knowledge*. The "facts" upon which our decisions rest merit the closest scrutiny, and we suggest that only attendance to a rigorous concept of knowledge can guarantee that the best decisions will be reached. For this reason, we ought to keep our conceptual houses in order when considering and using terms like *knowledge, opinion, belief, certainty, consensus,* or any of the other linguistic symbols that have epistemological implications.

BELIEF, TRUE BELIEF, RATIONAL BELIEF, AND KNOWLEDGE

Our three criteria for knowledge allow us to distinguish among various degrees of conviction and also to develop a useful distinction between *opinion* and *knowledge*. This distinction is important. Without recognizing the difference between opinion and knowledge, and between knowledge and several other degrees of conviction, one runs the risk of ascribing the status of knowledge to ideas that are conjectural and/or erroneous. History is replete with instances where dignification of mere *opinion* had tragic consequences. As we argued earlier, communicators lacking an epistemological substruction have no warrant for preferring, let alone advocating, one course of action or belief over another. When we speak of knowledge, we couch in language a certain stature; we dignify ideas, theories, or notions when we assign them the quality knowledge. Furthermore, we hold in awe those in society who we believe possess knowledge. It is precisely because the concept of knowledge possesses such practical linguistic and conceptual distinctiveness associated with evaluation of social, political, scientific, moral, and ethical claims, that knowledge is a concept crucial to maintaining civilization. These are reasons we should not abandon traditional distinctions between opinion and knowledge. The definition of knowledge we have proposed is valuable because it permits us to distinguish between knowledge and several levels of opinion. Following others, we shall term these levels of opinion: *belief, true belief,* and *rational belief.*

Beliefs are the most elementary of our opinions. They are characterized by two qualities: first, they may be either true or false; second, they may be arrived at either rationally or nonrationally. Most would agree that the witch doctor who performs a chant in order to drive out smallpox infection from a member of the tribe holds a false notion about effective ways to cure smallpox. Nonetheless, the medicine man believes his chant is curative. Similarly, one who reads the daily horoscope may genuinely believe that by attending to its predictions the course of life may be enhanced. Others of us may say that this belief is not rational, but despite its nonrationality, the other person's faith in astrology constitutes a belief.

A second level of opinion is *true belief.* The term "true belief" implies a conviction that is, in fact, true. True belief is similar to mere belief in that it may be arrived at either rationally or nonrationally. An ancient Pythagorean may have asserted that because all things are inherently mathematical it is possible to say that in all cases the square of the length of the hypotenuse of a right triangle equals the sum of the squares of the lengths of the other two sides. In our time we might argue that the Pythagorean's reason for confidence in his conclusion was nonrational, but we would concur that his conclusion was true. His conclusion is thus properly labeled a *true belief* however nonrationally arrived at.

A third level of opinion is *rational belief*. Although rational belief is like mere belief in that it may be either true or false, its defining characteristic is the presence of rationality.

Rationality is an ambiguous concept unless formally defined. We shall apply the term to ideas that can withstand critical inquiry. That some ideas are more reasonably held than others is familiar in philosophical literature. Chisholm, for example, asserts that "one belief is *more reasonable than* another, or, more exactly . . . one belief is more reasonable for a given person at a given time than is another belief."20 By way of illustration, Chisholm cites St. Augustine replying to a challenge to demonstrate why one ought to believe the testimony of one's senses. Augustine argued that it was more reasonable for most of us to act on the cues provided by our sense perceptions than it is to believe that we should not. 21 Bertrand Russell similarly justified the special reasonableness of believing sense perceptions, saying that "beliefs caused by perception are to be accepted unless there are positive grounds for rejecting them."22 The notion of what makes one belief more reasonable than another has been developed by at least one philosopher who writes within the context of rhetorical studies.

In defining how it is that one position may be judged more rational than another, Henry W. Johnstone, Jr. asserts the role rhetoric plays in determining reasonableness in philosophical argument. According to Johnstone's analysis, "the rationality of the philosophical enterprise consists in the use of a rhetoric."23 It is to be noted that Johnstone writes of *a* rhetoric. The particular variety of rhetoric he has in mind is one that serves to examine philosophical theses critically. 24 Such a rhetoric is employed by a critic *con amore* according to Johnstone. "He [the rational, philosophical critic] is like the inspector of products coming off the assembly line, who discards items only in order to raise the standards of the manufacturing process."25 For Johnstone, then, a belief is rational to the extent that it survives vigorous, critical, argumentative inspection. We accept this basic view of what is rational.

Rational belief, therefore, has as its defining characteristic the fact that, to some significant degree, persons holding such beliefs have allowed the beliefs to be subjected to criticism. In other words, opinions withstanding a degree of critical inspection are rational beliefs. Perhaps Toulmin, Rieke, and Janik put it best when they write: "Anyone participating in an argument shows his *rationality*, or lack of it, by the manner in which he handles and responds to the offering of reasons for or against claims. If he is 'open to argument,' he will either acknowledge the force of those reasons or seek to reply to them, and either way he will deal with them in a 'rational' manner. If he is 'deaf to argument,' by contrast, he may either ignore contrary reasons or reply to them with dogmatic assertions, and either way he fails to deal with the issues 'rationally.' "26

Such rationality does not necessarily allow us to attain knowledge. That is, critical examination of our convictions may not be of sufficient probative power to uncover error and validate the belief as knowledge. It is for this reason that rational beliefs, like mere beliefs, may be either true or false.

Mere belief, true belief, and rational belief cannot fairly be called "knowledge," Mere belief and rational belief fail to attain the level of knowledge because they may be false. True belief does not invariably meet standards of rationality and therefore cannot be termed "knowledge." However, there is a category of conviction we may justly label "knowledge."

Knowledge is a kind of belief in the sense that both belief and knowledge can have the same object. The witch doctor may possess *mere* belief that the moon is reborn each day in the east, perishes each day in the west, and is replaced anew the following day. The Pythagorean may entertain the *true* belief that the moon orbits the earth, yet for reasons explained by mathematical mysticism. Galileo may have held the *rational* belief that there is life on the moon, since his telescope revealed that the moon's surface had mountains, plains, valleys, and other features indicating to him an environment similar to earth's. Knowledge may have objects in common with these modes of acceptance, but knowledge meets one criterion affording it epistemological distinction, namely *sufficiency* of evidence. By sufficiency of evidence we mean evidence yielding demonstration of the truth of a claim. As we have indicated, demonstrations of sufficiency must withstand rigorous critical assessments, but an important qualification must be made clear: sufficiency of evidence is, in part, a matter of *degree*. Sufficiency of evidence obtains at the point where the level of support required to justify (in the sense of "persistent justification" discussed above) the claim "I know X" occurs. It is at this juncture that we may make claims like "I am certain of X." "X is true," and "I am sure that X."

Given this explanation of "sufficiency of evidence," one may be prompted to ask at what point, precisely, sufficiency of evidence obtains for any given knowledge claim. One may demand a formal principle for determining that point at which something transcends the bounds of true belief and may be elevated to the status of *justified* true belief, i.e., knowledge. We

33

do not believe such a demand can be met. Some might counter that if one cannot judge sufficiency reliably, then one cannot have knowledge. We think there are a number of replies to this conclusion.

It is clear that we all have knowledge that we would or could defend as justified true belief where "justification" is equivalent to the concept "sufficiency of evidence." For example, all who look dispassionately at the available evidence come to the conclusion that the earth is roughly spherical. Further, none in possession of a good Western education in the liberal arts would deny that there is irony in the Platonic dialogues. If asked why he or she held such beliefs to be knowledge, a person so questioned would at some point reply that there is an overwhelming sufficiency of evidence to justify holding the beliefs as true.

In our first example, a respondent might speak of flying high-altitude jet aircraft where he or she had many times *seen* clearly that the earth is round because at high altitudes the curvature of the horizon is evident. This kind of direct experience together with other confirming kinds of evidence would lead the respondent, as it leads us, to conclude that there is sufficient evidence to support the truth of the proposition under consideration. Unlike individuals in Ptolemy's age, who had *some* evidence supporting belief in a flat earth, we in the space age have such overwhelming evidence supporting the conception of a roughly round earth that it is incomprehensible that we could be wrong. Critics of concepts such as justified true belief are fond of using the example of those who believed the earth is flat to support the claim that we can never have knowledge as justified true belief, but we contend that there is a fundamental difference between the "knowers" of Ptolemy's day and one who has been in a high-altitude plane and is familiar with indirect evidence of the earth's spherical shape. Few, perhaps not even many of Ptolemy's contemporaries, would claim to have sufficient evidence to support a flat-earth view were the notion carefully explained to them. In the present age, and with the idea of sufficiency of evidence in mind, we are in a much different position from that of Ptolemy's contemporaries. Given the array of evidence available to us, there is simply no question but that we have sufficient evidence for the judgment that the earth is roughly spherical.

It is impossible to say at what *point* sufficiency is attained in respect to the question of the earth's geometric shape, or any other. Nonetheless, it is important that this factor not be taken to mean that human knowledge as justified true belief is impossible. The criteria for knowledge serve not simply as tools to tell us when we have knowledge, but they function as well to assure us what it is *we have* when we have such unassailable truths as that the earth is roughly spherical. For readers who still have doubts as to the accessibility of the sufficient-evidence criterion, more will be said in Chapters 5 and 6 with respect to how the rhetorical process illuminates our understanding of this requisite element in knowledge acquisition.

CERTAINTY AND KNOWLEDGE

Many thinkers who have written about "knowledge" have offered as its defining characteristic the notion of "certainty." Allan Wheelis, for example, claims that "knowledge is the name we give to those of our opinions to which certainty is ascribed."27 Similarly, Richard Cherwitz, in one of his early formulations of rhetorical epistemology, echoed Wheelis' view that knowledge is equatable with certainty,28 where certainty is defined as the absolute impossibility of mistake. It is our contention that this account of certainty is doubtful and that its use as a defining characteristic of knowledge is mistaken.

An initial problem with the concept of certainty evolves from the question of whether or not certainty is merely another term for knowledge itself. Once the constituents of knowledge obtain, it appears that certainty obtains as well. It is our contention, however, that the term "certainty" is ambiguous; the term may be taken in at least two different senses. In one sense certainty is a term referring to the result of *rational judgment*. In another sense, it denotes a *dogmatic state*, describing one's commitment to a particular proposition or belief. In the former case, certainty corresponds, perhaps, to rational belief, where "good reasons" may be given in support of a judgment. The informed citizen who studies the issues and the candidates during a political campaign may, in this sense, make the claim, "I am certain Jones is the best man for the job." Certainty as here employed is a result of a rational judgment, even though we might not wish to say, in light of our definition of knowledge, that our informed citizen *knows* Jones is the best man for the job. In the latter case, where certainty identifies a dogmatic state, certainty becomes wholly a case of commitment wherein emotional or other nonrational considerations can predominate. The witch doctor, imbued with mere belief, may be certain that secret potions are curative; his belief probably derives from mysticism, religious rite, and fear. The informed citizen, having rationally arrived at a conviction that Jones is the best candidate, may then become so taken with Jones' charisma that he or she continues to be certain of Jones' political viability even after serious and unethical political practices by Jones are exposed. In the last two cases, whether beliefs are arrived at rationally or nonrationally, they may yield a dogmatic tendency to cling to convictions even when good reasons against them have been presented.

Thus, there emerge clear differences between at least two senses of the term certainty. A major problem results: Even though certainty may be employed as a term referring to the consequence of rational judgment, it is not so used in all circumstances. Not all certainties arise from rational belief. Moreover, we have shown that rationally arrived at beliefs can be nonrationally preserved as certainties and such certainties do not deserve the status of knowledge.

There is still a sense in which it seems intuitively attractive to equate knowledge with certainty. It remains tempting to argue that "I know X" is equivalent to "I am certain that X." What is needed, we believe, is a reformulation of the concept of certainty, one that addresses the *relation* between certainty and *knowledge*.

Though we recognize that the term "analytic" has other technical meanings in philosophy, we propose to use the phrase *analytical certainty* to refer to certainty that obtains when all three criteria of the definition of knowledge have been satisfied. That is, there is certainty that we shall call analytical when one has attained knowledge as justified true belief. For one to say "I am [analytically] certain that X," one must believe that one possesses knowledge of X in terms of the justified true belief criteria; one cannot possess belief of any sort short of knowledge and claim analytical certainty.

This distinction uncovers an important fact about the concept of certainty. It demonstrates that one kind of certainty results from attaining knowledge, but even analytical certainty is not a defining characteristic of knowledge. Analytic certainty can only occur after and as a result of attaining knowledge. To view certainty, in any of its senses, as identical to knowledge is, as we said earlier, mistaken.

This view of the relationship between knowledge and certainty generates at least one further important implication that has not escaped philosophers: The doctrine of analytical certainty entails that once such certainty regarding an object of knowledge has been achieved, we can forego prudent fear that we have erred. We are justified in closing argument. According to John Dewey, because knowledge provides us with the right to be sure, it "terminates inquiry." He concludes, "That which satisfactorily terminates inquiry is, by definition, knowledge; it is knowledge because it *is* the appropriate close of inquiry."29 Or, as A. J. Ayer stated, knowledge implies "having the right to be sure."30

Chisholm correctly observes, however, that this "view leads . . . to a kind of dogmatism and infallibilism that is inconsistent with the spirit of free inquiry . . ."31 For this reason one must be cautious in claiming that analytical certainty has been attained. Part of the responsibility incumbent on us when claiming the right to be sure is that we maximize the possibility that if our knowledge claims are in error we can correct our mistakes. We should never close the door to criticism or further inquiry, for to do so would be to contend that we are infallible. In Chisholm's words, " . . .it is one thing to have the right to use a certain proposition in calculating probabilities; it is another thing to have the right to close one's mind to the possibility that one might be wrong."32

At this point readers may feel uncomfortable with the attenuation of analytical certainty that we have just presented. If, as we argue, truth, belief, and sufficiency of evidence yield knowledge, then it is fair to ask how one who attains knowledge could ever be in error. The definition of knowledge arrived at in this chapter seems to make the requirement of free inquiry otiose.

That line of thought misses the point of our argument. The three criteria themselves are not fallible, though people are. Anyone who has attained knowledge fulfilling the three criteria cannot be wrong. Continual inquiry is not important because it can add nothing to a genuine piece of knowledge, nor can it be of any aid to the knower who simply has knowledge in Dewey's sense of the right to be sure. Free inquiry is, nonetheless, crucial for the epistemic *process* because inquiry serves as a check on the inherently fallible nature of humankind. No matter how careful an investigator is in seeing that the criteria for knowledge are adhered to, he or she may err. A physicist may blunder in deciding the point at which sufficiency of evidence occurs. A historian may fail to realize that the work of an important ancient chronicler is apocryphal. Errors like these underscore the frailties of the human mind as an instrument in the search for truth. This does not, however, render useless the concept of knowledge as we have specified it. In trying to say what deserves the name knowledge, we are not dealing with the pragmatics of attaining knowledge but with the criteria that knowledge, *if* attained, must meet. What we have said about analytical certainty deals with the pragmatic question: How do we know what we know? We *know analytically* when error becomes unthinkable. Whether at that point we *have knowledge* must be decided, not by our certainty, but by whether that of which we are analytically certain meets the criteria of truth, belief, and sufficiency. We shall return to these topics in Chapter 5, but for now we are provisionally concluding that the concept of analytical certainty can be rendered useful if it is equated with unthinkability of error. Analytical certainty, like all other varieties of certainty, is a psychological term, not a term of epistemic judgment.

PRAGMATISM AND KNOWLEDGE

Before concluding discussion of our definition of knowledge as justified true belief, it is necessary to examine one further philosophical line of thought that appears to undermine our conception of knowledge. We are referring to recent interest among philosophers in what might be described as a "pragmatist" approach to epistemology, strongly represented by the writings of Richard Rorty. 33

Although Rorty does not specifically take issue with the traditional definition of knowledge as justified true belief, he does question many assumptions regarding the treatment of "truth" that are typically made by philosophers in the Western tradition. In *Consequences of Pragmatism*, Rorty argues for a pragmatic interpretation of truth, one he believes avoids the traditional ontological pitfalls associated with the term. On his analysis, the history of philosophy underscores our inability to come to grips fully with the concept of truth, in large measure because attempts to document how particular utterances correspond to reality have proved futile and have been undermined by continuous philosophical criticism. 34 Given this philosophical stalemate (i.e., our inability to demonstrate when an item of belief may be judged true), Rorty claims that the pragmatists' "suspicion that there is no interesting work to be done in this area" is supported. 35 Therefore, instead of exploring the notion of truth from the standpoint of correspondence to reality, Rorty opts for a *semantic* understanding of the term. Viewed in this way, "truth is just the name of a property which all true statements share." 36 Traditional philosophical questions about truth, then, are for Rorty "pseudo questions."

We wish at the outset of our discussion of this pragmatist viewpoint to emphasize that Rorty is not endeavoring to argue against the concept of truth. He is not, for example, suggesting that truth does not exist:

> When they [pragmatists] suggest that we not ask questions about the nature of Truth or Goodness, they do not invoke a theory about the nature of reality or knowledge or man which says "there is no such thing" as Truth and Goodness. Nor do they have a "relativistic" or "subjectivist" theory of Truth or Goodness. They would simply like to change the subject. They are in a position analogous to that of secularists who urge that research concerning the Nature, or the Will, of God does not get us anywhere. Such secularists are not saying that God does not exist, exactly; they feel unclear about what it would mean to affirm His existence, and thus about the point of denying it. 37

Some hold that Rorty and others have exposed an inherent limitation of attempts to treat truth (as part of the definition of knowledge) in its traditional formulation—a formulation assumed and argued for throughout

38

these pages. To accept this analysis, however, would be to miss the very point of Rorty's argument. As noted above, the pragmatists' discussion of truth merely shifts ground, but it does not specifically refute traditional accounts of truth. In one sense, therefore, pragmatism is not inherently nor entirely incompatible with traditional analytical formulations of knowledge; the questions raised by traditional epistemologists and by pragmatists are simply different. For this reason it would be inaccurate to classify traditional epistemology and pragmatism as opposite poles on a philosophical continuum. Given their different foci, one ought to say that these two approaches to truth and knowledge do not exist on the same continuum.

There is a sense, however, in which our acceptance of the assumptions of traditional Western epistemology must be juxtaposed to Rorty's brand of pragmatism. The rationale for his preferring a pragmatic conception of truth stems from his conclusion that prior historical debate has not gotten us very far toward understanding truth in its traditional ontological and epistemological senses. It seems to us that what such pragmatist philosophers are claiming is that it is unlikely that further debate will enhance our understanding of truth, hence the *question* must be changed.

The theory of rhetorical epistemology that we propose rejects this conclusion. We do not deny that philosophical debate regarding the concept of truth has been complex. It may be true that debate has not resulted in final resolutions of controversial issues, but we take exception to any conclusion that these shortcomings justify discontinuing inquiry. Given the history of philosophy, such terminations of discussion are unjustified. For example, philosophers do not change the subject or cease asking age-old questions in ethics, theology, or political philosophy just because final resolutions of problems in these areas have not been found.

Differences of taste and interest may provoke us to raise different questions, but we ought not put alternative questions into view by closing out inquiry into pertinent but so far unresolved matters. We do not offer our theory of rhetorical epistemology as a final answer to what writers like Rorty feel is unproductive debate. On the other hand, we think it would not be fair or even reasonable to say in advance of the arguments that our theory or any other is predictably unproductive because of the *kinds* of questions raised. Our approach to epistemology—which is grounded in the contention that communication and argument are instrumental in producing knowledge—would characterize Rorty's brand of philosophy (epistemology) as premature at best and impatient at worst. Later, we shall offer an account of reality and truth that attempts to make progress in the areas of epistemology that Rorty assumes are stalemated.

The argument we raise against Rorty and his followers is not a philosophical one, since he does not indict the position that knowledge is justified true belief on *philosophical* grounds, as Gettier does. Our complaint against Rorty's arguments is grounded in aesthetic considerations. Rorty and those of his persuasion feel compelled to reject traditional analyses of truth and justification because they have tired of the dreary trudge that constitutes effort to answer questions from a traditional philosophical standpoint. However, there is at least one consequence of abandoning the traditional approach that we believe argues in favor of continued, concerted efforts in traditional epistemological investigation. The consequence is this: To abandon any inquiry is essentially to cut off argument about the issue. One cannot say with confidence that questions will *remain* unanswerable, however long they may have remained opaque to understanding or may have frustrated attempts to make philosophical or other inroads toward their clarification. We contend that to attain knowledge we must have continued inquiry and debate. If a line of inquiry does not result in final answers, that is hardly damning. It would be more curious, and therefore suspicious, were our theory or any other to gain credit for resolving, in a final sense, a major philosophical issue. Rarely can philosophical theories lay claim to final resolutions. Finality defies the nature of philosophical enterprise. Continued debate and patience are essential to philosophical progress and refinement.

To what we have just said one might reply (and, indeed, Rorty does retort, but only by repeating his initial position) that precisely because a philosophical method fails to answer questions about truth, that method ought to be abandoned in favor of more pragmatically based inquiry. To this we respond that philosophical issues, especially those dealing with the concept of truth, are too important and harbor too many implications for daily conduct of our lives to be dismissed because they become tiresome. As we argued in our Introduction and first chapter, philosophical questions need to be broached in order that we may see the underlying, rational currents of human inquiry and decision making, as well as to identify the problems that confront us routinely. More specifically, practical problems relating to communication and rhetoric justify posing philosophical questions, especially questions pertaining to the concept of truth. The central theme of this book is that we cannot understand, let alone "cope" with, the discourse that surrounds us unless we attend first to the philosophical questions subsumed within theories of truth. Ironically, this is Rorty's argument on behalf of abandoning philosophy!

The importance of raising questions about the truth of discourse is separate from whether or not definitive answers are forthcoming. It is at least

40

arguable that the *processes* of asking and endeavoring to answer are more important than the potential outcome of those processes. It is the process—the employment of the philosophical method, we would say—that displays our rationality and allows us to cope with the world around us. Lack of definitive answers to questions does not lead to the conclusion that the questions themselves are unimportant, as contemporary pragmatists suggest when they argue from the purely historical premise that attempts at answers have proven fruitless to now.

In summary, we are suggesting that pragmatist epistemology: (1) does not logically contradict the traditional conception of knowledge as justified true belief; (2) may be premature, if not impatient, in its quest to overthrow or ignore questions raised in Western philosophy regarding the concept of truth; (3) may be naive in assuming that a lack of resolution to philosophically problematic issues justifies discontinuation of debate; and (4) can itself only be advanced and evaluated through employment of the philosophical method, with the attendant implication that some claims are true because they accurately portray reality.

LANGUAGE AND KNOWLEDGE

We wish now to advance and defend the contention that all knowledge claims are inherently linguistic. We propose that all epistemic judgments, as well as the analyses one might offer of them, are inherently bound up in the relation of knowledge and language. We do not claim that language forms a criterion of knowledge, but we will argue that language is a feature common to all knowledge claims. The point to be highlighted is that questions of knowledge are bound up with questions of language and its use, which is to say, with *rhetoric* broadly conceived. 38

The first evidence that questions of knowledge and questions of language are intimately related is the commonsense fact that language is the vehicle for all intellection. Regardless of the nature of the thinking activity one engages in, a common feature of each process is the presence of language or languages.

But what are the outstanding features of language when employed in the process called thinking? Perhaps the most important quality of all intellection is that it is *propositional*. Examples of propositions are: the sky is blue; the cow jumped over the moon; the product of two and five is ten; $2 + 3 = 5$; if you heat water, it will boil; and $p \supset q$.

The sense in which we are using the word propositional is akin to a familiar usage employed by philosophers in traditional epistemology. Specifically, we hold that a proposition is a postulated meaning-content inextricably associated with a specific declarative sentence or sentences. Individual propositions may be associated with a variety of ordinary language components, including: (1) several articulated sentences that are synonomous; (2) several sentences in different languages or dialects each of whose meaning is synonomous; (3) sentences directly implied; or (4) meaningful expressions that are not in themselves declarative sentences, but which are amenable to translation into declarative sentences. At base, the notion of proposition serves as a basis for the inherently *linguistic* nature of knowledge.

For the specific purposes of our inquiry, it is useful to distinguish among three varieties of propositions, exemplified in the illustrations just presented. First, there are propositions describing what a state of affairs will confirm as true. Second, there are propositions that, while reporting a state of affairs, do so erroneously; these are what we would label false propositions. A third variety reflects relationships among abstract entities, as do mathematical concepts and formal logical systems. Common to these types of propositions is their claim to express the truth about a state of affairs. A further common feature that will be important in later discussion is that epistemic claims will always be in, or be reducible to, one of the three propositional forms we have just identified.

Some readers may object to our inclusion of mathematical and logical symbol systems in a discussion of epistemology, but our contention is that there is good reason for doing so. Although mathematical and logical systems employ special symbolizations rather than ordinary linguistic expressions, such systems are inherently dependent upon and use language. This is demonstrated by the fact that the inception of formal systems of mathematics and logic proceeds *from language* to *special symbolization*. Even the highest mathematical abstractions are conceived in language, explained in language, understood in a language, and expressed in language. A classic example of the process by which higher abstractions proceed in language is found in Plato's *Meno*. There, Socrates elucidates the mathematical relationships among various segments of a square for a supposedly ignorant slave. The elucidation is intended as an argument for the Platonic theory of recollection, but it illustrates how mathematical concepts are acquired via language. Socrates' mathematical proof is accomplished through language, for although Socrates draws in the sand to illustrate the relations he is concerned with, the relations themselves are discovered and rendered analyzable linguistically. The importance of language to the proof is called to our attention by Plato himself when Socrates requires that the slave, to whom the mathematical proof is directed, speak Greek. 39 The implication is manifest; without language the proof could not be expressed let alone understood. It is for just this reason that mathematical treatises necessarily begin with linguistic explanations of their starting points, and the introductions of new mathematical concepts within the texts are presented linguistically. The equation $E = MC^2$ is a vacuous notion when unaccompanied by the linguistic explanation within the pages of the *Special Theory of Relativity*. A cursory inspection of any textbook in higher mathematics, physics, or logic confirms our central claim here: Language is requisite to all modes of intellection. It is reasonable, then, to assert that the propositions of even mathematics and logic are reducible to propositions in ordinary language, and that both systems find their inception in language.

The propositional nature of knowledge highlights our contention that abstractions must initially be encoded and decoded in language before they can be apprehended by or even taught to others. A distinction we wish to make is between "knowing" as a conscious, relfective, and therefore linguistic activity and mere perception, an activity not dependent on language. There may be awareness or perception prior to linguistic coding, but the activities associated with this kind of awareness are not reflective and thus they are not equivalent to knowledge. For example, when a one-year-old infant touches a hot stove for the first time, the child may perceive, that is, experience, pain, even though the perception occurs prior to linguistic coding. But this is not to say that in this experience the child *knows* that "the stove is hot" or knows that it is experiencing pain. To *know* would require the infant to reflect consciously about the experience, an activity requiring language. Thus we say the child learns *from* experience that stoves are hot and that they should not be touched. This knowledge results from languaged relfection on what was originally stimulus-response behavior: touching the stove, experiencing pain, repeating the experience, avoiding stoves in the future. When we speak of knowledge as justified true belief, we refer to a *reflective* (as opposed to a *reflexive*) activity that is dependent on language and that stands in contrast to less sophisticated varieties of cognition and affection.

There is another reservation that a philosopher might have about the claim that all knowledge is inherently linguistic. It has been argued that there is a distinction between *knowing how* and *knowing that*.[40] The claim is that a proposition such as "Smith knows how to roller skate" describes only a *capacity* or skill and not knowledge. As one philosopher says, "Puppies are not classified as dull or bright according to their ability to swim. Nor need *knowing-how* be the result of training or instruction. Puppies know how to swim without having received instruction in the subject."[41] Likewise, a master chef might be said to know how to cook vichyssoise; that is, the chef has a particular skill that makes it possible to tell at precisely what moment the dish is at perfection. The expertise is a matter of taste, we might say, and not a matter of knowledge. It might be contended that such examples prove that there are areas of knowledge where language is not a primary, nor even a major fact of experience.

This argument against the linguistic nature of *knowing how* is plausible at first sight, but it is mistaken for two reasons. First, such innate capacities as a dog's ability to swim, or a monkey's facility in climbing, or even a newborn human's attraction to the breast of its mother can hardly be construed as constituting knowledge in the sense in which the term is generally understood by philosophers or other careful users of language. Rather, we should use the term *skill* to characterize these innate capacities. Such skills are undoubtedly the results of lower biological functions of the stimulus/ response variety. Even in the case of a clever dog on whom we might even bestow the distinction "intelligent," it is doubtful whether such a basic feature of intelligence as self-awareness obtains; that is, it is doubtful that the clever dog knows that it *knows*.

The second reason the argument against the linguistic nature of knowing how is mistaken turns on the fact that some cases of knowing how are really disguised examples of *knowing that*. We may say, for example, that the chef's skill in making vichyssoise or the young person's skill in roller skating are cases of knowing how, and undoubtedly there is a measure of skill involved. However, one's ability to perform these activities, at least initially, is contingent upon possessing a number of propositions constituting "knowledge that." These include, in the case of the skater, knowledge that a certain shaped skate belongs on a certain foot, knowledge that one cannot skate on shag carpeting, and knowledge that for locomotion the skates must be in contact with the skating surface. In all likelihood, these items of knowledge were explained to or observed by the novice skater before he or she ever arrived at the skating rink. Though a skater may need to possess certain innate capacities, such as balance, before becoming a skillful skater, *knowledge that* is also requisite to such skill. And, knowledge that is essentially propositional, and, *a fortiori*, linguistic.

We will have more to say about the relationship of knowledge to language in Chapters 4 and 5 wherein elementary epistemological functions of langue and meaning are detailed. For the present, it is enough to have argued that all knowledge is linguistic. This modest claim is of seminal importance to rhetorical epistemology, since language is the basic feature of rhetoric as well as of knowing.

As we move to discussion of the nature, scope, and function of rhetoric, we caution readers that our claim that rhetoric is of epistemological significance is *not* equivalent to the just-arrived-at contention that knowledge is linguistic. Though the proposition that rhetoric is epistemic issues from the relation between knowledge and language, it involves much more.

NOTES

1. Evander Bradley McGilvary, *Toward a Perspective Realism*, ed. Albert G. Ramsperger (La Salle, Ill.: The Open Court Publishing Company, 1956), p. 11. For a discussion of the solipsistic problem as it relates to rhetoric, see Earl Croasmun and Richard A. Cherwitz, "Beyond Rhetorical Relativism," *Quarterly Journal of Speech*, 68 (1982), 1–16.

2. Robert L. Scott, "On Viewing Rhetoric as Epistemic," *Central States Speech Journal*, 18 (1967), p. 17.

3. The first systematic and extended treatment of epistemological issues is found in Plato's dialogues, especially works such as *Theaetetus*, though his predecessors (most notably Socrates and certain of the Sophists) raised epistemological issues. *Theaetetus* explores a variety of questions in the theory of knowledge, some of which are of direct consequence to rhetorical epistemology and are treated in this book. Perhaps the most accessible exposition of the doctrines in the dialogue is still the commentary of Francis M. Cornford, trans., *Plato's Theory of Knowledge, The Theaetetus and the Sophist of Plato* (London: Routledge and Kegan Paul, 1960).

4. Panayot Butchvarov, *The Concept of Knowledge* (Evanston, Ill.: Northwestern University Press, 1970), p. 25.

5. A. J. Ayer, *The Problem of Knowledge* (Baltimore: Penguin Books, 1956), pp. 31–35; Roderick M. Chisholm, *Perceiving: A Philosophical Study* (Ithaca, N.Y.: Cornell University Press, 1957), pp. 5, 17; Keith Lehrer, *Knowledge* (Oxford: Oxford University Press, 1978), pp. 1–23. Lehrer seeks to establish what the criteria of knowledge are without regard for whether we do, in fact, know anything. In an earlier essay, "Why Not Skepticism?" Lehrer argued that, in fact, we do not know anything, a claim that is, of course, entirely independent of the question of whether or not justified true belief constitutes knowledge or would constitute knowledge *if we had any knowledge*. Lehrer's skeptical position is presented as Chapter 21 in George S. Pappas and Marshall Swain, eds., *Essays on Knowledge and Justification* (Ithaca, N.Y.: Cornell University Press, 1978), pp. 321–63. Lehrer's arguments in favor of skepticism are treated by Dan Turner in the same volume, pp. 364–69.

6. Edmund Gettier, Jr., "Is Justified True Belief Knowledge?" *Analysis*, 23 (1963), 121–23. Gettier's argument was anticipated by Bertrand Russell, *The Problems of Philosophy* (London: Oxford University Press, 1959), pp. 131–32.

7. Keith Lehrer, "The Fourth Condition of Knowledge: A Defense," *Review of Metaphysics*, 24 (1970), 122–28. See also, Lehrer, *Knowledge*; Irving Thalberg, "In Defense of Justified True Belief," *Journal of Philosophy*, 66 (1969), 795–802; and Keith Lehrer and Thomas Paxton, Jr., "Knowledge: Undefeated Justified True Belief," *Journal of Philosophy*, 66 (1969), 225–37.

8. Anthony Quinton, "Knowledge and Belief," *The Encyclopedia of Philosophy*, 1967, Vol. 4, p. 345. Hereafter referred to as "Knowledge and Belief."

9. The laws of thought traditionally include the principle of identity (A is A), the principle of contradiction (A is not not-A), and the principle of excluded middle (everything is either A or not-A). Since classical times, the laws of thought have survived attempts to undermine their validity. The most serious inroads made against them originate in the field of mathematics, where their applicability to theories of arithmetic is questioned; yet, no final argument against their soundness has emerged even here. Moreover, in the realm of discourse, including nonmathematical philosophy, the laws of thought seem incorrigible. See Arthur Pap, "Logic, Mathematics and Knowledge of Nature," in A. J. Ayer, ed., *Logical Positivism* (Glencoe, Ill.: Free Press, 1959), pp. 147–61 and Bertrand Russell, *The Problems of Philosophy* (Oxford: Oxford University Press, 1959), pp. 72, 88, 89.

10. The distinction between "knowledge" and "opinion" is a familar one in ancient Greek philosophy and most prevalent in the works of Plato. It is a distinction we think absolutely essential for the preservation of a nontrivial formulation of the doctrine that rhetoric operates in epistemologically significant ways. As will become clear in later chapters, recent research claims, especially in communication studies, operate to blur the distinction between opinion (belief) and knowledge, a move we believe entails a thoroughgoing skepticism.

11. Quinton, "Knowledge and Belief," p. 356.

12. The apodictic/contingent distinction has had major importance in the development of rhetorical theory, almost since its initial articulation by Aristotle in his *Rhetoric*. We argue in Chapter 6 that its usefulness in distinguishing classes of knowledge is doubtful.

13. Auguste Comte, in providing the first full-blown formulation of positivism, suggested that the only valid knowledge is that generated by science and scientific method and that the only meaningful questions were those which could be empirically verified. Since Comte, the theory has become somewhat attenuated to allow that a meaningful subject of inquiry may be *potentially* verifiable, even if the means to do so are not immediately at hand. Hence, in 1950 the question of whether there are mountains on the dark side of the moon was a meaningful question because we could conceive of a way to verify it potentially even though space technology had not developed a rocket which could actually circumnavigate the moon. Questions such as the existence of God, the justness of capital punishment, or the value of a Van Gogh would, on the positivist's analysis, be cognitively meaningless questions unless one could devise a method of at least potentially verifying them. Of course, one might object to the positivist's critique that regardless of whether such questions can be verified empirically, their truth or falsity is still a legitimate issue: either there is or is not a God, either capital punishment is or is not just, and either Van Gogh's paintings are or are not valuable. This is to say, for example, there might exist an entity with the attributes of the Christian God, whether or not such an entity can be dealt with empirically. Some might even argue that the lack of empirical verifiability is a necessary attribute of being a God. The definitive critique of logical positivism appears in Carl G. Hempel, "Problems and Changes in the Empiricist Criterion of Meaning," *Revue Internationale de Philosophie*, 11 (1950), 41–63. This essay is reprinted in L. Linsky, ed., *Semantics and the Philosophy of Language* (Urbana: University of Illinois Press, 1952).

14. The inception of Greek atomic theory occurs in the fifth century B.C. The originator of the doctrine was Leucippus (a. 450 B.C.), but Democritus (c. 460–370 B.C.) greatly expanded the theory. Greek atomism is, however, best known through its popularization in Lucretius' *De Rerum Natura*. See Cyril Bailey, *The Greek Atomists and Epicurus* (Oxford: The Clarendon Press, 1928).

15. Butchvarov, p. 25.

16. We use the term "evidence" here as elsewhere in its broadest sense, as *that which counts in favor of any proposition* (or of any belief capable of being framed in propositional form).

17. Gettier, n. 6.

18. These two qualifications of the justification criterion assert that justification must be both relevant *and* sufficient or complete *to in fact be justification at all*. The reader can test these qualifications against such Gettier-inspired examples as provided by Lehrer, *Knowledge*, pp. 19–20.

19. Lloyd Bitzer, "Rhetoric and Public Knowledge," in *Rhetoric, Philosophy, and Literature*, ed. Don Burks (West Lafayette, Ind.: Purdue University Press, 1978), p. 91.

20. Roderick Chisholm, *Theory of Knowledge* (Englewood Cliffs, N.J.: Prentice-Hall, 1977), pp. 6–7.

21. See Saint Augustine, *Against the Academicians* (Milwaukee: Marquette University Press, 1942), passim.

22. Bertrand Russell, *An Inquiry Into Meaning and Truth* (New York: W. W. Norton & Co., 1940), p. 166.

23. Henry W. Johnstone, Jr., "Rationality and Rhetoric in Philosophy," *Quarterly Journal of Speech*, 59 (1973), p. 388. See the very similar assertion of A. J. Ayer in his *The Problem of Knowledge*, p. 30.

24. Johnstone, p. 388.

25. Johnstone, p. 388.

26. Stephen Toulmin, Richard Rieke, and Allan Janik, *An Introduction to Reasoning* (New York: Macmillan Publishing Co., 1979), p. 13.

27. Allen Wheelis, *The End of the Modern Age* (New York: Harper and Row, 1971), p. 81.

28. Richard Cherwitz, "Rhetoric as 'A Way of Knowing': An Attenuation of the Epistemological Claims of the 'New Rhetoric,' " *Southern Speech Communication Journal*, 42 (1977), p. 208, n.5.

29. John Dewey, *Logic: The Theory of Inquiry* (New York: Henry Holt & Co., 1938), p. 8.

30. A. J. Ayer, *The Problem of Knowledge*, pp. 31–35.

31. Chisholm, *Theory of Knowledge*, p. 116.

32. Chisholm, *Theory of Knowledge*, p. 118.

33. See, for example, Richard Rorty, *Philosophy and the Mirror of Nature* (Princeton, N.J.: Princeton University Press, 1979). While there have been a number of philosophical accounts of pragmatism offered in this century, Rorty's position seems to be among the most cogent and clear. For another contemporary rendering of pragmatist philosophy, see Nicholas Rescher, *Methodological Pragmatism: A Systems-Theoretic Approach to the Theory of Knowledge* (New York: New York University Press, 1977).

34. This argument is made in Richard Rorty, *Consequences of Pragmatism (Essays: 1972–1980)* (Minneapolis: University of Minnesota Press, 1982), pp. xiii–xlvii.

35. Ibid., p. xiv.

36. Ibid., p. xiii.

37. Ibid., p. xiv.

38. Again we anticipate the definition of rhetoric to be offered in Chapter 3. Yet, the sense in which we employ the term here is rather obvious.

39. Plato, *Meno*, 82a–85d.

40. Butchvarov, p. 17.

41. Butchvarov, p. 17.

RHETORIC

Since the fifth century B.C., theorists have attempted to explain the defining characteristics of the activity called rhetoric. 1 Definitions have not agreed, yet without a precise formulation of what the term means there is no possibility of understanding this activity's relation to the process of acquiring knowledge or to any other kind of human experience. Moreover, failure to define what we mean by rhetoric would leave our inquiry at the mercy of ambiguities associated with the term in both academic and popular usage. Accordingly, in this chapter we shall examine past definitions of rhetoric and formulate what we take to be the most useful meaning of the term. In that process we must deal with such perennial questions as: What is the relationship of rhetoric to the other arts and sciences? What is the relationship of rhetoric to "discourse," "communication," and kindred concepts?

To distinguish among concepts is not to define them; it is only to separate them in exclusionary ways. If we say that a treatise on history is not like a treatise on physics, biology, or mathematics, we shall not by that process uncover the distinctive characteristics of "doing" history. To say what rhetoric is or may be, we shall have to identify the necessary and sufficient qualities that make something *rhetorical*. Few definitions of rhetoric offered in the past have done this. Consequently, we shall sketch the postulates of leading theories of rhetoric but shall direct most of our attention toward contemporary definitions of what rhetoric is, chiefly because only in relatively recent times has the complexity of rhetorical activity been recognized.

DEFINITIONS OF RHETORIC

Among those unfamiliar with the history of rhetoric there exists a host of misconceptions about the subject and about the phenomena associated with it. In English dictionaries one finds as synonyms and characterizing modifiers for *rhetoric* such terms as: "elocution," "drool," "rave," "rhapsody," "bombast," "highfalutin," "style," "grandiloquent," "pompous," "tumid," and "aureate." Indeed, one need only tune to the evening news to hear broadcasters refer to a politican's statement as "mere rhetoric."

That these definitions and connotations are simplistic and often inaccurate comes into view as soon as one explores the definitions and theories of rhetoric offered by serious scholars across the centuries. Since the time of the ancient Greeks, rhetoric as discipline or art has received serious, sympathetic, though often controversial discussion by scholars concerned with the importance of human discourse.

"One of the principal interests of the Greeks was rhetoric,"2 but the earliest literature on the subject did not include treatment of its definition. Although early Sophists taught and wrote about the *practice* of rhetoric, they produced little that can be termed scholarly analysis of the term "rhetoric." This is understandable inasmuch as the Sophists were concerned with rhetoric for pragmatic reasons primarily and theoretical ones only secondarily. As George Kennedy observes, "they were primarily teachers of political excellence whose aims were practical and immediate."3 Because Greek society was "oriented to the spoken word,"4 and because no tradition of theory existed as a point of departure for defining the characteristics of rhetoric, the earliest treatises on the subject were addressed to practitioners of the art and not to those who might speculate about the nature and scope of rhetorical activity.

Our earliest extant treatment of rhetoric's characteristics came into being when the practice of rhetoric gained Plato's attention. That treatment was hardly a flattering one. In *Gorgias*, Plato defined rhetoric as an "art" akin to cookery, having no subject matter rightly its own.5 His analysis of what rhetoric was became a discussion of what it was not: it was not a true art; it did not involve knowledge of the subjects it treated; it was not designed to seek truth; it often made the poorer case seem the better; and those caught up in its practice should abandon their rhetorical studies and pursue more noble enterprises such as philosophy.

Later, in *Phaedrus*, Plato returned to the subject of rhetoric, providing his readers with some notion of what would be required before he would consider rhetoric respectable. In particular, he contended that rhetoric was "the art of enchanting the soul with words."6 Some scholars have concluded from their readings of the *Phaedrus* that Plato conceived of a genuine rhetorical art contrasting with the concept of rhetoric he held earlier in the *Gorgias*, but the consensus, with a few notable exceptions, is that Plato was no friend of rhetoric.7

Plato's contribution to rhetorical theory, though viewed negatively by most rhetoricians, was the first attempt through analysis (as opposed to mere illustration) to sort out what rhetoric was, as well as what it should be. As we shall show later, Plato did contribute to development of rhetorical theory, but it was chiefly by criticism that he advanced the defining process. His pupil, Aristotle, was first to formulate a genuinely cogent definition of rhetoric as art.

Aristotle's rhetorical theory, developed in *Rhetoric*, defined the art as "the faculty of discovering in the particular case what are the available means of persuasion."8 His analysis of communication and the ways in which it occurred led Aristotle to distinguish between scientific and philosophic discourse (which he called dialectic) on the one hand, and the common topics of public discussion and deliberation (rhetoric) on the other.9 For Aristotle, rhetoric was that art employed in the realm of public discussion for the purposes of daily social intercourse, including speeches of praise and blame, politics, and law. It was, in short, the discourse of the common person that constituted rhetoric and distinguished it from other modes of discourse such as demonstration, dialectic, and poetic. While, conceivably, rhetoric and dialectic might be used to argue any question or problem, Aristotle believed that the average Greek citizen was unaccustomed to and unprepared for scientific or philosophical disputation.10 The citizens needed—and actually employed—less technically rigorous discourse.

Although his exposition represented a significant advance over anything that came before it, Aristotle's analysis of rhetoric was incomplete. By restricting rhetoric to the realm of public discussion for the purposes of daily social intercourse, Aristotle excluded many areas of human thought and inquiry involving deliberation and discussion. Political, legal, and epideictic speeches certainly fall within the province of rhetoric, as Aristotle observed, but these modes of discourse are not the only important patterns of thought for informed citizens of the twentieth century. Today, questions of scientific and philosophical importance form a significant portion of our discursive life, and they are not always discussed dialectically. The editorial pages of newspapers and magazines, for example, contain extensive and sometimes technical discourse. Furthermore, a wide variety of issues enter into daily decision making: Should I smoke in light of the relevant scientific evidence? Do nuclear power plants present a clear and present danger? If I take an airplane trip from Los Angeles to New York, what are the probabilities that I will be involved in an accident? Should I support a nuclear freeze? Should the U.S. build an S.S.T.? Is the B-1 bomber a viable weapons system? These and dozens of other semi-technical, moral, and at least quasi-philosophical issues arise in modern citizens' thought and talk. The level of sophistication required for intelligent citizenship casts further doubt on Aristotle's conception that distinctions of kind can be made between popular discourse which he called rhetoric and scholarly discourse which he called dialectic. A good many modern scholars—scientists as well as rhetoricians—now contend that the *methods* of pragmatic discourse are the same in scholarship and popular communication. Those methods, it is often argued today, are fulsomely rhetorical, though there may be differences in complexity and stylistic conventions. It is also clear that Aristotle's definition of rhetoric as discovery of the available means of persuasion was too limited in his own time and is much more so today. We cite only one shortcoming: Aristotle did not account for inquiry through discussion, except insofar as that activity was illustrated by the question-answer process he designated dialectic. This shortcoming renders the Aristotelian definition of rhetoric especially inadequate for our purposes, for it is precisely the role of private and public discourse in pursuit of knowledge that is our subject.

Important advances toward a more comprehensive understanding of rhetoric occurred in the Roman world in the first century B.C. and the first century A.D. The most notable contributions were made by Cicero and Quintilian, two theorists who advanced roughly comparable accounts of the essential features of rhetorical discourse. Cicero viewed rhetoric from the pragmatic standpoint used by the early Sophists; rhetoric was "the art of effective persuasion."[11] But Cicero's explanation of the art went considerably beyond the implications of this terse statement. As Ralph Micken has said, "To Cicero, rhetoric was training for leadership. The product of that training was a man learned in all fields, a philosopher skilled in the arts of speaking."[12] It appeared to Cicero that the arts and products of philosophy, statecraft, and science were socially moribund until given public life and meaning through rhetoric. Rhetoric as interpretation and activation of received knowledge was the very glue of social experience. Cicero even regretted—though he did not remedy the omission—that no one had yet developed a theory of inquiry through discourse. Throughout his writings, Cicero focused on the nature and functions of an *orator's* rhetoric, even while recognizing that rhetorical principles were relevant to informal as well as formal discourse.

The Ciceronian contribution that has most bearing on our present inquiry was his insistence that the functions of philosophy and rhetoric cannot be disentangled. As Richard McKeon has put it:

> The relation of philosophy to rhetoric . . . is the relation of content to expression, and mastery and use of the one depend on competence in the other. . . . Since style is inseparably joined with subject matter, the relation between the two may be discussed in either rhetoric or philosophy; for philosophers face the problems of style, and orators problems of proof.[13]

As McKeon's statement indicates, Cicero posited an interrelationship between philosophical and rhetorical activities, but he did not penetrate beneath their mutual dependence on expression.

Quintilian defined rhetoric much as Cicero did. Rhetoric was "the science of speaking well."[14] Quintilian emphasized the notion of a "good man skilled in speaking." He undertook, in short, to deal with the moral dimensions of rhetoric, but his analysis became circular. He would deny the noble name of "orator" to anyone he was unwilling to credit with "good" ends. As George Kennedy has said, the major fault with Quintilian's attempt to discern how morality relates to rhetoric and rhetorical influence was that "he believes that what is good is self-evident."15 Quintilian saw one of the gaps in traditional definitions of rhetoric—they took no account of the moral qualities of communicative actions; but his mind was so much on the practitioner's skills that he filled the gap with terms, not premises. And, like Cicero's, Quintilian's rhetoric was almost exclusively a rhetoric of oratory.

In sum, both Cicero and Quintilian took notice of philosophical dimensions of rhetorical activity, but neither pursued the topic to the point of clearly defining the interface between philosophy and rhetoric. Moreover, since both focused their attention on the orator, as person, neither was inclined to probe the non-oratorical aspects of rhetoric as art.

With the fall of the Roman Republic soon after Cicero's death in 43 B.C., freedom of speech gradually became more and more constrained. Kennedy believes some of the narrowness in Quintilian's philosophical observations may be attributable to the repressive conditions under which he lived in the first century A.D.16 In any case, it was not until Augustine's conversion to Christianity in 387 A.D. that we can say a fresh attack was made on the problem of defining rhetoric. A practitioner and teacher of sophistic rhetoric, Augustine-turned-Christian quickly addressed the problem of developing a theory of Christian communication. The results were a philosophy of teaching (*The Teacher*) and, over succeeding years, his major rhetorical work, *On Christian Doctrine*. Taken together, these two works constitute a penetrating analysis of Christian teaching and preaching, but, of course, the converted Augustine was no longer interested in rhetoric in general. His major secular contribution was his showing that where rhetoric is dominated by allegiance to authoritative works, interpretation of authorized sources becomes the dominant inventional activity of rhetors. In short, Augustine produced definitive analyses of the subspecies of rhetoric we call homiletics.

The medieval world inherited Augustine's theory of preaching and teaching, Cicero's most narrowly conceived work, *De Inventione*, and the *Rhetorica ad Herennium*, mistakenly attributed to Cicero. From these works and certain sophistic writings, European scholars gradually began to reconstruct an understanding of that ubiquitous set of phenomena the ancients had called rhetoric. The process was slow, partly because the more comprehensive ancient works were recovered only gradually, partly because the Roman tradition of treating rhetoric as an art of legal pleading had little relevance in the post-Roman world, and partly because for several centuries scholarship was predominantly religious rather than secular. Rhetoric was an inherited *term*, but its significance was difficult to see. The conceptual baseline from which medieval thought about rhetoric began can be illustrated from Cassiodorus Senator's *An Introduction to Divine and Human Readings*, written sometime after 551 A.D. for the instruction of monks. It was a compendium of presumably useful, inherited knowledge, a digest and bibliographical guide. Among many other things, the book enumerated the liberal arts, in which the *trivium* consisted of grammar, rhetoric, and logic. Grammar dealt with figures of speech and syntactic matters; rhetoric with molding discourse according to certain organizational and stylistic considerations; and logic with discovery of knowledge and truth. Rhetoric, Cassiodorus wrote:

> Is said to be derived *apo tou rhetorieuein*, that is, from skill in making a set speech. The art of rhetoric, moreover, according to the teaching of professors of secular letters, is expertness in discourse on civil questions. The orator, then, is a good man skilled, as has just been said, in discoursing on civil questions. The function of an orator is speaking suitably in order to persuade. 17

Cassiodorus' work was a significant sourcebook in southern Europe and perhaps beyond in the sixth through eighth centuries. What it said about rhetoric illustrates that to the eighth century at least, the accepted definitions of rhetoric were basically Roman, narrow, and for early medieval Europe largely irrelevant since religious rather than civil questions were the dominant concerns.

Change came when secular communication was given increased importance by growth in commerce and by the emergence of a legal profession. Then, in works of such scholars as Alberic of Monte Cassino, the diluted Ciceronian rhetoric that had been inherited began to be applied to *written* discourse, especially to letter writing. 18 Alberic and his contemporaries unwittingly stumbled on an important discovery: *The principles of rhetoric transcend the communicative forms employed in a given case*. Whatever rhetoric was, it now emerged that it was characteristic of both written and spoken discourse and alternative forms thereof.

The intermodal nature of rhetoric was only implicitly argued for by rhetoricians such as Alberic. It was suggested rather than developed as a theme; hence, at the dawn of the Renaissance, rhetoric remained an ill-developed concept.

It is dangerous to generalize about the status of rhetoric in the Renaissance. A minor reason is that students of the period disagree about when the Renaissance began and ended. A more serious reason is that scholars of the Renaissance period held quite different views of the nature of rhetoric and of its significance. To suggest the poles of thought about rhetoric in this period, we shall cite Giovanni Battista Vico (1668–1774) as a spokesman for the Italian Humanist tradition of the fourteenth to eighteenth centuries and Petrus Ramus (1515–1572) as a representative of an essentially anti-rhetorical stream of thought influential in northern Europe and the British Islands. We choose Vico as an example because there has been a new twentieth-century surge of interest in his conceptions of rhetoric, philosophy, science, and history; and we choose Ramus because of the influence he had on the organization of late Renaissance education. Of Vico, Samuel Ijsseling has written:

> Language has a prominent role in the realization of the state and politics, religion and culture, the moral order and legal system, and is the design of modern science. According to Vico the human spirit (*ingenium*) did not form language, but was formed by it. Man is assigned the task of passing on and refining language: the world in which we now live has been unlocked by the mythical, poetic and later the objective, rational word. Outstanding speakers are those able to preserve, develop and transform this world. . . . Vico made a plea for rhetoric and formulated a number of objections against the Cartesian ideal of science and education. 19

As was the case with many Italian Humanists, Vico saw in philological exploration of language an avenue to discernment of how humans *discover*; the rationalism of Descartes could only confirm or disconfirm linkages among human discoveries. Rhetoric, for Vico, and a number of Humanists, was the study of human expression through study of language, the repository of human wisdom.

Of course, humanism in the strong form expressed by Vico lost out in the competition among seminal ideas in the gradually emerging scientific age. Petrus Ramus, a teacher of rhetoric and logic who also claimed to be a Humanist, thought of rhetoric in a way more congenial to emerging Western philosophy and science. Ramus insisted that rhetoric and logic (hence philosophy) must be distinct and separate arts. Logic he assigned the functions of discovery and judgment and rhetoric the function of presentation. Rhetoric was thus sundered from any but aesthetic and ornamenting concerns; and since his educational reforms were popular in northern Europe and England, equation of rhetoric with style became normative. 20

A major point needs to be made concerning the status of rhetoric in the Renaissance. Whether rhetoric, as a concept, was associated with philology as in the hands of the Italian Humanists or was confined to the function of presentation as in the hands of Ramus, the effect was to associate rhetoric with *style*. This association is still reflected in several of the defining synonyms we have quoted from modern dictionaries.

It was not until the ascendancy of science and scientific method that significant rigor was introduced into the quest for a definitive explanation of the concept "rhetoric." Rhetoricians and some philosophers then placed emphasis on the new science of mind. Douglas Ehninger fittingly labeled the seventeenth and eighteenth centuries as an era of "psychological" concern with rhetoric. 21

In philosophy and science Francis Bacon was a major transition figure in the movement of thought from Renaissance Humanism to modern scientism. He reflected emerging theories of faculty psychology when he defined the art of rhetoric as the application of "reason to imagination for the better moving of the will." 22 His vision of rhetoric as an art of adapting communication to subject matter and to audience in order to achieve influence was developed in detail by George Campbell, avowedly drawing on Bacon, Locke, and Hume for psychological concepts. 23

Campbell reflected his allegiance to the traditions of faculty psychology and to the new theories of associative processes in *Philosophy of Rhetoric,* where he equated *eloquence* with *rhetoric,* defining eloquence as "that art or talent by which the discourse is adapted to its end." 24 His aim was to discern the processes by which such adaptation was achieved in "the grand art of communication, not of ideas only, but of sentiments, passions, dispositions, and purposes." 25 To "canvass those principles in our nature to which the various attempts are adapted" would, he said, "bring us into a new country, of which, though there have been some successful incursions occasionally made upon its frontiers, we are not yet in full possession." 26 The "new country" was the territory of psychological analysis of the cognitive, affective, and conative processes subsumed under the general study of "the nature of the human mind, and more especially in the principles of the imagination." 27 As Vincent Bevilacqua has observed,

> The new rhetoric of the eighteenth century . . . while embracing many elements common to the Ciceronian, Ramian, and stylistic patterns, broke sharply with antecedent rhetorical theory in both treatment and emphasis. The result was an experimentally oriented rhetoric that further reformed historical views of invention, arrangement, and style on a basis comparable to that sustaining the reformation of philosophy inspired by Bacon and Locke nearly a century earlier. 28

For a variety of reasons the conception of rhetoric that emerged from the eighteenth century and came to dominate nineteenth-century thinking was a conception of rhetoric as *management* of previously discerned ideas—psychologically grounded management of verbal structures for the purpose of evoking emotional and logical responses in readers or auditors. Rhetorical *invention*, classically considered under such headings as commonplaces, *topoi*, enthymeme, example, and syllogism, substantially disappeared from consideration in what was called rhetoric. Discovery of general ideas and of truth was treated as the business of logic or, more broadly, of the scientific method.

It is plain that such conceptions tended to posit that *all* knowledge and intellection are governed by experience and sense data—an assumption we shall criticize in later chapters. In their ultimate forms these conceptions produced radical limitations on rhetorical concerns in the nineteenth century. Alexander Bain (1818–1903) was the Scottish logician/rhetorician who had widest influence in England and the United States during the latter half of the nineteenth century. His definition of rhetoric held sway in theory of writing until the time of World War I; he wrote:

> The direct bearing of Rhetorical art is, of course, not Invention, but Correctness; in other words, polish, elegance, or refinement. It deals with curable defects and faults, and with such merits as can be secured by method. It aids, without superseding, the intuitive perception of what is excellent in a literary performance. 29

This general view of the scope and functions of rhetoric dominated Anglo-American thought until such specialists in oral composition as Charles H. Woolbert and James A. Winans challenged it on psychological grounds, and their contemporaries began to resuscitate classical theories. 30 Even so, in theory of writing Bain's definition remained widely accepted.

To assume that communication has no inventional function, no status in processes of discovery, is to assume that the objective character of reality is umproblematic, requiring little or no refinement, interpretation, and discussion. That there *is* a problem here was recognized by David Hume in an Appendix to *A Treatise of Human Nature*:

> Having thus loosened all our particular perceptions, when I proceed to explain the principle of connection, which binds them together, and makes us attribute to them a real simplicity and identity, I am sensible that my account is very defective. . . . If perceptions are distinct existences, they form a whole only by being connected together. But no connections among distinct existences are ever discoverable by human understanding. 31

Most eighteenth-, nineteenth-, and early twentieth-century rhetoricians assumed that discourse has nothing to do with the connecting and attributing processes that "Hume's problem" isolated. The terms in which we pose that problem throughout this book are suggested by this question: When and how are our daily experiences and sensory perceptions brought to the state that we are willing to call "knowledge"? We will argue that only when data of experience are subjected to critical analysis and debate are they deserving of the designation "knowledge."

Against the definition of rhetoric worked out by modern rhetoricians and philosophers, we would lodge a further complaint. In their attempts to accommodate developments in science, these scholars focused on *processes* rather than defining what rhetoric *is*. They provided excellent clues to how rhetoric *operates*, but they did not search for the most basic and intrinsic *qualities* of rhetoric. This is partly because most students of rhetoric in the last three centuries were more interested in the practice of rhetoric than in rhetoric's theoretical and philosophical roots.

Though many definitions of rhetoric have been offered in the twentieth century, a minority have come from philosophically inclined rhetoricians and rhetorically inclined philosophers. The minority have sought to locate the attributes or qualities that distinguish rhetorical *discourse* from other modes of influence and transmission. They have focused on the *discursive components* of rhetorical discourse. Even so, a good many such definitions designate rhetorical phenomena as phenomena chiefly of language and symbols. In fact, I. A. Richards, a pioneer theorist of the twentieth century, argued that rhetoric is "a study of misunderstanding and its remedies."32 The contemporary definitions we shall now detail reflect this pattern of thought, though they come closer than earlier definitions to isolating uniquely rhetorical features of discourse.

Donald C. Bryant is a contemporary rhetorician who has attempted to locate attributes of discourse that are inherently rhetorical. He originally defined rhetoric as "the rationale of informative and suasory discourse."33 Later Bryant reformulated his definition to recognize that it is not *discourse itself*, but certain elements or *constituents of discourse* that become potentially persuasive and informative. In his altered version, Bryant suggested that rhetoric is "the rationale of informative and suasory *in* discourse."34

Bryant's effort to locate the qualities that render discourse rhetorical is not without problems. First, Bryant's definition does not directly specify the rhetorical properties of communication. The notions of suasory and informative do not identify specific components of discourse; they name broad characterizations of the *intent* and/or *effect* of discourse. In short, Bryant's definition hinges upon such problematic concepts as a speaker's motives and an audience's reactions. For that reason, the definition is reminiscent of earlier statements that focused on ends, processes, and psychological constituents pursuant to and assumed in rhetorical action. His definition falls short of isolating necessary and sufficient properties that make discourse rhetorical. One might attempt suasion but fail to persuade. Would the discourse still be rhetorical?

A more specific problem with Bryant's definition evolves out of his distinction between information-giving and persuasion. Not only is it difficult to determine the distinguishing features of each, whether through an analysis of a speaker's intent or an audience's response, but such distinctions may be unnecessary. The literature in recent rhetorical theory provides ample grounds for suggesting that the difference between what is informative and what is suasory is negligible. Richard M. Weaver, for example, contended that all language is sermonic; that is, all discourse entails communication of values, beliefs, and judgments because of its reliance on language.35 It is certainly difficult to conceive of purely objective, neutral, or scientific language devoid of persuasive overtones or undertones. In our view, Bryant's definition fails to explain *what* the rationale of informative and suasive in discourse *is*, and it implies a perhaps impossible bifurcation between suasion and information-giving.

The definition of rhetoric espoused by Karl Wallace illustrates another kind of discursive explanation. On his analysis, rhetoric deals "with the substance of discourse, as well as with structure and style."36 According to Wallace, rhetors and rhetoricians engage in the activity of giving and appraising "good reasons."37 But while substance, style, structure, and good reasons are no doubt discursive constituents of whatever one would call rhetorical, these may not be defining characteristics of rhetoric. The presence of substance, style, and structure does not tell us why a given specimen of discourse is rhetorical. There are many kinds of human interaction and activity that possess substance, style, and structure but which it would seem odd to designate as *rhetorical*. Music, for instance, may be seen as having substance, style, and structure. But the substance, style, and structure of music are certainly of an order different from what appears in discourse. It remains, then, to locate the ingredients or forms specified by each of Wallace's three criteria and to assess what it is about them that renders discourse rhetorical.

One of the more encompassing and systematic definitions of rhetoric was presented by Ehninger. Arguing, after Burke, that rhetoric "is the art of symbolic inducement," Ehninger noted that rhetoricians should study "all of the ways in which men may influence each other's thinking and behavior through the strategic use of symbols."38 We are sympathetic with Ehninger's suggestion that rhetoric involves manipulation of symbols, but his definition suffers from some of the same problems riddling previous treatments of the concept. To begin with, symbols are not unique ingredients of rhetorical discourse. Unmistakably, symbols function at times in non-persuasive ways. Coercion, for example, may use symbols in order to instigate action, but coercion is frequently not discursive, as when it assumes the form of direct, blatant force. Coercion forces or mandates; its principal character is not that it convinces and persuades.

Second, Ehninger's definition, like many others, rests on a determination of motives and intent. Thus, although we do not disagree with Ehninger's contention that rhetoric may include attempts to convey information, instigate action, or influence belief, we insist that these are not practically or conceptually useful *defining* qualities. They only name symptoms, describe a speaker's motives for engaging in something to be called rhetoric, and identify effects that such efforts may have on an audience. A complete definition must identify the ways symbols function uniquely in whatever we call rhetorical discourse. Merely to conclude that rhetoric uses symbols is not to isolate the basic constituents of symbolic manipulation that indicate an enterprise is rhetorical and not otherwise. Information, action, and influence are entailed by rhetorical communication, but they are not paradigmatic of the art or the action.

A final representative definition is that presented by Chaim Perelman. For him, rhetoric includes only the "discursive techniques" for obtaining a "mind's adherence."39 Our objection to this view is not that the definition is incorrect; it is simply incomplete. The phrase "discursive techniques" is vague, alluding to, but not indicating what are the discursive characteristics of what is to be called rhetoric. Furthermore, the contention that rhetoric seeks the adherence of minds is less than definitional. Like previously discussed qualities associated with discourse, "adherence of minds" refers only to a symptom of the rhetorical process; it does not advance definitional attributes. In other words, "adherence of minds" provides an answer to the question: What is *involved* in rhetoric? But it does not address the more fundamental question: What *is* rhetoric?

The preceding pages provide a cursory inspection of the history of definitions of rhetoric. This is not to be confused with a history of rhetorical theory—a topic beyond the scope of this book. Each epoch's definitions of rhetoric have attempted to correct deficiencies assumed to exist in prior treatments. There have been progressive refinements and increased philosophical sophistication. Yet, even the best of the major definitions so far proposed fail to identify the fundamental constituents that set rhetoric apart from other products of human activity. Each definition suffers from one or more of the following problems:

1. Failure to accommodate collective activities of practitioner, critic, and theorist;
2. Failure to recognize that rhetorical discourse may occur in either written or oral mediums;
3. Isolation of symptoms, processes, motives, and ends of rhetoric to the neglect of necessary and sufficient features;
4. Failure to recognize inventional as well as managerial aspects of the concept;
5. Failure to recognize the diverse areas of human thought and inquiry where rhetoric can inform discussion and deliberation;
6. Presupposing that ethical malpractice occurs in all rhetorical acts;
7. Exhibiting overriding concern with showing rhetoric's relationship to other arts and sciences or definition by exclusion rather than inclusion; and/or
8. Failure to recognize that principles of rhetoric transcend the modes of rhetoric employed in given cases.

A REFORMULATION OF THE DEFINITION OF RHETORIC

Having underscored the failures of traditional definitions to locate rhetorical features of discourse, we propose an alternative definition. Our definition is advanced as an extension of previous thinking. We begin with the assumption that persuasion is a vital feature of discourse that can reasonably be called rhetoric. This claim is justified in part by the general historic agreement that persuasion is the ultimate aim of rhetorical discourse and in part by the general, modern agreement that language is itself fundamentally "sermonic." Our definition is sympathetic to and consistent with most major treatments of the term, but our aim is to frame a definition that is responsive to the eight problems previously listed. The most basic of these problems is failure to expose the necessary and sufficient constituents of rhetorical acts. Its solution is essential if a definition of rhetoric is to have philosophical viability and relative accuracy.

The contemporary theorists who have come closest to detailing the rhetorical attributes of discourse focused their definitions on such processes and intentions as suasion and inducement. On that kind of analysis, what makes a given specimen of discourse rhetorical is its potential to evoke persuasion or, more broadly expressed, symbolic inducement. These features of rhetoric, however, are only symptomatic and not indicative of what rhetoric *is*. To uncover the basis for such symptoms or more accurately to specify the discursive components responsible for potentially persuasive dimensions of rhetoric, we offer the following definition: *Rhetoric is the art of describing reality through language.*

Under this definition, the study of rhetoric becomes an effort to understand how humans, in various capacities and in a variety of situations, describe reality through language. To act rhetorically is to use language in asserting or seeming to assert claims about reality. At the heart of this definition is the assumption that what renders discourse potentially persuasive is that a rhetor (e.g., a speaker or writer) implicitly or explicitly sets forth claims that either differ from or cohere with views of reality held by audiences (e.g., a specific scholarly community, a reader of fiction, or an assembly of persons attending a political rally).

It deserves special notice that rhetoric is *not* herein defined by the *accuracy* of the claims about reality. Nor is rhetoric contingent on the rhetor's *intent* or the subsequent *effect* and *impact* of his or her discourse. Not all rhetorical messages portray reality accurately. They are nonetheless explicitly or implicitly assertive. Many examples of discourse *purport* to describe reality but do so inaccurately. Such discourse may even entail innumerable ethical malpractices. But as such cases attest, the *potential* for persuasion does not derive exclusively from accuracy. On the contrary, the potential for inducement rests upon the claims' *consistency* with views maintained by the audience. A rhetor who in describing the political world violates the audience's expectancies, failing to espouse an interpretation of reality in tune with theirs, may realize a less than satisfactory rhetorical response; in fact he or she may dissuade rather than persuade. Conversely, a speaker or writer who depicts reality in harmony with an audience's expectations may be able to produce a favorable response, eliciting adherence. The advice echoed in most speech textbooks that a rhetor should begin with what is known or accepted in order to persuade or convert a less than sympathetic audience issues well from our definition of rhetoric. All of this is to suggest that *accuracy* of description is not an essential feature of rhetoric.

Our conception of rhetoric is not predicated on identification of intent or effect. Whenever a rhetor has described reality through language, the discourse is necessarily rhetorical. There are many examples of discourse where without conscious intent a speaker or writer implicitly or explicitly described reality and thereby attained potential for persuasion. A poet or writer of fiction may produce potentially rhetorical work without intending to do so. Good illustrations of this are found in poems recited by protesters during the Vietnam War. Some of the poets' intentions seem to have been to entertain or please, but to the extent that their work made statements that were pertinent to the struggle in Indochina the work was open

62

to rhetorical use. There are also many instances in which a speaker or writer had persuasive intentions but, because of failure to use available means of persuasion or because of overriding situational constraints, the creator's desired effect went unrealized. To call either kind of discursive effort nonrhetorical because the outcomes were other than those intended is to oversimplify. The efforts were rhetorical because they were descriptions of reality through language; whether those descriptions evoked responses hoped for by their creators cannot alter the works' internal, assertive character. Effect and impact are not definitional criteria for rhetoric. Descriptions of reality may "fail" or "succeed," but they are rhetorical in either case if in substance and form they have the *potential* to persuade or induce. That potential resides in linguistic description.

A familiar, specific example will clarify our distinction further. It is agreed by all that John Milton's *Paradise Lost* was created as *both* theological persuasion and as a fictive work of imagination. The poem asserts as reality a struggle between good and evil in the universe. The struggle, however, is portrayed as personalized warfare between Satan and God. In its own time, the theological quality of the poem could scarcely be missed by any reader, but in our own day many readers lack knowledge of the theological issues and so approach the poem as a wholly imaginative portrayal of a fictive world. The major point we wish to make is that *Paradise Lost* was and remains a rhetorical work because its substance and form are potentially persuasive—whether a given modern reader recognizes those potentialities or not.

To summarize, whenever humans include within discourses (whether scientific, political, philosophical, or other) characterizations of reality asserted through language, there is the possibility of persuasion. Under the terms of the definition we propose, such characterizations of reality should be called rhetorical. To use Bryant's locution, describing reality by means of language is *the rationale* of suasory discourse. Describing reality through language is the discursive feature that is paradigmatic of rhetorical action. Such description is not a symptom of rhetorical discourse; it is *the* defining feature.

Some may think our proposed definition of rhetoric is too broad. It includes a host of human enterprises within the domain of rhetoric. This we grant, replying first that potentially persuasive phenomena simply are pervasive and that any attempt to categorize such phenomena according to their forms or the situations in which they occur evades answering the fundamental question: What *is* rhetoric? Second, we think it is unsound to assume that rhetoric is a limited enterprise, characteristic of only a few human activities. In our judgment rhetoric, or persuasive potential, is an integral part of nearly all verbal activity. As several philosophical theorists of rhetoric have pointed out, whenever we describe, assert, discuss, deliberate, or debate we make claims, and those claims have at least potential persuasive qualities. Inducement may not be the primary objective of all our remarks about what is, but the potential for inducement is almost always present. Scientists, historians, philosophers, and others are engaged in rhetorical activity to whatever extent they assert or imply that reality is as they say it is. This being so, we contend that any discourse that invites or demands its audience to see the world in a certain specified way is potentially persuasive and therefore must be denominated rhetorical.

It follows from our analysis that the job of a rhetorician is to investigate both the pragmatic aspects and the philosophical implications of discourse purporting to describe reality. A rhetorical *critic* would examine the techniques and strategies employed by speakers or writers in their descriptions of reality. A rhetorical *theorist* would explore psychological, ethical, epistemological, ontological, and other implications of characterizations of reality. It is an advantage of our definition of rhetoric that the tasks of practitioners, critics, and theorists are all anticipated within the definition.

Our position is that need exists for rhetorical analysis of many human, verbal enterprises. We do not imply, however, that only rhetorical analysis is pertinent in studying discourse. We can illustrate the role of rhetorical analysis *vis à vis* other kinds of analysis by considering rhetorical study of scientific discourse.

A rhetorical investigation of scientific discourse would not necessarily be a scientific analysis. Each science has its own subject matter, requiring specific training and expertise if it is to be examined on scientific grounds. A rhetorician looking at scientific discourse would not be competent to discuss critically, say, an astronomical theory or the mechanics of a sophisticated scientific method. He or she would be capable of assessing the pragmatic and philosophical potentialities of the ways scientists describe reality through language, and the persuasive potentialities of these invitations for response from the scientific community or any other community into whose presence the discourse might come. Rhetoric, as we define it, is not synonomous with science, but rhetoric has a role in science as enterprise. We shall discuss this point in greater detail later, but for now it is enough to say that rhetoric invites a kind of thought and inquiry that is distinct from other forms of thought and inquiry, although those other activities employ rhetoric insofar as they describe reality through language.

To present more fully the implications of our definition of rhetoric, we wish to consider other terms often used synonomously and interchangeably with rhetoric. Two of the more frequently used terms are "communication" and "discourse." By saying that rhetoric is describing reality through language, we can stipulate several important differences among rhetoric, communication, and discourse. To begin with, communication is a process-oriented concept; it implies the transmission of messages among people, through written, oral, or nonverbal mediums. We agree with David Mortensen that "communication occurs whenever persons attribute significance to message-related behavior."40 In other words, the concept communication encompasses all verbal and nonverbal messages resulting in at least a minimal level of awareness. Compared with "rhetoric," "communication" is the broader term. The phrase "rhetorical communication" can make sense precisely because "rhetorical" modifies "communication," indicating that rhetoric is the species and communication is the genus.

The term "discourse" usually names a subset of communication. That is to say, discourse is not a kind of communication but a part of some types of communication. All communication is composed of messages, but discourse refers to but one kind of message. Discursive messages, for example, may be contrasted and compared to nonverbal messages; both are kinds of communication to the extent that people attribute significance to them. In addition, both nonverbal and discursive messages may have the same designata; that is, both may represent the same objects, ideas, and relationships. However, their manners of expression differ; nonverbal communication exploits cues and gestures, but discourse uses spoken and written words.

As we have defined the term, *rhetoric* refers to a particular kind of discourse. In the phrase "rhetorical discourse," the term rhetoric indicates the kind or type of discourse spoken of. Rhetorical discourse is whatever discourse describes reality through language, but there are kinds of discourse in which reality is not described. Much fiction, for example, does not purport to describe reality. The same could be said of much poetry. Where this is true, the words "poetic" and "fictive" become appropriate modifiers of the term *discourse*. There are, however, many instances where poetic and fictive discourses do, in whole or in part, describe reality, and to that extent *rhetorical* also becomes an appropriate modifying term, as when we are inclined to refer to a poem or novel as "rhetorical poetry" or "rhetorical fiction."

Some readers may be uncomfortable with our exclusion of nonverbal messages from the messages we would call rhetorical. Our response is that nonverbal "languages" cannot *in and of themselves* be rhetorical unless and until the relationships among extralinguistic phenomena for which nonverbal symbols stand are translated into words. Then the verbal translations gain rhetorical status if they allegedly describe reality. To the extent that nonverbal cues make us think and then talk or write, their outcomes can be rhetorical. As sheer conditioned response or as a signal identifying or emphasizing data or conditions yet to be linguistically formulated, nonverbal phenomena cannot describe reality. Once given linguistic transformation, their meanings can become rhetorical in the sense in which we apply the term. At this juncture we leave open the question, What proportion of nonverbal elements are transformed into language and eventually become rhetorical?

Before leaving the definition of rhetoric, it is desirable to anticipate several of our arguments in later chapters regarding the relationship of rhetoric to dialectic. The rhetoric/dialectic distinction has been an important topic of discussion since the classical era. Theorists have attempted to explain this relationship in numerous ways, and there have been at least three schools of thought: the view of rhetoric as less rigorous, hence subservient to dialectic;[41] the view that rhetoric is the counterpart of dialectic;[42] and the view that rhetoric, as the study of actuality rather than possibility, is a particular application of dialectic.[43] Common to each position is the contention that dialectic peculiarly involves the practice of defining and examining statements to establish logical acceptability, as by question, answer, and comparison of opposites. In one of the most thorough expositions of this concept, Mortimer Adler views dialectic as a rationally, rather than empirically, sustained enterprise.[44] Echoing this interpretation, Richard Weaver suggested that: "Dialectic is that stage which defines the subject satisfactorily with regard to the *logos*, or the set of propositions making up some coherent universe of discourse; and we can therefore say that a dialectical position is established when its relation to an opposite has been made clear. . . ."[45]

The definition of rhetoric we have chosen implies a relationship between rhetoric and dialectic that is not captured in any of the three schools of thought just cited. We said that rhetoric describes reality through language, so we cannot accommodate the position that rhetoric is subservient to dialectic, nor the positions that rhetoric is a counterpart or an application of dialectic. On the contrary, we must claim that dialectic is a kind or form of rhetoric. We shall later argue that dialectic is the purest form of rhetoric, owing to the fact that it is intentionally a faithful description of reality through language. *Intentionally* and *faithful* are key terms here. Rhetorical discourse can occur without those attributes, as when a speaker or writer purports to describe reality, but the description is accidentally or deliberately unfaithful to reality as the rhetor understands it.

We reserve the phrase *dialectical rhetoric* for those descriptions of reality that are presented as intentionally faithful to the rhetor's own conception of reality. This conception squares with the widely accepted meanings of dialectic advanced by Adler, Weaver, and others who hold that dialectic involves definition, question and answer, and juxtapositions of opposites. Where we differ from Adler and the others is in insisting that because dialectic involves descriptions of reality through language, it consists of statements with at least a potential for persuasion and hence dialectic must be considered a rhetorical enterprise.

CONCLUSION

We have examined leading definitions of rhetoric and have proposed a reformulation of the concept. We suggested that there has been a general failure to locate the necessary and sufficient constituents of what can fairly be called rhetorical activity. We have proposed to define rhetoric as *description of reality through language*. In defense of this definition we claim that it solves or avoids eight problems not resolved by prior investigation. We contend that our definition:

1. Accommodates not only the practitioner of the art, but the theorist and critic as well;
2. Recognizes that rhetoric may be transmitted through either written or oral mediums;
3. Instead of isolating symptoms, processes, motives, and ends of rhetoric as definitive, it identifies purported description of reality through use of language as the definitive feature of the art;
4. Presumes that use of rhetoric requires inventional as well as managerial activity because to describe reality through language it is necessary to search for the most substantive bases on which to rest claims and to search for the best methods of their expression;
5. Recognizes the role of rhetoric in all human thought and inquiry involving discussion and deliberation, without implying that rhetorical activity is identical with thought and inquiry;
6. Makes clear that inaccuracy and ethical malpractice, while often present in rhetorical discourse, do not definitively characterize rhetorical activity;
7. Permits one to discern relationships among rhetoric and other knowledge-seeking enterprises without positing that such connections are primary, definitional attributes of rhetoric per se; and
8. Makes manifest that principles of rhetoric transcend principles that govern particular modes of rhetoric employed in given cases.

NOTES

1. For a lucid discussion of the emergence of classical rhetoric, see James J. Murphy, *A Synoptic History of Classical Rhetoric* (New York: Random House, 1972), pp. 3–15.

2. George Kennedy, *The Art of Persuasion in Greece* (Princeton, N.J.: Princeton University Press, 1963), p. 3.

3. Kennedy, p. 13.

4. James L. Golden, Goodwin F. Berquist, and William E. Coleman, *The Rhetoric of Western Thought* (Dubuque, Iowa: Kendall/Hunt Publishing Company, 1976), p. 21.

5. Plato. *Gorgias*, 462e–465d.

6. Plato, *Phaedrus*, 261a.

7. The majority view is represented by, among others, Oscar L. Brownstein, "Plato's *Phaedrus*: Dialectic as the Genuine Art of Speaking," *Quarterly Journal of Speech*, 51 (1965), 392–98 and Everett Lee Hunt, "Plato and Aristotle on Rhetoric and Rhetoricians," *Studies in Rhetoric and Public Speaking in Honor of James Albert Winans* (New York: Appleton-Century-Crofts, 1925), p. 42. Among those who argue that Plato held an acceptable form of rhetoric to be both possible and desirable is James W. Hikins, "Plato's Rhetorical Theory: Old Perspectives on the Epistemology of the New Rhetoric," *Central States Speech Journal*, 32 (1981), 160–76.

8. Aristotle, *Rhetoric*, 1355b.

9. Aristotle, *Rhetoric*, 1354a.

10. Aristotle, *Rhetoric*, 1356a–1357b.

11. Cicero, *De Inventione*, I.5.

12. Ralph A. Micken, "Introduction," to *Cicero on Oratory and Orators*, trans. or ed. J. S. Watson (Carbondale: Southern Illinois University Press, 1970), p. xiv.

13. Richard McKeon, "Introduction" to Marcus Tullius Cicero, *Brutus, On The Nature of the Gods, On Divination, On Duties* (Chicago: University of Chicago Press, 1950), p. 23.

14. The phrase *bene dicendi scientia* (a knowledge of speaking well) is a bit misleading. The modern reader may take *scientia* to imply the exactitude of science. Likewise, *bene*, though usually indicating a dimension of moral or ethical goodness, is also misleading within the context in which Quintilian uses it. Quintilian wrote about rhetoric from the position of a chair financed by the Roman government; the "good man" in Quintilian's eyes would likely be the ideal Roman public official. Needless to say, many Roman citizens would have other ideas about what it meant to exercise "a knowledge of speaking well." See, for example, George A. Kennedy, *Classical Rhetoric and Its Christian and Secular Traditions From Ancient to Modern Times* (Chapel Hill, University of North Carolina Press, 1980), pp. 100–13. Hereafter referred to as *Classical Rhetoric*.

15. George Kennedy, *Quintilian* (New York: Twayne Publishers, 1969), p. 125.

16. Ibid., pp. 125, 127.

17. *Divine and Human Readings*, trans. L. W. Jones (New York: Octagon Books, 1966), pp. 148–49.

18. See Kennedy, *Classical Rhetoric*, pp. 185–87.

19. *Rhetoric and Philosophy in Conflict* (The Hague: Martinus Nijhoff, 1976), p. 58.

20. For a cogent analysis of Ramus and his impact on rhetorical theory, see Walter J. Ong, *Ramus: Method, and the Decay of Dialogue* (Cambridge: Harvard University Press, 1958).

21. Douglas Ehninger, "On Systems of Rhetoric," in *Contemporary Rhetoric: A Reader's Coursebook*, ed. Douglas Ehninger (Glenview, Ill.: Scott, Foresman and Company, 1972), p. 51.

22. Hugh C. Dick, ed., *Selected Writings of Francis Bacon* (New York: Modern Library, 1955), p. 309.

23. See George Campbell, *The Philosophy of Rhetoric* (Carbondale, Southern Illinois University Press, 1963).

24. Ibid., p. 1.

25. Ibid., p. xlix.

26. Ibid., p. 1–1i.

27. Ibid., p. xlix.

28. Vincent M. Bevilacqua, "Philosophical Influences in the Development of English Rhetorical Theory: 1748–1783," *Proceedings of the Leeds Philosophical and Literary Society, Literary and Historical Section*, Vol IXX, Part IV, p. 192.

29. Alexander Bain, *English Composition in Rhetoric* (London: Longmans, Green, 1888), pp. x–xi. Originally published in 1866.

30. See James Winans, *Public Speaking: Principles and Practices* (New York: Century Company, 1917) and Charles Woolbert, *The Fundamentals of Speech* (New York: Harper and Row, 1920). For a discussion of Winans and Woolbert, see William P. Sandford and W. Hays Yeager, *Principles of Effective Speaking* (New York: T. Nelson and Sons, 1930); see especially p. 263.

31. Antony Flew, ed., *David Hume on Human Nature and Understanding* (New York: Collier Books, 1962), p. 284. George Campbell in *Philosophy of Rhetoric*, Bk. II, ch. 7 sought to resolve the problem by saying that "a particular idea often serves as the sign of a whole class" and, similarly, words as signs may come to "represent" classes of particulars, all by "abstruse and dark" operations of the mind.

32. I. A. Richards, *The Philosophy of Rhetoric* (London: Oxford University Press, 1936), p. 3.

33. Donald C. Bryant, "Rhetoric: Its Functions and Its Scope," in Ehninger, *Contemporary Rhetoric*, p. 18.

34. Donald Bryant, *Rhetorical Dimensions in Criticism* (Baton Rouge: Louisiana State University Press, 1973), p. 14.

35. See Richard L. Johannesen, Rennard Strickland and Ralph T. Eubanks, *Language Is Sermonic: Richard Weaver on the Nature of Rhetoric* (Baton Rouge: Louisiana State University Press, 1970).

36. Karl R. Wallace, "The Substance of Rhetoric: Good Reasons," in Ehninger, *Contemporary Rhetoric*, p. 75.

37. Ibid., p. 82.

38. Douglas Ehninger, *Contemporary Rhetoric*, p. 3.

39. Ch. Perelman and L. Olbrechts-Tyteca, *The New Rhetoric*, trans. John Wilkinson and Purcell Weaver (Notre Dame: Notre Dame University Press, 1969), p. 4.

40. C. David Mortenson, *Communication: The Study of Human Interaction* (New York: McGraw-Hill Book Company, 1972), p. 14.

41. See, for example, Plato's *Phaedrus*. Among those who interpret Plato in this way is Oscar L. Brownstein, "Plato's *Phaedrus*: Dialectic as the Genuine Art of Speaking," *Quarterly Journal of Speech*, 51 (1965), 392–98.

42. Aristotle, *Rhetoric*, 1354a.

43. See, for example, Richard M. Weaver, *The Ethics of Rhetoric* (Chicago: Henry Regnery, 1953), especially Chapters I and II.

44. See, for example, Mortimer Adler, *Dialectic* (New York: Harcourt, Brace, & Co., 1927), especially p. 75.

45. Weaver, p. 27.

MEANING: THE INTERFACE
BETWEEN KNOWLEDGE
AND RHETORIC

We have said that a symbiotic association exists between rhetoric and knowledge. This implies that there is some characteristic or quality in virtue of which the two concepts are related. In Chapter 1 we argued for the existence of such a relationship by examining instances of ordinary discourse illustrating that knowing and communicating are associated. In Chapter 2 we hinted at the nature of this relationship when we claimed that the kind of knowledge that is of interest to an epistemologist is "knowledge that"—knowledge that is essentially propositional and, thus, *linguistic*. In Chapter 3 where rhetoric was defined as the description of reality through language, the common thread connecting rhetoric and epistemology was implicitly located in the reliance of both on language. We shall now undertake to give a full account of how rhetoric and epistemology are kindred because of their common reliance on language.

To explain the rhetoric/knowledge relationship it is necessary to treat the nature and functions of language. To do so is of practical as well as theoretical importance. For example, a clear and precise conception of language is requisite to statement of and argument for or against any philosophical position. But more pragmatic uses of clear conceptions of language are common. Consider the legal system. One need not have legal training to comprehend the importance of clarity and precision in legal language. And even the most pedestrian disputes among individuals are often results of misunderstandings or misapplications of language in social relationships.

Such considerations have led both rhetorical and philosophical scholars to explore the relationships among rhetoric, language, and knowing. It was I. A. Richards' contention that through examination of language and its use we can comprehend the nature of communication and improve communicative enterprises. Richards conceived rhetoric as a "study of misunderstanding and its remedies," and through analysis of meaning and how it changes as discourse occurs he hoped to decrease misunderstanding.[1] Similarly, James Cornman contended that an analysis of language is of concern to philosophers because "language has an important and perhaps even unique role to play in future attempts to resolve ontological problems."[2] Corresponding questions regarding the basic role of language in any field of inquiry may be raised if that discipline purports to produce epistemic judgments.

In our analysis of language we take as our starting point the observation that language is the interface between communication and knowing. Identification of the precise character of this interface requires that we define what language is, and as background for that task we shall survey some theories of language that have appeared potentially useful for finding the theoretical relationships between rhetoric and epistemology. Our task here is to illustrate the directions such theories have taken, not to provide an exhaustive survey of theories of language.

TRADITIONAL THEORIES OF MEANING

Research focusing on the nature of language and meaning has come from a variety of scholarly disciplines. Yet despite recognition that "as the main vehicle of human communication, language is indispensable" and despite the promise of books and monographs with such auspicious titles as *The Meaning of Meaning*, "The Concept of Meaning," and *Understanding Understanding*, there is little consensus about the nature and functions of language and meaning. 3 In what follows we shall examine several leading avenues of thought about the nature and functions of linguistic meaning.

Traditionally, three kinds of theories of meaning have been presented: (1) referential theories, (2) ideational theories, and (3) stimulus-response or behavioral theories.

REFERENTIAL THEORIES OF MEANING

The most common approach to meaning contends that units of language (words, phrases, or whole sentences) designate particular objects or ideas in the world. Put another way, this point of view holds that the meaning of a linguistic expression is a function of something that stands apart from or exists outside of the expression itself; such things are "picked out" or "named by" some conventional form of expression. 4

This commonsense notion of what it means to mean has long been plagued by serious difficulties. Foremost among these is what we might label the argument from several meanings. This objection, first advanced by Frege, demonstrates that there are objects or ideas (i.e., referents) to which more than one nonsynonomous locution can be correctly ascribed. 5 For example, "The Great War" and "World War I" are expressions both of which accurately refer to the same object. Because phrases of this sort may also mean differently when ascribed to a single referent, the quality of possessing a particular meaning cannot be explained by specifying *the* object a term or other linguistic unit refers to. The most basic formulation of the referential theory, then, appears inadequate.

Another objection to the referential view arises from existence of what have been called "syncategorematic" terms. Many words, such as conjunctions (e.g., and, but, or), prepositions (e.g., about, for, with), and others appear to have no referents at all. Therefore, it cannot be from extralinguistic objects that these locutions derive their meaning.

Finally, it has long been recognized that there are more basic units of meaning than words or terms. The most basic units of meaning have of late been termed "morphemes," and they may include units as small as syllables or even individual sounds. For example, the term "syncategorematic" contains the syllable "syn," which, like the Greek term from which it is derived, means "with" or "together with." Likewise, the first letter in the term "atheist" gives the word a meaning diametrically opposed to "theist." Yet it is difficult to formulate a referential theory that would analyze "a" or "syn" as deriving meaning from any extralinguistic entity.

Not all formulations of the referential theory define meaning as a function of simple ascriptions of locutions to objects. More sophisticated referential theories have sought to define meaning as a function of the *relationship between* a particular locution and the object to which it refers. Philosophers such as Russell, Frege, Church, Lewis, and Carnap have all contributed to this conception by suggesting that use of language be viewed, in one way or another, within the context of broader *semantic systems*.6 In this way, the "meaning" of, for example, such syncategorematic terms as "and," "but," "if" is to be gleaned from the context of the term's appearance in sentences. However, it appears that to make this claim is to generate a separate sense of meaning for syncategorematic terms and, hence, to complicate the theory of meaning without justification. Such a nonparsimonious solution should be suspect.

In sum, the referential theory has not been generally judged to offer an adequate account of the nature and function of meaning.

IDEATIONAL THEORIES OF MEANING

Ideational theories posit that meaning is not a function of designating extralinguistic entities by linguistic units, but the meaning of a particular locution is determined by a corresponding idea in the mind of the rhetor.7 Thus the term "book" would be held to derive its meaning from the idea of book to which the word *book* corresponds.

Three major objections have been raised against this account of meaning. First, the view must hold that thought is independent of language in order to explain the generation of language (meaning) from thought. Yet as our discussion in Chapter 2 indicated, it is impossible to conceive of thought as universally independent of language; we wish to say, all thought is inherently linguistic in character. Hence, the claim that ideas occur first and meanings derive therefrom is objectionable.

A second serious problem is that within the ideational theory it is implicit that there must be an idea that corresponds to every meaningful linguistic expression. Even worse, there must be an idea that corresponds to every *sense* in which any expression could be meaningful. Not even in relatively simple locutions does the speaker or listener have ideas that correspond to every meaningful possibility of every unit of utterance. Additionally, in the case of those units of a given utterance that do correspond to an idea in the mind of the speaker or listener, it is almost always true that the idea refers not to one thing, but to several. In other words, there could be no one-on-one mapping of even a single word onto a unique idea possessed by the speaker/listener; generally, even the simplest ideas have numerous alternative meanings. The very existence of multiple possible meanings for simple ideas renders the ideational theory problematic.

A third objection to the ideational view stems from the theory's incapacity to provide a consistent explanation of what an idea is and from whence it comes. If one contends that meaning is an outgrowth of ideas, a definition of what an idea *is* and a set of criteria by which to know when an idea exists are requisite. Otherwise, there would be no way to evaluate the particulars of any one ideational theory, let alone to distinguish the theory at appropriate levels of analysis from other theories of meaning. Some ideational theorists have recognized this need to provide a philosophically encompassing explanation of ideas, but their accounts are often predicated on the argument that independent physical objects stand in relation to thoughts or ideas. The result is that such an ideational theory becomes no more than a form of referential theory, and it then becomes subject to the problems we identified above.

We should note finally that some students of communication have claimed that meaning resides in people, not in things. They are in essence subscribing to a form of ideational theory. 8 In light of what we have already said, this position is questionable. Other meaning-resides-in-people theorists, including those who follow Wittgenstein, take a somewhat different position with which we shall deal below.

STIMULUS-RESPONSE THEORIES OF MEANING

A third traditional way of conceiving meaning argues that a locution is meaningful because of the response which the utterance, as stimulus, occasions in the listener.9 According to this view, meaning is not to be found in extralinguistic referents, nor in ideas in the mind; meaning is a function of human *behavior*. Consider the word "fire." According to stimulus-response theory, the meaning of the locution "Fire!" is a product of both the situation in which the term is uttered and the response the word evokes in an auditor. Responses to language are, of course, presumed to be conditioned, learned responses.

The stimulus-response view cannot survive critical inspection, for it leads to the absurd conclusion that a given word has virtually a limitless number of meanings because any one word may elicit a number of different responses depending upon context, time of utterance, and audience. Thus, in the example of the locution "Fire!," a reader may conjure up visions of a crowd fleeing from a movie theater upon the discovery of smoke. However, one can just as easily interpret the utterance in quite different ways. Perhaps some unfortunate is about to be executed by a firing squad. Or, the command could be signaling the end of a long countdown prior to the lift-off of a rocket. Still other meanings could be associated with this term, and all could produce distinctive kinds of responses.

This view entails consequences that render impossible both meaningful definition of meaning and meaningful definition of communication. If we say meaning is always at least partly dependent on context, we must add that context is never strictly the same on any two occasions; it follows that no term can ever mean precisely the same thing in successive uses. Yet it is clear that there is a measure of stability in our uses of language. A measure of stability exists and allows us to use a term meaningfully on different occasions. That stability cannot stem from context, time, audience, or stimulus-response behavior. This is because regularity and stability issue from some fixed source unaccounted for by the thoroughgoing process notion that is the foundation of contemporary stimulus-response theories. Regardless of what that source is—whether extralinguistic referents, or ideas in the mind, or something else—human behavior is often a result and not a cause of meaning.

A second observation relevant to the stimulus-response theory concerns what it is to provide an account of meaning in the first place. It seems to us that what the stimulus-response approach provides is not a theory of *meaning* but some rather general remarks better characterized as sociology or psychology. One indication that this observation has merit is that a person could hold either of the two views earlier discussed—the referential view or the ideational approach—and *also* hold most of what is advanced by the stimulus-response school of thought. In other words, stimulus-response theorists seem not to be *raising* the kinds of issues that bear directly on what it is for something to mean. Baldly stated, meaning and behavior are two radically different concepts.

CONTEMPORARY THEORIES OF MEANING

Numerous thinkers have recognized the problems inherent in each of the traditional theories of meaning. Especially since the end of World War II, a great deal of energy has been expended on framing theories of meaning that avoid these problems. The same general solution appears to have been adopted by a large group of recent theorists, and for this reason we shall discuss the various treatments collectively. In general, we may label the recent approach to the problem of meaning a "linguistic-use approach."

The most celebrated theorist to formulate the linguistic-use approach to meaning is certainly Wittgenstein. In an effort to provide an analysis that did not view meaning as a "thing" or "entity," Wittgenstein adopted a radical vantage point. He treated meaning as a function of the pragmatic use of language. In *Philosophical Investigations*, Wittgenstein admonished us to "Look at the sentence as an instrument, and at its sense as its employment."[10] According to Magee, while Wittgenstein was of the opinion that what philosophy is concerned with "is the understanding of meaning," nonetheless, "to understand meaning we have to see what people actually do in what they take to be the meaningful use of terms."[11]

A view closely allied to Wittgenstein's—and in large measure influenced by him—is *speech-act* analysis of language. Like Wittgenstein, speech-act philosophers look to the *act* which is being performed to explain how it is that utterances mean. As members in a language community, individuals engage in certain routinized ways of speaking. It is this routinization that is the object of study for speech-act theorists. Austin's familiar distinctions among an utterance's locutionary, illocutionary, and perlocutionary employment form a basis for analysis of meaning focusing attention on the performance aspect of language-use.[12] In the illocutionary act—the employment of an utterance to achieve some effect (to *do* something)—theorists claim to have discovered an important means by which to explain what linguistic utterances mean. As Alston describes it, "We must look for general trends in linguistic behavior if we are to exhibit the meanings of words as functions of what speakers do with them."[13]

76

Austin's pioneering work was expanded by Searle and others. All sought to provide a more encompasssing analysis of speech acts than Austin had attempted. This was achieved by analyzing speech acts into a highly taxonomized categorization of rules for usage (e.g., constitutive vs. regulative rules). The primary contribution to a theory of meaning was to strengthen the contention that meaning is a function of linguistic usage. 14 The linguistic-use approach to meaning has enormously benefitted study of the nature and function of language; however, as a theory of *meaning*, the resulting view is subject to what we believe are serious objections.

First, it is not clear that the linguistic-use approach has provided a theory of *meaning* at all. This difficulty was appreciated by Searle himself, when he wrote:

> Linguistic philosophers of the period I am discussing had no general theory of language on which to base their particular conceptual analyses. What they had in place of a general theory was a few slogans, the most prominent of which was the slogan, "Meaning Is Use." This slogan embodied the belief that the meaning of a word is not to be found by looking for some associated mental entities in an introspective realm, nor by looking for some entity for which it stands, whether abstract or concrete, mental or physical, particular or general, but rather by carefully examining how the word is actually used in the language. As an escape route from Platonic or Empiricist or Tractatus-like theories of meaning, the slogan "Meaning Is Use" was quite beneficial. But as a tool of analysis in its own right, the notion of use is so vague that in part it may lead to the confusions I have been trying to expose. 15

Objection to speech-act theory as a theory of meaning runs: because of the "vagueness" that Searle alludes to, the linguistic-use philosophers confused the question "What does X mean?" with the question "How is X used?" Put another way, the former is not only irreducible to the latter, the latter is wholly unenlightening as an *account of* the former. This objection asserts that whatever information an answer to "How is X used?" provides, the answer in no way tells us what X *means*.

A related objection concerns the inability of speech-use theories to account for stability in language use. Merely to suggest that certain rules underlie language use is not to account for the regularity with which linguistic utterances have common references through time and across situations. Rather than positing *explanations*—explanations that traditional theorists tried to offer as solutions to the problem of meaning—linguistic-use theorists beg the question. At best, these theorists provide a psychological/sociological, that is, a *behavioral* account of how language is used; they do not analyze how language means.

In summary, traditional approaches to the problem of meaning have raised the kinds of questions necessary for an analysis of the problem, but their answers confront serious theoretical difficulties. Contemporary theorists appear singularly reluctant to broach the traditional questions. Thus, although contemporary theories yield important insights into language use, they circumvent the problem of meaning. What is required is a return to the basic issues of meaning addressed by traditional theorists. In what follows we shall attempt to confront directly the traditional question about the nature and function of meaning.

TOWARD A NEW THEORY OF MEANING

Let us begin by considering an example of everyday discourse. One of us some years ago discovered the following passage on the bathroom wall of a major American corporation: "Thursday is April 5th this year, so we can all relax—at least for a little while."

What does this mysterious piece of graffiti *mean*? Though he was an employee of the corporation on whose bathroom wall these words were inscribed, the discoverer had no idea what the words meant when he first noticed them. Were they meant as an expression of relief by some segment of the work force that had realized a particular deadline was pushed back a day? Was the message some kind of code? Or was this a tongue-in-cheek scrawling, the prank of a practical joker who intended to puzzle whoever happened to read the lines? If this last explanation were true, the graffiti would not mean anything. Yet in what sense could one possibly say that such a grammatically well-formed expression, including familiar language elements, means nothing? The lines have a great deal of meaning that a reader can grasp "at first blush." For example, any reader could notice: the day of the week on which April 5th supposedly falls, the imputation that *someone* may "breathe a little easier" for a short time because April 5th falls on Thursday, the implication that the reprieve may be short-lived, or the simple fact that the message must mean something.

Furthermore, one can conceive of contexts in which the message could carry a great deal of additional meaning. For instance, what if the graffiti had been found inscribed on an ancient prison wall just excavated in Athens? Archaeologists, after translating the message, might be just as perplexed about its meaning as we are. But if the translators were familiar with Plato's *Phaedo,* a likely meaning of the message would suggest itself. The message was perhaps written by a prisoner awaiting execution. Using this hypothesis, the reader could construct the following meaning: The condemned realized the Athenian custom of not executing prisoners dur-

78

ing the period when a ceremonial ship was en route to the island of Delos. The prisoner realized that the ship (hypothetically scheduled to leave on the 5th of April) would be gone on the day he was scheduled to die (Thursday). For such reasons he chose to scrawl the laconic message on the wall of his prison cell.

The mystery message illustrates the importance of *context* in the problem of meaning. It reveals a context/meaning symbiosis. On one hand, the message points "beyond itself" to some context that the reader or listener immediately inquires about or searches for, *and which in large measure determines the message's meaning.* On the other hand, the message seems also to point inward "toward itself," since the very fact that one takes the message as meaningful and inquires about or searches for context suggests an intrinsic meaning. Here too a large measure of the message's meaning is determined. In a similar vein, it seems obvious that the very *act* of message formulation infuses a message with meaning. (One must be careful here not to confuse the *act* of message formulation with the notion of *speech acts* treated above.) Finally, even if what we have been assuming was a message were, in fact, merely a chance collection of marks that by coincidence appeared to be a message, the fact that the message appears meaningful would still need to be accounted for. Now, another dimension of the problem of meaning confronts us: The message is meaningful as a function of its form.

Our four-fold assessment of the dimensions of meaning is not exhaustive; some theorists identify as many as seven senses of meaning.16 But we have carried the analysis far enough to demonstrate that a theory of meaning that accounts for all the nuances of the meaning functions of language is *a*, if not *the*, fundamental requirement of theories of communication. How else can we hope to acquire anything like an in-depth understanding of the phenomena of messages and communicative behavior? The question that suggests itself is: What general features must such a theory embody in order to account for the various dimensions of meaning that any given utterance may exhibit?

GENERAL FEATURES OF A NEW THEORY OF MEANING

In attempting to resolve the inadequacies of theories of meaning already discussed, it will be useful to make two general observations about those theories. First, with the exception of the speech-act theories, the approaches to meaning we have reviewed have either been explicitly referential or they have been reducible to a referential form. Further, even the speech-act theorists have begun to recognize the vacuousness of analyzing meaning wholly as a function of *action*. Searle, for one, was compelled to repair to a more traditional referential conception of meaning as a starting point for his reconsideration of early speech-act theories. In his most recent work, *Intentionality*, Searle notes that a successful explanation of meaning must range far beyond the concept of the speech act and "requires an account of how the mind/brain relates the organism to reality."[17]

What these facts point to is that a reassertion of the referential view, in some guise or other, is perhaps a requirement for some portion of any theorist's framework. Why this is necessary is explained by the limitations of the speech-act approach. One example that Searle mentions will remind us of Searle's own self-critical awareness and will suggest a point we are moving toward. In *Speech Acts*, Searle makes what we take to be a critically important observation. With respect to Wittgenstein's touted analogy between games such as chess and the "language game," Searle notes that there is an important difference between the analogues.[18] In the language game the "moves"—be they considered as morphemes, words, sentences, or even larger units—*have meaning*, regardless of how one uses the term. In chess, however, we do not say that each piece has meaning, nor each move, except respecting the overall strategy we are employing or the final outcome of the game. Thus, even those subscribing to a language-use conception of meaning must eventually return to a referential account of discourse in order to explain how individual units of language have meaning apart from the larger contexts in which they are used. The illocutionary act of lying, for example, is composed of numerous language units—just as the mystery message with which we began this section was formed. The units, when taken together, count as the act of lying. To a significant degree, the chess analogy makes sense. It is the cumulative bringing together of individual units (whatever they are taken to be) that counts as the act in question. However, unlike the chess move, each language act is formed of individual components that *themselves* have meaning below, above, and beyond the larger act. We suggest that this is why even language-use (speech-act) theorists have retrenched in one degree or another to adopt some measure of referentiality in their theory building.

Given our purposes, it deserves notice, too, that communication scholars of logical-empiricist orientation have been unable to escape some degree of referentiality even through use of operational definitions.[19]

Another observation with respect to past theories of meaning is that they almost always treat language as fundamentally *symbolic*. Discourse is held to be a collection of symbols that *stand for* something, whether that something be an object, idea, or an action. John Stewart's observation about communication studies is as true now as it was when offered in 1972:

> A review of over four hundred issues of speech journals published between 1953 and 1970, thirty-six selected speech communication textbooks, and fifteen works frequently cited by text authors revealed that speech scholars view language as fundamentally a system of symbols, and meaning as a matter of symbols representing or naming objects, ideas, or behavioral responses. Speech communication scholars almost unanimously agree that language is fundamentally a system of symbols and that a symbol is generally "anything that represents something else."[20]

Now if *referentialism* and *symbolicity* lie at the heart of contemporary theories of communication and if such theories are unable to account satisfactorily for meaning, it makes sense to try to reformulate the basic tenets that have been tacitly accepted. We begin by eschewing these heretofore accepted groundings for a theory of meaning. What seems called for is a radical reconception of what language is and how it functions.

We propose that referential theories of meaning and those that imply referentiality have succumbed to the difficulties we have cited because of what we shall call the *ostensive* fallacy. Utterances are held to *point out* things in the world; that is, language is used to REFER TO. An accurate description of the activity of referring will allow us to avoid the consequences of the ostensive fallacy. We wish to say that linguistic utterances REFER WITH. The term "with" is not an allusion to the wherewithal of the utterance (the nouns, verbs, phrases, morphemes, etc.). To say that a term refers *with* and by doing so has meaning is to assert that employment of any term will occasion recognition in a conscious entity of the existence of certain *relationships*. It will not bring recognition of the existence of *objects*. So interpreted, language acts principally to make relationships conspicuous to selves through an occasioning process. Language does not function to point out things in the world; it creates awareness of *relations* and their *terms*, where "terms" means relational conditions among extralinguistic phenomena.

An example will illustrate the manner in which language refers *with*. Consider the familiar sentence, "The cat is on the mat." A commonsense way of describing how language functions in this example is to say that language is being employed to *point out the location of the cat*. This is the referential view in small. Yet, regardless of one's theory of language, a problem immediately arises about such a view: How is it possible to give the location of anything just by pointing? The notion of location requires establishment of a point of reference *from which* to point. According to our reformulation, the sentence in question—like all meaningful units of language—serves to make clear a *relation*. The discourse has meaning precisely because it makes an auditor aware of a relationship among self, utterer, and extralinguistic phenomena, in the present case the cat and the mat.

On this view, it is incorrect to say that "The cat is on the mat" makes conspicuous the relationship between only two extralinguistic phenomena—cat and mat. This aspect of the relational function of language is secondary in the sense that it is based on the more primary function of underscoring the relations among rhetor, tacit auditor, and extralinguistic entities. Strictly speaking, the utterance does not make us conscious of a relation between cat and mat; fundamentally, the utterance makes us aware of a more primary relation between rhetor *and* cat and mat. Put differently, the relation between cat and mat which the locution seeks to capture and make conspicuous is always predicated on the more primary relation between or among rhetor, tacit auditor, and extralinguistic phenomena.

The primary relationships among rhetor, tacit auditor, cat, and mat, and the secondary relationship between cat and mat, do not exhaust the richness of meaning conceived relationally. A host of additional relationships may be made conspicuous by the simple locution "The cat is on the mat." For example, an array of implicatures, each a product of relationality, may obtain. Some of the more immediately obvious ones are: "The cat is not in the garage, or the kitchen, or in the yard, or. . ."; "The mat is under the cat"; "The cat is above the mat"; and so on. Here "levels of meaning" are defined in terms of relations, made conspicuous through their embodiment in language.

It is clear that individual utterances never entirely capture the relations even among the extralinguistic phenomena. A particular rhetor's usage underscores his or her relationship within a vastly complex world of relationships (where "relationship" is understood in the technical sense). Such a conclusion implies something about meaning and language, and also about how the world is composed and how we come to apprehend and know it. In fact, it might be argued that this view of language is itself predicated on a particular theory of ontology and epistemology. For this reason we shall need to treat the notion of "a relation" technically in the following chapters. However, for now, we can conclude that a primary function of language is to *refer with*, that is, to underscore *relationships*. 21

82

Our discussion of relationality also contributes to a reformulation of the second tenet of most theories of meaning in communication. This is the proposition that there is a symbolic dimension of language. From the relational perspective we are developing, it is untenable to say that words (or any other meaningful units of language) refer to *things* or symbolize objects. We contend that meaningful units of language operate solely to describe relations. A more appropriate description of meaningful elements of linguistic utterances, whether morphemes, words, sentences, or other discernible units of meaning, would be that the utterances *embody* the relationships they occasion in the mind of the auditor. This is the case whether the auditor is one's interlocuter or the self. In the manner of Burke's notion of "entitlement"[22] (yet in contrast to his position on the symbolic nature of language), terms are not symbols that stand deputy for things; they are relata that contain, encompass, reflect, and embody one or more relationships. The apperception of linguistic terms, then, establishes for any self a set or purported set of relationships in which the self is contextualized. To "have meaning" is to participate in this contextualization, as the rich ordinary-language use of the term "meaning" betrays. To mean is, in a sense, to raise consciousness, anew or in greater degree, of oneself, of others, and of one's relationships to extralinguistic entities.

Words and the relations they embody are inseparable. Once a word is coined and comes to embody a particular relation or set of relations, the two cannot, even by agreement, be completely separated. A word may continue to embody its relation for as long as there remains in the memory of one conscious entity an affinity with a portion of the term's original or subsequent relational embodiments. It is this feature of meaning that makes etymology possible. Likewise, it is to the relational analysis of referentiality and symbolicity that we must attribute the possibilities of meaning we earlier ascribed to the mystery message that perplexes us still. Whatever the historical explanation for its existence, what that scrawl means in any sense is a function of how, as a collection of symbols, it *embodies* a particular, finite, collection of relations.

One may extend this relational analysis of meaning not only to such everyday examples of discourse as "The cat is on the mat" and curious messages like the graffiti, but to fictive discourse as well. In general, relationality offers a productive way to account for what is the product of what we call "the arts." It is commonplace to say that a work such as Rabelais' *Gargantua and Pantagruel* is *fictional*. Moreover, people are inclined to distinguish between such fictional linguistic *creations* of reality and other linguistic *descriptions* of reality. In practice most of us draw this line between the fictions we create through language and the reality we try to describe through language. Such distinctions seem to argue against the thesis that all of reality is socially created through language. That thesis renders paradoxical the practice of making fiction / reality distinctions and even the conceptual criteria upon which any such distinction must rest. If, however, we accept the fact of these distinctions, certain questions follow: What are we to say about the worlds of poetry, drama, and literature? How are we to account for these domains that clearly result from linguistic *creation*? How are we to account for the meaningfulness of anything that we all agree is a fiction?

The answer must be framed in terms of relationality. One of the foremost contemporary students of literary analysis, Kenneth Burke, expresses our point of view in his description of how we analyze a work of art:

> If we are analyzing such a structure, we look first of all for key terms. (Thus, "Hamlet" would certainly be a key term in *Hamlet,* and "Emma Bovary" in *Madame Bovary.*) Then we look for their transformations (as when we ask what sufferances and changes a character undergoes). But, however we analyze such material, the main thing is that we are first of all vowed to let the words have their say. At this first stage at least, we should not heckle. Thus, if a novelist writes a story with Australia as his background, we could not reasonably heckle him at the very start, even if we wanted to do so at the end, because he had placed his story in Australia rather than Norway or New Zealand. Even if we were preparing eventually to demur, our first step would require us to note (insofar as we are able) how the writer's words proceed. And in this sense, a Dramatistic approach to language vows us first of all to considerations of pure verbal internality, as we seek to chart the transformations within the work itself (for that's what we get, even in a superficial outline of a story's plot, and in a placing of the main characters with relation to one another, though newspaper reviewers may not care to recognize in their report of a book such a sheer terministic enterprise).23

Burke's conclusion warrants emphasis: "In this sense, the most haphazard of reviewers indexes a book, noting what he considers notable relationships and transformations among the work's key terms."24 It makes sense to say that a work of fiction is understood as a complex of meanings, and that such meanings are the products of the complexes of relationships in which those complexes stand to one another and the relational transformations that occur *through the use of language.* Burke, of course, would include act, scene, agent, agency, and purpose as central complexes of relationships to be examined.

It is relevant at this point to ask whether from such an analysis of art we learn any lesson that applies to our general understanding of meaning. Are not the meanings of objects of experience functions of relations and transformations that are given salience by an artist's imagination—by his or her *words*—in fiction or poetry or drama? Such a view was in Burke's mind. At one point he mentions Malinowski's notion of "context and situation" and introduces the idea of "circumference."25 His idea here is that one can "locate" oneself relationally in a number of different ways. One might say that she or he is "'writing these words in Florida this January,' or 'during a lull in the bombing of North Vietnam,' or 'in a period following the invention of the atomic bomb but prior to a landing of electronic instruments on the surface of the moon.'" The relational character of such contextual explanations is clear. The degree to which Burke was influenced by relational thinking is apparent in remarks he makes about Spinoza, remarks clearly exhibiting the concept of relationality. He continues a paragraph later:

> As I see our problem, we shall here be radically involved with variations on Spinoza's concept of substance (as overall situational context). Thinking along such lines, we ask: In the last analysis, how could even some one tiny pinpoint exist, or be "determined," except insofar as the entire context of the universe lets it be there, in exactly the conditions by which it is conditioned (or lets it be determined in exactly such terms as do define its existence)? 26

What "defines" the existence of "even some one tiny pinpoint" (what Burke calls "the entire context of the universe") is the *relation*. If we grant this and believe that we use language in anything like the ways experience tells us we use it, it is difficult to see how we can account for meaning apart from what we have called its primary function, namely, to make relations conspicuous to selves.

We shall next undertake to show how a relational theory of meaning avoids the shortcomings of other theories of meaning.

ADVANTAGES OF THE RELATIONAL THEORY OF MEANING

The first problem with the referential account of meaning is what we termed "argument from several meanings." If many terms can describe the same object, it makes no sense to say that a term derives its meaning from referring to a particular object. Our relational view of meaning copes with this problem in the following way. We said that the phrases "World War I" and "The Great War" refer to the same object. From a relational perspective the two phrases have in common the fact that each embodies a defining characteristic of a larger aggregate. "World War I" embodies a chronological characteristic of the complex of characters and events that the war comprised. "World War I" was precisely that; it was the first *world* war, and it is to be distinguished relationally from all other wars fought previously and subsequently. On the other hand, "The Great War" calls to mind the same aggregate of events, and it too describes relationally a particular aspect of that larger complex; it embodies the feature of magnitude: "greatness." This second phrase focuses on the enormity of the war, in its scope and perhaps in the principles fought for. In short, the two locutions share some common referents, but their different meanings can be explained by the fact that they embody separate relationships among rhetor, tacit auditor, and extralinguistic phenomena.

A relational view of meaning recognizes what we know intuitively: What appear to be similar or synonomous locutions are in fact distinct because of the unique relational features that each occasions. The reason a person can recognize that two locutions refer to a common object is that each locution calls forth in the interlocutor's mind a more or less complete aggregate of aspects that collectively constitute the "object" in question. The point to be seen is that the two phrases we have explored do not refer to the *same* thing; they define parts, aspects, or characteristics of a large, common aggregate. It is the parts, aspects, or characteristics that serve to call up or occasion awareness of the larger totality.

A second objection to the referential theory of meaning stems from the fact that words such as conjunctions and prepositions do not refer to particular objects, so the referential view of meaning makes little sense with respect to them. Relational theory does not face this objection at all because it is asserted that words never stand for objects. Syncategorematic or any other terms *embody relations*. Relational theory also offers a consistent and parsimonious explanation of meaning applicable to all categories of words and all categories of meaningful linguistic units. In this respect relational theory solves problems faced by sophisticated varieties of referentialism that, in unduly complicated ways, assert that broad semantic systems explain the appearances of words in various frames of context.

Relational theory also avoids a third problem of referential theories. Referential theories cannot account for the meanings of linguistic units such as prefixes and suffixes. Relational theory avoids this difficulty by highlighting how even morphemes are units that embody relations and thereby have meanings. To recur to our earlier example, the term "atheist" is meaningful and distinct from the term "theist" because the "a" embodies a particular relation, that of negation.

Ideational theory holds that meaning is determined by an idea in the mind of the rhetor. We objected that this view implies that thought is independent of language. No such implication occurs in relational theory because relational theory holds that thought is inherently linguistic. To say that language *embodies* relations among extralinguistic referents, rhetor, and tacit auditor does not imply that thought is separate from language; it asserts an identification of thought and language *in* the reference to interrelationships.

A relational theory of meaning also avoids the ideational problem that it is impossible to locate and specify a unique thought that is coextensive with the meaning of each individual unit of language. Within relational theory there is no reason to assume that language units must be associated with individual ideas. The individual relation may occasion a number of meanings. It is true that one must make a distinction between an aggregate of relations known proximately and an aggregate of relations known remotely, but this is a distinction with which we are all familiar. When a child is developing language, it is necessary for the child to be cognizant of a number of very elementary "ideas." These are later taken up by the mind, not as individual notions but as parts of larger collectivities. In teaching a child language we carefully articulate even the simplest words contained in two- or three-word phrases; e.g., "Go beddy bye." If the child attunes his or her perception to such elemental phrases, the child eventually learns the meanings of those phrases. Within a few months or years, it is no longer necessary for the child to hear each term as a distinct element; the phrases will be processed and used as wholes. By the time of young adulthood we process large chunks of language without any need to call up individual ideas. A word or two will now occasion an array of relationships much as the first few words of a well known song bring to mind the entire verse and melody. Given what is known about language acquisition and about learning second languages, there seems no obstacle to the relationalist's thesis that units of language mean in multiple, relational ways, at least for anyone who commands the syntactical constructions of a language.

A further objection to the ideational theory of meaning is that no cogent analysis of the concept "idea" is provided. The relational theory posits an inherent interconnectedness among the extralinguistic referent, rhetor, and tacit audience. It holds that "ideas" are themselves products of the relational nature of all that exists in awareness of the universe. Ideas are not to be regarded as strange, other worldly, ephemeral constructs produced in the life of the mind; "ideas" are conceived of as natural phenomena arising out of perceptions of the world of relations.

We objected to stimulus-response theories of meaning that any word may have a number of uses, depending on context, time of utterance, audience, and the like. We further objected that a stimulus-response account or even one that posits "mediated" responses fails to explain the inherent stability and regularity we can observe in the uses of language. Consider again our example of a person who shouts "Fire!" According to S-R theorists, the conditioned response of the audience determines the meaning of the term. According to Hullian S-O-R theorists, the meaning of the term is the "habit strength" associated with the term. But "Fire!" does not *mean* "crowds fleeing from a theater" or habituated fear of fire. Nor does it mean the launching of a rocket or the shooting of a condemned prisoner. We suggest that the consequences of such a speech act are to be accounted for on the basis of an underlying stability of meaning. This stability, we believe, follows from the relation(s) that a term or phrase embodies. As language users we generate the word "fire" to embody a certain *range* of relations that encompasses a limited number of events in the world. Those events come into view as products of the relations permissibly embodied in the word "fire." On this analysis, use of the word "fire" occurs only under stable, specifiable conditions; that is, only when certain stable (that is, persistent over time), identifiable relations obtain between members of the language community and the world of which they are a part.

We have already dealt with how a relational theory of meaning escapes the charge that behavior and meaning are not equivalent. In order to account for behaviors "produced by words," it is necessary to account for how one word is more or less stable in use. This stability is a function of the stable relations that linguistic units embody. Thus, relationality, in explanation of the phenomenon of stable meaning, accounts for regularities in behavior. Put differently, in answering the question, What does "fire" *mean*? relational theory helps us understand the *behavior* that results from uttering the locution, "Fire!"

Objectors to the speech-act approach to meaning focus on two issues. First, these theorists fail to distinguish clearly between meaning and use. Second, they do not provide an account of the stability underlying *rules* of language in use. As we have seen, a relational theory does account for the natures of meaning and use and, in so doing, it explains the stability of language in use. Again, this solution is accomplished by focusing on the notion of *the relation* and its *embodiment* in linguistic units.

CONCLUSION

We have identified the interface between rhetoric and epistemology as *language*. We have also developed an account of the concept of *meaning*. We have argued that meaning is a function of a linguistic unit's *embodiment* of relations among rhetor, tacit audience, and extralinguistic phenomena. Using these premises, we can now investigate how rhetoric, as a body of linguistic units embodying relations, functions to generate knowledge.

NOTES

1. See I. A. Richards, *The Philosophy of Rhetoric* (London: Oxford University Press, 1936), p. 3ff.

2. James W. Cornman, "Language and the Future of Metaphysics," in Robert E. Wood, ed., *The Future of Metaphysics* (Chicago: Quadrangle Books, 1970), p. 151.

3. Herbert H. Clark and Eve V. Clark, *Psychology and Language* (New York: Harcourt Brace Jovanovich, 1977), p. 3. B. Aubrey Fisher contends that "Book titles such as *The Meaning of Meaning* and *Understanding Understanding* are rather provocative but tend to promise more than they deliver." Yet his own essay "The Concept of Meaning," in which this criticism is launched, does not go much farther in exploring basic issues in meaning theory. See Fisher's *Perspectives on Human Communication* (New York: Macmillan Publishing Co., 1978), pp. 249–64.

4. Classic statements of the referential view of meaning appear in John Stuart Mill, *A System of Logic* (New York: Harper and Brothers, 1952), pp. 11–15; and Gottlob Frege, "On Sense and Reference," in Peter Geach and Max Black, eds., *Philosophical Writings* (Oxford: Oxford University Press, 1952). Contemporary formulations of the referential perspective are presented in Alonzo Church, "The Need for Abstract Entities in Semantic Analysis," *Proceedings of the American Academy of Arts and Sciences*, 80 (1951), 100–12, and C. I. Lewis, *An Analysis of Knowledge and Valuation* (La Salle, Ill.: The Open Court Publishing Co., 1946). For an essentially linguistic critique of referential theories of meaning see Gary Cronkhite, "Perception and Meaning," in Carroll C. Arnold and John Waite Bowers, eds., *Handbook of Rhetorical and Communication Theory* (Boston: Allyn and Bacon, 1984), pp. 112–14.

5. Frege's celebrated example of the Morning Star and the Evening Star is discussed by Panayot Butchvarov, *Being qua Being* (Bloomington: Indiana University Press, 1970), pp. 1–2ff.

6. The "semantic systems" approach is discussed in accessible form by William P. Alston, "Meaning," in *The Encyclopedia of Philosophy*, Paul Edwards, ed. (New York: Macmillan Publishing Co. and the Free Press, 1967), pp. 234–35.

7. Ideational theory derives ultimately from Greek conceptions of mind, including, for example, Plato's. Its most proximate early formulation is that of John Locke, *Essay Concerning Human Understanding*, Book III.

8. Fisher calls claims such as "meanings are in people," "meaning is perception," or "people, not words, mean," the "clichés of communication." (*Perspectives on Human Communication*, p. 256.) Cronkhite writes: "There may be an 'idea' behind the word, but what we display to explain the idea are other words, which certainly limits the utility of theories of this sort." ("Perception and Meaning," p. 115.) Still, much literature in rhetorical epistemology is sympathetic to, if

not derived from, observations such as Barry Brummett's: "Reality is meaning yet meaning is something created and discovered in communication." Context makes clear that emphasis belongs on "created" as opposed to "discovered." See Brummett's "Some Implications of 'Process' or 'Intersubjectivity': Postmodern Rhetoric," *Philosophy and Rhetoric*, 9 (1976), 29–30.

9. Among numerous formulations of stimulus-response theories of meaning are B. F. Skinner, *Verbal Behavior* (New York: Appleton-Century-Crofts, 1957); C. K. Ogden and I. A. Richards, *The Meaning of Meaning* (New York: Harcourt, Brace and Co., 1938); and C. C. Fries, "Meaning and Linguistic Analysis," *Language*, 30 (1954), 57–68. Cronkhite reviews "radical behaviorist" and "neobehavioral" theories of meaning, finding none that accounts for the "range or set of permissible semantic meanings in a given language" ("Perception and Meaning," pp. 112–24.

10. Ludwig Wittgenstein, *Philosophical Investigations*, trans. G. E. M. Anscombe (New York: Macmillan Publishing Co., 1953), p. 126e (421).

11. Bryan Magee, *Modern British Philosophy* (New York: St. Martin's Press, 1971), p. 9.

12. J. L. Austin, *How to Do Things with Words*, J. O. Urmson, ed. (Cambridge: Harvard University Press, 1962).

13. Alston, p. 238.

14. John R. Searle, *Speech Acts* (London: Cambridge University Press, 1969), pp. 136–56.

15. Searle, p. 146.

16. See Alston, p. 233.

17. John R. Searle, *Intentionality: An Essay in the Philosophy of Mind* (New York: Cambridge University Press, 1983), p. vii. See also his *Expression and Meaning* (New York: Cambridge University Press, 1979).

18. See Searle, *Speech Acts*, pp. 33–43, 63–64, and 123ff.

19. See, for example, Daniel J. O'Keefe, "Logical Empiricism and the Study of Human Communication," *Speech Monographs*, 42 (1975), 169–83.

20. John Stewart, "Concepts of Language and Meaning: A Comparative Study," *The Quarterly Journal of Speech*, 58 (1972), p. 124.

21. Kenneth D. Frandsen and Donald A. Clement have come to a conclusion similar to ours, along a very different route. After reviewing and synthesizing theories and research associated with semiotics, cybernetics, information theory, attribution theory, and information-integration theory, these scholars propose to define "information" as "any signal employed by a communicator in judging intentions, priorities, facts, statements, or persons. . . . This conception of information, by drawing attention away from the *stuff* of signals and directing attention toward the *interconnections* between persons and signals manifested in human processes of judgment and action, provides a basis for understanding the manner in which communicators decide *what* is signaled, *why* it is being signaled, *who* the signaler is, and what are the *consequences* of attending to the signals." See their "The Functions of Human Communication in Informing: Communicating and Processing Information," in Carroll C. Arnold and John Waite Bowers, eds., *Handbook of Rhetorical and Communication Theory* (Boston: Allyn and Bacon, 1984), pp. 338–99. (Quotations appear on p. 385; emphasis in the original.)

22. See Kenneth Burke, "What Are the Signs of What? A Theory of 'Entitlement,' " in *Language as Symbolic Action: Essays on Life, Literature, and Method* (Berkeley: University of California Press, 1966).

23. Burke, pp. 368–69.

24. Burke, p. 369.

25. Burke, pp. 359–60.

26. Burke, p. 360.

VIEWING RHETORIC AS EPISTEMIC

The purpose of this chapter is to show how rhetorical discourse describes reality through language and in doing so makes relations conspicuous to selves. We do not argue that rhetoric is "a way" of knowing distinct from other ways (e.g., distinct from philosophical epistemology, from science, or from theological insight). Rather, we contend that *all* ways of knowing are inherently rhetorical. 1 We do not argue, however, that all instances of rhetorical discourse are necessarily epistemic. We shall propose criteria by means of which an inquirer can advance and evaluate epistemic judgments and so achieve the greatest possible assurance that he or she has attained knowledge.

RHETORICAL CONSTITUENTS OF EPISTEMIC DISCOURSE

We said in Chapter 4 that meaning is a function of a linguistic unit's embodiment of relationships obtaining among rhetor, extralinguistic phenomena, and tacit audience. If that is true, we should be able to identify *ways* in which discourse is used to describe the world. We shall first explore the most basic products of using language and afterward examine more complex and sophisticated aspects of generating knowledge claims through use of language. Once these processes are understood, we will be in a position to say how and in what ways rhetorical discourse contributes to acquisition of knowledge as persistently justified true belief.

As we have said, we believe that one of the values of conceiving of knowledge as persistently justified true belief is that that conception frames a goal toward which we can seek to elevate our opinions. Accordingly, we will first direct our attention to how various rhetorical constituents of discourse contribute to acquisition of knowledge.

THE DIFFERENTIATIVE CONSTITUENT OF RHETORIC

As we have seen, linguistic units generate meaning by making relations conspicuous to selves. This most basic function of meaningful units of language implies difference. To establish in language a relationship among rhetor, extralinguistic phenomena, and tacit audience is to distinguish between, at minimum, two relata theretofore undistinguished. Thus, the primary epistemological function of discourse that is rhetorical is to differentiate among relata constituting the universe. For example, when one becomes conscious of a patch of color, several epistemic judgments are made in the first person. These might proceed as follows: "I am conscious of something;" "I am conscious of a visual something"; "I am conscious of an amorphous patch of color"; "I am conscious of an amorphous patch of color to which I affix the label 'red' "; "I am conscious of certain spatial relationships between the patch of color and other relata in the perceptual field"; "I am conscious that the stoplight has turned red." Of course, in such familiar complexes of perceptions one's appraisal occurs very quickly—in some cases, it might be claimed, automatically. However, a person just learning to drive a car must proceed carefully and methodically until driving habits become virtually spontaneous. In a similar way, an individual confronted for the first time with a new phenomenon must go through a step-by-step process in a methodical manner in order to incorporate the phenomenon into his or her stock of knowledge. One who travels to a jungle wilderness for the first time may, for example, hear an unfamiliar sound in the night. As the sound appears on the fringes of consciousness, the individual will name the phenomenon; that is, the person will *differentiate* the phenomenon linguistically as an entity standing in a relationship of otherness to him or her. This is the likely first thought that would run through the jungle visitor's mind. The raw awareness that is preconsciousness—the first affective cues at the most physiological level—intrudes to shake the person from other contemplation of surroundings. "I hear a sound" is a brief bit of intrapersonal communication; it differentiates the sound in question from countless other possible elements of immediate experience. Then, through progressively more discriminating propositions, the person will hope to arrive at a description that will assess the sound in terms that are both meaningful and useful from the standpoint of making relational distinctions: "I hear a sound that is nasal in character and very much like the sound I heard a toucan make one evening at the San Antonio Zoo. Toucans flourish in this part of the wilderness; therefore, I am probably hearing a toucan."

In each of the above cases, the person is reflecting on collections of relata that stand in consciousness as related to the knower. This process of reflection begins with naming and proceeds through a number of operations to as complete a description as is possible or desirable. The process is *rhetorical* by our definition of rhetoric, for it is "description of reality through language." Furthermore, as we have already noted, it is an instance of *intrapersonal* rhetoric in which differentiation, the primary epistemological function of rhetoric, is carried out. It is reflexive interaction between self and itself and is dialectical, as we have defined dialectic. We propose that this intrapersonal dialectic stands as the paradigm of epistemic, dialectical rhetoric. The rhetoric enables a thinker to raise possibilities about the nature of personal cognitions, and it ultimately permits the person to choose among possibilities. It is important to notice further that such intrapersonal rhetoric constitutes a search for knowledge as justified true belief. The processes can, of course, occur *inter*personally, but intrapersonal searching for knowledge as persistently justified true belief provides the most perspicuous instances of the basic processes.

In all epistemic judgments the differentiative function that is peculiar to rhetoric occurs, whether the judgments are primary, first-person, or derivative.[2] Consider the first-person epistemic judgment, "I have a headache." An epistemologist can give a partial account of the indubitable nature of such a judgment. That account would hold that linguistic descriptions of some physiological states such as directly experiencing a headache are indubitable, partly because one has direct awareness of that which is experienced (the headache). But to complete this account one must recognize the role of differentiation, which is a function of characterizing reality through language—a function of rhetoric. Noting this, our epistemologist can incorporate in his or her account the differentiative character of the verbalized judgment—in this case differentiative between a headache and other directly experienced phenomena. It is difficult to conceive how any such first-person epistemic judgments can be taken as knowledge without recognizing that their utterance in language—in rhetoric—differentiates. Such differentiation is a uniquely *linguistic* process, made feasible because language can embody relations and make those relations conspicuous. When language used purports to describe reality—when it becomes rhetorical—acquisition of knowledge as persistently justified true belief becomes possible, though not, of course, inevitable.

THE ASSOCIATIVE CONSTITUENT OF RHETORIC

Given the function of differentiation, the primary function of rhetorical discourse, more sophisticated aspects of acquiring knowledge become possible. This is true whether we are focusing on first-person epistemic judgments made intrapersonally or interpersonal generation of knowledge in such modalities as dyadic, group, or speaker-large audience communication. In all cases of human communication, generation of knowledge involves differentiation, but it involves more. A further knowledge-yielding function of rhetoric is *association*.

Because all knowledge is ultimately grounded in first-person epistemic judgments and because most of our knowledge claims move considerably beyond the intrapersonal domain, a significant proportion of our knowledge must be *derivative*.[3] The associative constituent of rhetoric accounts for the relationship between first-person epistemic judgments and derivative knowledge and for the relationship between one bit of derivative knowledge and another. These relationships are *associative*. Combination of one description of reality with another yields a third item of knowledge, and so on. The resulting knowledge we call derivative. Derivative knowledge may be, and frequently is, derived from other derivative knowledge. But the process is not entirely linear; an item of knowledge that is derivative may reveal more than the sum of the items from which it was obtained. This is because it is a feature of derivative knowledge that it often uncovers a complex of relationships (as opposed to a single relationship) between or among the items. For example, consider a patient's first-person epistemic judgments: "I am in pain"; "The pain is in my right side"; "The pain is most severe in my abdominal region"; "I have never had my appendix removed"; "I am nauseated"; "I am feverish"; "I cannot walk;" "My white-blood cell count is elevated"; "My physician believes I have a serious case of appendicitis." From these judgments one might derive the knowledge, "There is a good chance that I have a serious attack of appendicitis." The patient's knowledge regarding his or her malady derives from the first-person epistemic judgments cited, and also from other epistemic judgments such as: "Symptoms of appendicitis include nausea and fever," and "appendicitis is a serious condition." The patient's derivative knowledge reveals more than the sum of the items of knowledge from which it was derived. The association of differentiative constituents makes relationships conspicuous within a systematic relational complex—a relational complex that is what it is only by virtue of the relationships in which particular relata can stand to each other. 4

Regardless of how remote any item of derived knowledge is with respect to the first-person epistemic judgments from which it was generated, it is at least theoretically possible (although not always practically possible) to trace its lineage and arrive at the original judgments upon which the item of derived knowledge is based. Were it not that our derived knowledge rests ultimately on first-person epistemic judgments, the concept of knowledge as persistently justified true belief would be problematic. As Plato made clear in *Theaetetus,* one could always respond to a purported item of knowledge with the question, "How do you know that?" 5 If the response is an appeal to an additional item of purported knowledge, the question "How do you know that?" can be repeated, and so on *ad infinitum.* To avoid such infinite regress, there must be claims that are known to be true without appeal to additional judgments. Our contention is that these are first-person epistemic judgments, wherein the knower directly apprehends the object of knowledge. 6 The philosophical notion of "direct realism" which anchors this claim will be discussed fully in Chapter 6.

We have not yet dealt with how the process of association is rhetorical. It is most obviously rhetorical in that to arrive at any item of derived knowledge we must employ intermediate descriptions of reality. This rhetorical process is enhanced as associations among descriptions of reality allow us to see new relations embodied by our discourse. And this activity itself may be a catalyst prompting additional differentiation, additional association, and hence, generation of new knowledge claims.

Association is a rhetorical constituent of describing reality for yet another reason. Association occurs by virtue of "reasons," "inferences," "warrants," "enthymemes," "implicature," "the 'taken-for-granted'," and other connection-making processes. These are processes that have long been recognized as rhetorical. An example will illustrate. Almost from the inception of rhetorical theory, scholars concerned with discerning the principles of persuasion have found it necessary to explore the manner in which speakers and writers build persuasive arguments by drawing inferences.[7] It soon became apparent that effective persuasion depended not only on adherence to rules of validity and probability, but also on the ability of communicators to tap the beliefs, attitudes, and values assumed by their audiences. Associative processes are essential here. In discussions of Aristotle's "enthymeme," contemporary scholars have recognized that persuasive arguments are commonly constructed jointly by speaker and audience, with missing parts of arguments, left implicit by the speaker, supplied intrapersonally by the audience.[8] Similarly, Toulmin's conception of arguments as composed of "grounds," "warrants," and "claims," has underscored the vital role played by audiences in supplying portions of the material upon which the acceptability of an argument depends.[9] Examination of how communicators in our society effect persuasion, whether about mundane or philosophical affairs, will show that a majority of arguments involve "premises" or "conclusions" that have to be tacitly accepted because they are not articulated as propositions. It is especially common to find arguments for which the audience must fill in the necessary warrant or supply prior arguments as premises for the first link in a rhetor's explicit argument. The contemporary concepts of argumentative "chains" and "clusters" further illustrate recognition that actual practice in argumentation employs premises and warrants that are implicit and must be associatively supplied by audiences but are nonetheless operative.[10]

Association of one idea with another or of one inference with another is the fundamental process by which propositions become connected in discourse. The use of tacitly known propositions conveniently illustrates the presence of association in rhetorical discourse. There are, of course, circumstances in which all elements of arguments are articulated by rhetors;

then, association is guided or directed by the rhetor's language, but association is still the fundamental process of connection making.

With an understanding of how audiences are required to or are guided in associating ideas, we can see how derivative knowledge comes into existence: knowledge supplied by individuals other than the rhetor permits development of additional knowledge. Furthermore, justification for what is held as knowledge derives from knowledge claims (premises) supplied by or for an audience. We are not arguing that the supplying of reasons by an audience *guarantees* that a belief will be elevated to the status of knowledge. The audience could be wrong; it may supply false or inadequately established premises. Our point is that in many cases, without material supplied by the audience, knowledge as persistently justified true belief is unattainable.

Our claim here is best grasped by considering the distinction between validity and soundness, a distinction commonly drawn by rhetoricians and logicians alike.11 To be justified in making an epistemic judgment, one's argument must adhere to principles of logical entailment, that is, to principles of formal validity. Thus, for an argument to be formally valid, a requisite number of component parts must be present and be arranged (or arrangeable) in a certain order. Yet if one accepts the traditional rhetorical wisdom that the audience supplies vital links in the speaker's argument, it follows that validity is to an important degree audience dependent. In chains of reasoning audience dependence is the *rhetorical* ingredient accounting for the emergence of logical sorites.

To summarize, we contend that an argument cannot be valid unless a given number of premises arranged in a certain order according to the rules of inference are present. Further, when speakers confront audiences (including themselves) for the purpose of persuading, the audience will often be required to provide certain premises which the speaker does not articulate but which are requisite to "filling out" the form of the argument in order to render it amenable to tests of validity. In the case of sorites, the audience will provide intermediary inferences or conclusions. Therefore, where a speaker does not advance an explicitly articulated, formally valid argument (which happens in the majority of even philosophical arguments), formal validity of arguments depends on derivative knowledge provided by the audience.12

From this analysis we can see how, from at least one perspective, rhetoric is epistemic: derivative knowledge is dependent upon the associative constituent of rhetoric. When audiences and speakers recognize that the result of their interaction is an item of knowledge greater than what was stipulated by articulated parts, they reveal to themselves that through rhetorical interaction a new item of knowledge has been discovered jointly. We are not suggesting that the conclusion of a formally valid deduction somehow contains information not inferentially derived from the premises. What we *are* suggesting is that when speaker and audience come together in the world and engage in discourse, the result of that confluence is more than any one individual—speaker or audience member—brought to the rhetorical situation. If the interaction between speaker and audience is successful and productive, something is revealed to each party that was formerly merely suspected at best. And this is true in any situation where arguer confronts interlocutor, whether in scholarly or everyday discourse.

THE PRESERVATIVE CONSTITUENT OF RHETORIC

In addition to its differentiative and associative functions, rhetorical discourse also functions epistemically as *preservative*. It operates to insure that epistemic judgments are maintained in the marketplace of ideas where they may be subjected to the scrutiny of arguers. Frequently, rhetorical discourse keeps alive ideas whose time has not yet come. For example, had all linguistic descriptions regarding the possibility that the sun is the center of the immediate universe, and all statements impinging upon such a thesis, gone out of existence or had they never arisen in discourse, there might never have been a heliocentric theory. Scientific theories are couched in language that describes reality (faithfully or unfaithfully), and sufficient justification must be marshaled in their support before they attain the status of knowledge.

In explanation of this rather general overview of rhetoric's preservative function, consider a philosophical / rhetorical dimension of John Stuart Mill's *On Liberty*. In his book, Mill developed a conception of truth in opposition to the Aristotelian tradition in political philosophy. Aristotle had contended that "truth and justice are by nature more powerful than their opposites; so that, when decisions are not made as they should be, the speakers with the right on their side have only themselves to thank for the outcome."13 Mill, however, argued that truth holds no unique advantage: "It is a piece of idle sentimentality, that truth, merely as truth, has any inherent power denied to error." Mill regarded the dictum that truth always triumphs over error as "one of those pleasant falsehoods which men repeat but experience refutes." "Men," he said, "are not more zealous for truth than they are for error, and a sufficient application of legal or even social penalties will generally succeed in stopping the propagation of either."14 Mill denied any extraordinary power for truth, and he viewed the majority of individuals as no more disposed toward good than toward evil. Mill concluded that there is an important role for what we are calling rhetoric in determining the truth of a viewpoint. His conception of rhetoric held the art of discourse to be virtually synonymous with argumentation. Because he held that there was no advantage intrinsic to truth, Mill was preoccupied with explaining how one might distinguish truth from error.

Mill's solution was to posit that vigorous defense of ideas and opinions in free and open disputation was the best method to determine the merits of supposedly "true" or "good" claims. In "On the Liberty of Thought and Discussion," Mill advanced a three-part argument. First, "If any opinion is through the action of an individual, group, or entire culture, suppressed and condemned to silence, that opinion may, for aught we know, be true."15 Mill reasoned that views once considered dangerous or false were sometimes later found to be true. He presented as examples Socrates, Jesus, and Marcus Aurelius, all of whom espoused ideas originally challenged as falsehoods. 16 Second, Mill argued that "even if a received opinion be entirely true, unless it is suffered to be and actually is vigorously and earnestly contested, it will, by most of those who receive it, be held in a manner of prejudice, with little comprehension or feeling of its rational grounds."17 Here, Mill was suggesting that rigorous debate by informed opponents is essential to keep a belief alive as a practical force in the world; hence, competition among ideas is essential. Mill's final argument posited that, "Though a silenced opinion be an error, it may, and very commonly does, contain a portion of truth." This thesis rested on the premise that prevailing opinion rarely contains the whole truth: "It is only by the collision of adverse opinions that the remainder of the truth has any chance of being supplied."18

Central to all three arguments was Mill's contention that an idea is most likely to be correct, not because of consistency with past fact or received opinion, but when it can withstand continuous, rigorous, argumentative opposition in the marketplace of ideas. It is rhetoric that guarantees continuing life for a concept, or ultimately defeats it. Rhetoric functions positively or negatively as a preservative.

In discussing rhetoric as preservative it seems important to consider what some might see as a corollary: Rhetoric defeats competing notions, as it preserves others. This may seem implicit in what we have cited from Mill as well as our ensuing commentary. Rhetoric functions to preserve "truth" in the marketplace, but part of the way it does so is by attenuating the credibility of the "false." Ptolemaic cosmology was sustained by rhetoric, and it was defeated by rhetoric as the heliocentric theory was rhetorically made to predominate. The notion of preservative, therefore, identifies a kind of "screening" function sustained rhetorically.

Rhetoric preserves in a twofold way: by sustaining and strengthening whatever can be said *for* an idea and by providing the means by which "error" can be perceived as erroneous. When rhetoric performs the latter function of casting a view as erroneous, it does not remove the erroneous view from the marketplace of ideas. Quite the contrary. Where through rhetorical processes judgments are determined to be erroneous, there is an important sense in which those judgments are still rhetorically preserved. Through rhetoric such judgments are removed from the set of judgments we label "knowledge" and are placed within the set of propositions we label "doubtful" or, at worst, "false beliefs." This aspect of rhetoric's preservative function is critical; rhetoric does not explode allegedly false ideas in any final sense. Rhetoric sustains the falsity of a false idea by virtue of, among other things, rhetoric's differentiating function.

That rhetoric does not expunge even ideas alleged to be false is one guarantee against dogmatism. In the world of discourse-in-use, rhetoric's preservative function, even of ideas generally removed from the stock of knowledge but not from the marketplace of ideas, is often fostered by those who still hold to a discredited idea. For example, the "Flat Earth Society" still argues vigorously for a Ptolemaic view of the solar system. It is by resort to rhetoric that the Flat Earth partisans keep their idea alive, reminding those who find overwhelming reasons to doubt their claims that even knowledge itself has to be sustained by reassertive rhetoric. Where advocates for "false" ideas no longer exist, the rhetoric of historians and literary artists preserves the ideas; the myths about Zeus still exist for us, thanks to rhetorical preservation. This preservative function of rhetoric not only works against dogmatism, it tends to inoculate us against social, political, and intellectual intolerance.

Rhetoric's preservative function is further highlighted by George Campbell's notion of the lively idea. Briefly put, Campbell was concerned in *Philosophy of Rhetoric* to explain how individuals assess truth and falsity through discourse. His concern was epistemological. Following Hume, Campbell noted that rhetoric helps to make and keep ideas "vivacious." [19] Further, he held that bringing ideas clearly and forcefully to mind, with reinforcement from one's memories and experiences, is to a very large degree a function of linguistic choices.

Coupled with our earlier notion that meaning is linguistic embodiment of relations, Campbell's focus on vivacity allows us to say that at least one important epistemological function of rhetoric is to permit others (or ourselves) to understand, to take seriously, perhaps to embrace, points of

100

view expressed in discourse. Depending on word choices and syntactical formulations, language will be more or less successful in making conspicuous the relations among rhetor, extralinguistic phenomena, and tacit audience. The more rhetorically adept one is, the more likely it is that an audience will: (1) understand a speaker's or writer's intention; (2) assess the relative merits of arguments accurately and thoroughly; and (3) be aided in assessing the speaker's or writer's ideas *vis-à-vis* the respondents' own ideas.

If there is any validity at all to the judgment that knowledge is cumulative and that we do make progress in coming to know the way the world really is, it is the preservative function of rhetoric that makes possible such advancement. An idea is proposed, perhaps in an incomplete or even muddled fashion; the idea may at first be rejected by the majority of individuals; the thinker *qua* rhetor perseveres, perhaps formulating the ideas with increased accuracy and clarity; the idea may now win additional advocates but still not receive wide currency; still the thinker and his or her adherents can persist, arguing in favor of their hypothesis with increasing accuracy and definition; finally, the idea may achieve the status of knowledge because the preserving capacity of rhetorical discourse allows ideas to be repeatedly adjusted as proponents refine the view, ultimately allowing successful defense of it against critical inspection by others.

Whether viewed in the context of Mill's thesis of the marketplace of ideas or of Campbell's conception of the lively idea, the preservative function of rhetoric has implications for two of the three criteria of knowledge: truth and persistent justification. With reference to truth, if there is any chance that truth can be discovered, discovery will occur only if the preservative function of rhetoric can keep true opinions before us long enough to allow their evaluation and validation. Moreover, according to Campbell's concept of the lively idea, we can best guarantee that true opinion will be kept alive if its embodiment in language is accomplished so as to make the relationships concerned vividly conspicuous. With respect to persistent justification, one cannot justify (in the strictest rational sense) a knowledge claim without the use of language which, at minimum, makes conspicuous a set of relationships embodying the rationale for the epistemic judgment. The very notion of justification presumes the ability of rhetors to make clear (to make lively) their reasons for suggesting that a proposition is true. If an interlocutor is unable to understand, embrace, or otherwise grasp the relations embodied in a rhetor's linguistic usage, a fair assessment of reasoning and evidence is precluded and attainment of the persistent justification criterion is impossible. Likewise, if Gettier-type "exceptions" to the justification of a knowledge claim are encountered, it is through the preservative function of rhetoric that the claim may eventually be vindicated and *persistent* justification established.

THE EVALUATIVE CONSTITUENT OF RHETORIC

A fourth constituent of rhetorical discourse has important social as well as epistemological consequences. This is *critical evaluation*. All linguistic statements about reality are critiques and evaluations at least in the sense that they imply what is not or what is doubtful as they assert what allegedly is. In this sense at least, and often in much more explicit ways, discourse operates to critique and evaluate beliefs, privately and consensually. Through discourse one increases or decreases confidence that one is approaching the truth, and to the degree that our opinions or beliefs withstand the critical inquiry implicit in discourse we grow confident that what we hold approaches knowledge.

That rhetorical discourse contains a dimension of critical appraisal is important socially. Through energetic discourse we restrain consensus-based social movements, air points of view, and perhaps establish the social tolerance that stems from intellectual tolerance. For these reasons, Henry W. Johnstone, Jr., could conclude that "the rationality of the philosophical enterprise consists in the use of a rhetoric."[20] According to Johnstone, philosophical critics proceed by the form of rhetoric we have labeled *dialectical* to inspect intellectual products with an eye to raising the "standards of the manufacturing process."[21] This rhetorical function that Johnstone sees as central to doing philosophy is the function that Socrates espoused when he contended that those questions that are of importance to us in the everyday conduct of our lives *are* philosophical issues. Rhetorical discourse functions to describe reality through language; it is therefore epistemological rhetoric that serves us in searching for understanding and in discovering bases for action.

All rhetoric is evaluative, since rhetoric is differentiative; but not all evaluative rhetoric is epistemic. We need to ask, then, what criteria evaluative rhetoric must meet in order to be considered epistemic. We suggest that there are three such criteria.

First, rhetoric that is evaluatively epistemic must be *bilateral* in character. By this we mean that the participants in argument must have equal initiative and control in the course of the rhetorical encounter. Bilaterality means coercive and manipulative methods are eschewed. There is an "agreement of a special sort." As a result, whoever engages in argument, "instead of being an inert object or sink, is an active participant."[22]

Through tacit or explicit commitment to bilaterality, initiative and control in discourse pass back and forth among participants. This gives assurance that instead of being haphazardly launched, arguments will tend to cluster around points of stasis. *Stasis* is a term originating in Greek and Roman rhetorical theory. It refers to the points in an argumentative encounter where a "stand" must be made, where thesis and antithesis clash and where resolution must be reached before arguers can move on to further points in dispute.23 In what we call dialectical rhetoric, arguers focus reflectively on such points of clash or stasis; they know such points must be knowingly resolved before the argumentative process can move on. Rhetors move thus reflectively from stasis to stasis until all interlocutorial resources have been exhausted and the participants can make, or knowingly see that they cannot make, a final determination of legitimate knowledge claims about the issue in controversy. But without shared initiative and control it is not possible to proceed in this fashion; hence, in the absence of this special *procedural* agreement, it is hard to see how rhetoric can become epistemic.

Second, in order for one to gain knowledge from argument, rhetorical evaluation must be viewed as an activity of *correction,* wherein the clash of contradictory ideas exposes error. Correction may involve wholesale abandonment of a position formerly held, amending part of a former view, or adding knowledge discovered in the encounter in order to flesh out a prior position. Unless participants remain open to these possibilities we have only expression of attitudes based on dogmatically held positions. Rhetoric that is epistemic cannot be sheer self-expression; it must be a dialogic process of utterances and responses whose cumulative effect is achievement of or movement toward knowledge. It can only be achieved where the parties share willingness to correct opinions.

Third, and issuing from the two properties discussed above, unless rhetoric functions as an enterprise of person-risking, there can be no assurance that the attempts to acquire knowledge will be successful. This third aspect of the evaluative constituent of epistemic rhetoric we call *self-risk.* Douglas Ehninger defined self-risk: "By entering upon argument . . . a disputant opens the possibility that as a result of interchange he may be persuaded of his opponent's view or, failing that, at least may be forced to make alterations in his own."24 The result of self-risk is that one may depart from an argumentative encounter "a different 'self' or 'person' " since one's attitudes, beliefs, and values may be "remolded."25 The greater the degree of personal investment in a given argumentative position (say, for example, a religious or ethical stance), the greater the degree of self-risk which must be demonstrated by the arguers.

The importance of the self-risk criterion for epistemic rhetoric can be underscored by remembering that the "self" is at the core of all epistemic judgments. Language embodies relations between the self and other relata, and since all knowledge claims begin with and are predicated on this establishing of relations between self and other relata, it follows that all knowledge is essentially knowledge of self. Though he does not explicitly develop a relational conception of self, the philosopher Maurice Natanson arrives at a somewhat similar conclusion: "Self knowledge is the clue to as much of our comprehension of the world as man can gain."26

According to Natanson, we can be certain of very little; we can, nevertheless, attain apodictic knowledge of ourselves. If he is correct and our analysis of linguistic embodiment and meaning tends to confirm it, the quest for knowledge rests upon a crucial epistemological condition: Knowledge is a function of the conscious relationship of the person to all else. Learning entails confronting the self with the relations in which the self stands to everything else. Yet, as we have implied, this thesis is clearly not one that casts knowledge as subjective. How, then, does one gain knowledge of such relationships?

Only when an arguer exposes self to the possibility of being reshaped as a result of rhetorical encounter can the self be repositioned *vis-à-vis* the relata of a relational complex. Only then can rhetorical activity move one closer to knowledge. Relationships remain unrecognized, unarticulated, hence inconspicuous, until one is willing to open the self to critical inspection. And with that statement we come upon the vehicle for acquiring knowledge—controversy. It is through controversy that one exposes self, allowing others and the world to enter freely and to probe "the privacy of his cognitive and affective life." Natanson concisely describes the mode when he writes that philosophy "is the visitor who announces himself through the calling card of argumentation."27 The person-risking that is part of the evaluative constituent of rhetoric renders relations between the self and all else conspicuous. Here, linguistic embodiment allows the particular relations embraced by an individual self to be juxtaposed critically with all other possible relations observable in the relational complex. Only intrapersonal or interpersonal controversy evokes the self to contemplation of its relational possibilities, which may or may not command change.

Applying the criteria of bilateralism, correction, and self-risk to the evaluative component of rhetoric suggests that the only kind of rhetorical discourse that deserves epistemic status is that which we described in Chapter 3 as dialectical. We said that dialectic is the purest mode of rhetoric because it is intended to be *faithful* description of reality through language. The three criteria of evaluation that we have just discussed define intention to describe faithfully. Once these criteria are met consistently and systematically by an arguer, they constitute the original Greek sense of dialectic, namely, the pursuit of serious inquiry. 28

An additional concept relevant to our discussion of the evaluative constituent of rhetoric is "intersubjectivity" or "intersubjective validation." 29 Simply put, our claim is that when arguers fulfill the three criteria associated with the evaluative feature of rhetoric, they in essence transcend subjectivity—the embracing of one's own, privately held opinions and beliefs. They enter the more epistemologically productive realm of intersubjectivity. Thus, whether an arguer confronts his or her own private self in intrapersonal argument that meets the three criteria of evaluation, or whether an arguer confronts an interlocutor interpersonally in a similar way, the criterial dimensions of evaluation enhance the likelihood that the product of the argumentative process will be *knowledge,* as opposed to belief, true belief, or rational belief. In this way, intersubjective validation supplants subjectivity in dialectical rhetoric.

Our analysis of dialectic and intersubjective validation makes clear the relationship between the evaluative constituent of rhetoric and knowledge as persistently justified true belief. Without the three properties of bilateralism, correction, and self-risk, justification of one's knowledge is unattainable. In other words, while the confluence of the three criteria of evaluation does not guarantee that justification will reach the sufficiency of evidence required to demonstrate conclusively that a particular epistemic judgment is true, without the three properties constituting the evaluative component of epistemic rhetoric, persistent justification will certainly remain beyond the grasp of the inquirer. Even during those rare moments when a thinker suddenly realizes a new discovery apart from the presence of another arguer, we cannot conceive how that thinker would gain *justified* confidence in the veracity of the discovery without meeting dialectical rhetoric's evaluative criteria. 30

THE PERSPECTIVAL CONSTITUENT OF RHETORIC

Rhetorical discourse can perform the functions of appraising and making conspicuous the relations among objects of reality existing independently of conscious, thinking human beings. Yet one could easily point out that humans constantly disagree, especially in reference to the most vital and important issues of the day. Indeed, one could go on from this fact to contend that knowledge as persistently justified true belief cannot be attained through rhetoric of any sort. We have responded to this view by contending that disagreement among people does not preclude the possibility of attaining knowledge as we have defined it. Now, we wish to add that rhetorical discourse always has a *perspectival* dimension that accounts for the pervasiveness of disagreement but does not preclude attainment of *some* knowledge.

We begin our discussion of the perspectival function of rhetoric with a postulate: *When individuals differentiate, associate, preserve, and evaluate—that is, when they employ rhetorical discourse—they do so from a particular and unique perspective.* 31 We reserve for our next chapter a technical exposition of the particular ontological theory underpinning this postulate. For the present, we shall confine ourselves to explaining what we mean by a "perspectival constituent of rhetoric."

We have already defended our premise that objects of knowledge and conscious, rational beings besides our individual selves exist independently of ourselves. From this premise it follows that each person and each "thing" 32 in the universe *stands in some particular relation to every other thing.* It could scarcely be otherwise. Consider the opposite thesis, that something might stand wholly unrelated to anything else. Such a state of affairs is inconceivable. Let us take the quality *good* as an example. However we analyze the term, it seems inconceivable that the quality of goodness could exist as the only element in the universe. Even for a Platonist, good *in the world* exists in relation to the Form of good, and the Form of good exists *in relation to* a world of Forms. One can be more concrete. Contemporary ethicists tend to agree that good makes sense only in reference to particular acts that we designate as good or not good. Here, again, good exists in relation to specific human actions. In empirical matters also, each discernible item of experience is what it is only in relation to other things. For the lay person, for the logician, and for the scientist, each particular is distinct and is what it is only in relation to other things, and particulars often stand together in complexes; that is, they exist in interrelated ways. Moreover, such complexes can be made sense of only with respect to the context of particulars in which they stand. This is true whether we are considering an empirical example, an ethical claim, an aesthetic judgment, or whatever.

The implication for rhetorical enterprises is this: Because a rhetor is a conscious, perceiving entity, he or she stands within the world as a particular within a relational complex that is, itself, formed from other particulars. It is by being aware of the surrounding context of particulars and relational complexes that a rhetor is afforded capacity to change anything in the world, or that an audience can influence a rhetor. Yet the rhetor (or member of the audience) must view the world from some perspective;

106

only a small part of the whole can be perceived at any one time. Moreover, what is apprehended from one perspective will seem different from what is apprehended from another perspective. An all-inclusive description of reality through language is an impossibility. Perspectival differences are inevitable. There is the source of vast numbers of disagreements in the world of discourse.

If we recognize the perspectival character of all rhetorical discourse, we recognize that a world existing independently of a rhetor may be taken in different, even contradictory, ways. But each "way" will potentially constitute knowledge as persistently justified true belief. There may be *some* truth in the view taken. Let us return to an epistemic judgment considered earlier: "Richard Nixon was a good president." The object of knowledge here is Richard Nixon's "goodness" as president. It may appear at first that both an affirmation and a denial of this object of knowledge can be true. Using the same body of evidence, some individuals have claimed that "Richard Nixon was a good president" and others have said, "Richard Nixon was a bad president." However, it is logically and conceptually impossible to entertain both statements as knowledge at the same time and in the same way. How is it then that both statements can and are taken to be items of *knowledge*?

The answer lies in understanding each individual's perspective, in noting the particular relationship in which the subject stands to the context of particulars that includes the object of knowledge. The reason for apparently contradictory judgments lies in the fact that each commentator apprehends a different aspect of Nixon's presidency. One may focus on the former president's handling of foreign policy and the other on his actions associated with his reelection campaign. That an object of knowledge may have aspects is vitally important. An aspect of any object may be an elementary, indivisible quality such as goodness or justice or beauty, or it may be something divisible physically like size or shape, or it may be a collection of qualities divisible conceptually, as is Richard Nixon's foreign policy. In the last case, the collection of qualities may be divided further. It is not surprising to find disagreement regarding the effectiveness or ineffectiveness, or the rightness or wrongness, or the appropriateness or inappropriateness of Nixon's foreign policy. Recognizing the role of perspectives illustrates that disagreement between or among individuals is very often disagreement about the qualities or significance of different aspects of the object of knowledge. In our day-to-day discourse we often label this state of affairs "arguing on two different levels." In some of the literature on theory of argument it is called "not achieving stasis." In any case, it reflects either the subject's particular relation to the object of knowledge (commonly called one's "point of view") or the subject's unwillingness or inability to see the point of view of his or her interlocutor. In none of these circumstances does disagreement provide any reason to abandon the notion that knowledge is persistently justified true belief; indeed, given the rhetorical epistemology we have developed in this book, it would be very strange if the discourse we use to describe the world did not reflect and evoke disagreement and misunderstanding.

Rhetoric describes in language the way the world is *from the perspective of an individual rhetor.* This is a fact constantly employed by those who practice the rhetoric of social amelioration; they strive to make individual perspectives embraceable by others. They are not always successful in their attempts to explain different perspectives to their fellows, but creating appreciation and respect for alternative perspectives is the major aim of their rhetoric. Bigots, racists, or xenophobes may never accept the self-risk involved in accepting new perspectives; with them multi-perspectival rhetoric will fail. On the other hand, we can call some rhetoric *propaganda* because it is discourse that excludes consideration of alternative perspectives. The linguistic descriptions of reality that issued from the pen of Joseph Goebbels contained mixtures of statements that corresponded faithfully to some aspects of the world and other statements describing aspects of the world that were known to be other than as portrayed. What we can fairly call propaganda is discourse that strategically mingles supportable and unsupportable perspectives on reality. As Konrad Kellen has observed, 'it [propaganda] operates . . . with many different kinds of truth—half truth, limited truth, truth out of context."33 To employ vocabulary we have used earlier, propaganda operates to *exclude* free play of perspectives in the marketplace of ideas.

Noting that all rhetoric is perspectival and combining these observations with the other elements of rhetorical epistemology already outlined enables us to refine the concept of knowledge as justified true belief. We are now able to see that justified true belief results in *knowledge,* but usually of only some *aspects* of the world. Furthermore, because rhetorical discourse operates as perspective, one can have full knowledge of something only to the degree that one has embraced the perspectives of others as well as one's own. One can, of course, have limited knowledge of aspects of something, of a relational complex of particulars such as knowledge of Richard Nixon's presidential foreign policy. Knowledge can be complete, however, only to the degree all aspects of the object of knowledge have been viewed from all relevant perspectives. Those who search for truth through scholarship will find this concept familiar.

THE EPISTEMOLOGICAL RELEVANCE OF RHETORIC

We believe we have made clear that rhetoric is essential to the process of acquiring knowledge. We have emphasized, however, that not all rhetoric earns epistemic status. If knowledge is conceived as "persistently justified true belief," only some of our beliefs can be elevated to the status of knowledge. Our contention that rhetoric is epistemic is, therefore, a qualified claim. To be epistemic, rhetoric must meet several qualifying conditions, each building hierarchically on the others to produce the greatest humanly possible degree of assurance regarding the veracity of the knowledge claim in question. We can summarize the conditions to be met as follows:

1. *Epistemologically productive rhetoric must make conspicuous the relations obtaining among rhetor, extralinguistic phenomena, and tacit audience; it must differentiate among the relata constituting the universe.*

2. *Epistemologically productive rhetoric must draw valid inferences (associations) between first-person epistemic judgments and derived knowledge; in other words, it must be possible at least theoretically to trace the lineage between one description of reality and all others upon which any particular item of knowledge is based.* To attain the status of knowledge, rhetoric must motivate recognition of the missing, unarticulated premises on which the validity of the epistemic judgment rests. The conclusion of epistemologically productive rhetoric may be potentially capable of yielding an item of knowledge greater in sum than the individually expressed premises underlying the conclusion. But the conclusion must contain only that information that is inferentially derived from the larger set of premises, including such underlying, unexpressed, enthymematic features as implicature.

3. *Epistemologically productive rhetoric must be preserved in the marketplace of ideas for a time sufficient to establish its validity and truthfulness.* The rhetoric must be capable of withstanding rigorous argumentative opposition, and its expression must sufficiently accord with the principles of vivacity to bring its ideas clearly and forcefully to mind and to call up pertinent memories and experiences. This will maximize the possibility that the relations embodied in discourse can be understood and embraced by others, allowing assessment of the evidence and reasoning associated with the item or items of knowledge.

4. *Epistemologically productive rhetoric must be based on critical evaluation; it must be dialectically secured.* To achieve epistemic status, rhetoric must be bilateral, affording each rhetor equality for initiative and control over lines of influence. In addition, the rhetoric must be corrective, harboring the assumption that the clash of differing ideas is the best means of exposing error and yielding truth. This assumption is an expression of the principle that knowledge develops cumulatively. Epistemologically productive rhetoric must also involve self-risk, where knowers risk the possibility that their views will be altered as a result of argument. Rhetoric deserving the status of knowledge presupposes that the self can be repositioned *vis-a-vis* the relata constituting the comprehended universe. This in turn allows intersubjectivity to supplant subjectivity.

5. *Epistemologically productive rhetoric must make clear the particular perspective of the knower; it must begin with the recognition that everything in the universe stands in a particular relation to everything else, where all things are what they are because of the unique relationships in which they stand to all else.* For this reason, our knowledge is often partial or limited, embodying a relationship between the knower and one aspect of an object of reality. Rhetoric can result in full knowledge only when a knower has exploratively embraced the perspectives of all relevant others, permitting the richest understanding of the object in question.

This list of conditions reveals an important fact about rhetoric and about knowledge. Some lines of thought have treated rhetoric as a vehicle used by communicators to propagate truth, but that view overlooks an important creative function of rhetorical activity. If our analysis is sound, *rhetoric is more than embellishment added to alleged truths.* Rhetoric is more than a means of making truths effective. Rhetorical activity is itself a major part of the process of *discovery.* Each of the conditions set forth highlights the inseparability of propagation and discovery, whether rhetorical activity becomes fully epistemic or not. It follows that the familiarly posed dichotomies between content and form and between invention and disposition are not dichotomies at all. Embedded in these alleged distinctions is an assumption that truth and knowledge exist prior to the rhetorical enterprise, that rhetoric serves only to impart discovered knowledge to audiences. Yet each of the constituents of rhetoric indicates that rhetoric is more than a vehicle of transmission. Part of rhetorical functioning can be and often is *exploration.* Through the combined processes of differentiating, associating, preserving, evaluating, and viewing in perspective we *discover* the world we live in. Even when rhetorical activity falls short of the listed conditions, discovery of possibilities occurs; and when our discourses attain the level of sophistication and rigor that can meet the criteria fully, that rhetoric is epistemic.

NOTES

1. Our claim here is that rhetoric is essential to knowing regardless of the particular content of a given knowledge claim. This thesis is distinct from the claim advanced by some that rhetoric is only one way of generating knowledge, that is, that rhetoric is "a" way of knowing and not "the" way of knowing. For a discussion of the "a" way of knowing position, see Robert L. Scott, "On Viewing Rhetoric as Epistemic: Ten Years Later," *Central States Speech Journal,* 27 (1976), 258–66; Thomas B. Farrell, "Knowledge, Consensus, and Rhetorical Theory," *Quarterly Journal of Speech,* 62 (1976), 1–14; and Richard Cherwitz, "Rhetoric as a 'Way of Knowing:' An Attenuation of the Epistemological Claims of the 'New Rhetoric,' " *Southern Speech Communication Journal,* 42 (1977), 207–19. Our claim that rhetoric is "the" way of knowing departs significantly from other similar claims. See, for example, Walter M. Carleton, "What Is Rhetorical Knowledge? A Reply to Farrell—And More," *Quarterly Journal of Speech,* 64 (1978), 313–28.

2. The distinction among "primary," "first-person," and "derivative knowledge" is discussed by Panayot Butchvarov, *The Concept of Knowledge* (Evanston, Ill.: Northwestern University Press, 1970), pp. 4, 21 33–36, 41–42, 61–96. Primary epistemic judgments are of the form "A knows that p" and do not require justification by appeal to other epistemic judgments. Derivative knowledge, by contrast, is in need of such justification; that is, derived knowledge relies upon other items of knowledge as an integral part of justification. An example of a first-person epistemic judgment would be: "I have a headache." For reasons developed throughout this book, we are in agreement with Butchvarov that first-person epistemic judgments have a kind of "logical priority" over third-person judgments (e.g., "Jones knows that p").

3. Ibid., pp. 34–35, 95. Butchvarov claims that "derivative epistemic judgments . . . are subject to justification by reference to other epistemic judgments."

4. The notion of a "relational complex" is treated technically in Chapter 6 which presents and defends a theory of relationality. Our claim is that everything that is, is what it is by virtue of its relationship to all else. Our use of the term "relational complex" is consistent with the treatment of relationality offered by Evander Bradley McGilvary, *Toward a Perspective Realism,* Albert G. Ramsperger, ed. (La Salle, Ill.: Open Court Publishing Co., 1956).

5. This question raised by Plato in *Theaetetus* is an important one. In order to avoid an infinite regress, there must be some sort of knowledge that can be justified in the absence of appeal to other items of knowledge. As we have maintained, such judgments requiring no appeal to additional items of knowledge are called "first-person epistemic judgments" and are known by virtue of direct experiencing.

6. Readers should be aware that there are those who have questioned the concept of "first-person" epistemic judgments as a foundation of knowledge. See, for example, Donald Scherer, "Incorrigibilist Dilemmas," *Southern Journal of Philosophy,* (Fall, 1973), 237–39. Scherer's thesis is in contrast to that presented by Roderick M. Chisholm, *Theory of Knowledge* (Englewood Cliffs, N.J.: Prentice-Hall, 1966), pp. 28, 40–55.

7. The importance of "inferences" in human communication is most frequently seen in discussion of theory of argument. See, for example, Stephen Toulmin, Richard Rieke, and Allan Janik, *An Introduction to Reasoning* (New York: Macmillan Publishing Co., 1979), pp. 3–20. See also, Douglas Ehninger, *Influence, Belief, and Argument: An Introduction to Responsible Persuasion* (Glenview, Ill.: Scott, Foresman and Company, 1974); and Richard D. Rieke and Malcolm O. Sillars, *Argumentation and the Decision Making Process* (New York: John Wiley & Sons, 1975).

8. Aristotle, *Rhetoric,* I.1, 1355a. For Aristotle, the enthymeme was a rhetorical syllogism, that is, a form of logical reasoning employed in the realm of contingent affairs. The concept of "enthymeme" has been widely treated in the literature on rhetorical theory. See, Lloyd F. Bitzer, "Aristotle's Enthymeme Revisited," *Quarterly Journal of Speech,* 45 (1959), 399–408; Charles S. Mudd, "The Enthymeme and Logical Validity," *Quarterly Journal of Speech,* 45 (1959), 409–14; and Richard L. Lanigan, "Enthymeme: The Rhetorical Species of Aristotle's Syllogism," *Southern Speech Communication Journal,* 39 (1974), 207–22.

9. These terms are those used by Stephen Toulmin, *The Uses of Argument* (Cambridge: Cambridge University Press, 1958), pp. 97–107. In 1958 Toulmin employed the vocabulary of "data," "warrant," "claim." He has since modified the terminology used in his argumentative model. See Toulmin, Rieke, and Janik, pp. 25–27.

10. The concepts of "chains" and "clusters" are discussed clearly by Ehninger. According to him, "When arguments are arranged in a series or chain, each unit of proof save the first one is preceded by a similar unit, the conclusion or claim statement of which serves as evidence for the argument that follows." On the other hand, "a number of independent arguments or chains of arguments may be grouped together into a cluster, or bundle, or proofs, the cumulative effect of which is to support the claim in question." Douglas Ehninger, *Influence, Belief, and Argument: An Introduction to Responsible Persuasion,* pp. 14, 15.

11. A valid argument is one whose premises, if true, logically lead to the specified conclusion. Thus, an argument which correctly conforms to the rules of logic would be said to be valid; that is, we would say its conclusion is entailed. A sound argument must not only meet the standards of validity but, in addition, such an argument must contain all true premises. This distinction between validity and soundness is best captured in an example: All liberals are honest; you are a liberal; therefore, you must be honest. While such an argument is, by definition, "valid," we could certainly question whether or not it is a "sound" argument. In short, its conclusion logically follows if we suppose the truth of the premises. To suppose the truth of the individual premises, though, is suspect in this case.

12. This is precisely the point made in Henry W. Johnstone, Jr., "Rationality and Rhetoric in Philosophy," *Quarterly Journal of Speech,* 59, (1973), 381–89. On sorites, see Irving M. Copi, *Introduction to Logic* (New York: Macmillan, 1972).

13. Aristotle, *Rhetoric,* I.2, 1355a.

14. John Stuart Mill, *Autobiography and Other Writings,* Jack Stillinger, ed. (Boston: Houghton Mifflin, 1969), p. 377.

15. Ibid., p. 400.

16. Ibid., pp. 366–83.

17. Ibid., p. 400.

18. Ibid.

19. The notion of "vivacity" is treated in George Campbell, *The Philosophy of Rhetoric* (Carbondale: Southern Illinois University Press, 1963), pp. 285–384 (Book III).

20. Johnstone, p. 388.

21. Ibid.

22. Douglas Ehninger, "Argument as Method: Its Nature, Its Limitations, and Its Uses," *Speech Monographs,* 38 (1970), pp. 102, 103.

23. The concept of *stasis* has been examined extensively in speech communication. See, among others, Otto Alvin Loeb Dieter, "Stasis," *Speech Monographs,* 17 (1950), 345–69; Ray Nadeau, "Some Aristotelian and Stoic Influences on the Theory of Stases," *Speech Monographs,* 26 (1959), 248–54; and Ray Nadeau, "Hermogenes' *On Stases:* A Translation with an Introduction and Notes," *Speech Monographs,* 31 (1964), 361–424.

24. Ehninger, "Argument as Method," p. 104.

25. Ibid.

26. Maurice Natanson, "The Claims of Immediacy," in *Philosophy, Rhetoric and Argumentation,* Henry W. Johnstone, Jr., and Maurice Natanson, eds. (University Park: Pennsylvania State University Press, 1965), p. 16.

27. Ibid.

28. The conception of "dialectic" herein presented is consistent with Plato's use of the term. In *Republic,* Plato conceives of dialectic as the supreme philosophical method; it is the highest of all human arts. Says Plato, dialectic is "the coping-stone, as it were, placed above the sciences" (*Republic,* 534e). In *Cratylus* Plato describes the dialectician as "the man who knows how to ask and answer questions" (*Cratylus* 390c). For a good discussion of Plato's view of dialectic, see Julius Stenzel, *Plato's Method of Dialectic,* trans. and ed. by D. J. Allan (Oxford: Oxford University Press, 1940). A clear exposition of the concept from classical to present times appears in Roland Hall, "Dialectic," *The Encyclopedia of Philosophy,* 1967, pp. 385–89.

29. The concepts of "intersubjectivity" and "intersubjective validation" are treated in Barry Brummett, "Some Implications of 'Process' or 'Intersubjectivity': Postmodern Rhetoric," *Philosophy and Rhetoric,* 9 (1976), 21–51; and Richard Cherwitz, "Rhetoric as a 'Way of Knowing': An Attenuation of the Epistemological Claims of the 'New Rhetoric,' " *Southern Speech Communication Journal,* 42 (1977), 207–19. We urge readers not to equate our remarks here with the views developed by these authors or others in, for example, the phenomenological tradition. Our exact position regarding intersubjectivity will be made clear in Chapter 6.

30. Our claim here suggests the possibility of intrapersonal rhetoric. The implication is intended. With our comments pertaining to the "differentiative" function of rhetoric we are once more contending that intrapersonal rhetoric may be the paradigm of epistemic rhetoric. For fuller treatment of this perspective, see

James W. Hikins, "The Epistemological Relevance of Intrapersonal Rhetoric," *Southern Speech Communication Journal,* 42 (1977), 220–27.

31. The terms "perspectival," "perspective," and "perspectivism" appear frequently in the literature in communication studies, most recently in Wayne Brockriede, "Constructs, Experience, and Argument," *Quarterly Journal of Speech,* 71 (1985), 151–163. See also, B. Aubry Fisher, *Perspectives on Human Communication* (New York: Macmillan, 1978). While these sources use such terms at times in ways consistent with the view developed in this book, none of these authors acknowledge the philosophical grounds of perspectivism in the work of McGilvary or others. Nor have scholars in communication pursued the concept of perspective in terms of its ontological foundations and/or implications.

32. We use the term "thing" to denote the independent objects of reality and not to refer to what have traditionally been described as "physical objects." More will be said on this subject in Chapter 6.

33. Jacques Ellul, *Propaganda: The Formation of Men's Attitudes,* Konrad Kellen, trans. (New York: Knopf Books, 1965), p. v.

ONTOLOGY AND RHETORICAL
EPISTEMOLOGY

We have now outlined a rhetorical epistemology. We have defined knowledge as justified true belief. We have defined rhetoric as description of reality through language, and we have detailed the interface between knowledge and rhetoric, locating the symbiotic relationship between knowing and communication in the use of language to make relations conspicuous to selves. In Chapter 5 we discussed five properties which, when present in discourse, permit rhetoric to function in an epistemologically productive way. In short, the preceding chapters have focused on "rhetoric" and "epistemology," arguing that the two domains of human activity are inherently interconnected. Implicit within our theory of rhetorical epistemology, however, is a host of assumptions regarding the character of the world about which we endeavor to know. Completing our treatment of rhetorical knowledge requires that these assumptions be made explicit and be explored systematically because, unless the foundations upon which a rhetorical epistemology rests are carefully and thoroughly delineated, one can have little confidence in the theory's veracity.

In this chapter we shall investigate the ontology both assumed in and implied by our rhetorical epistemology. The kinds of questions we must explore have been touched on earlier. In Chapter 2 we posited the existence of an independent reality, that is, a reality independent of individuals' beliefs, attitudes, and values. This was called an assumption at that point, as was our contention that reality impinges upon a knower in such a way as often to validate or disconfirm claims to knowledge. Similarly, in Chapters 4 and 5 we asserted that the most basic ontological concept, from which all of reality arises, is "the relation." Additionally, we argued that *consciousness,* a foundational notion in our theory of knowledge acquisition, is itself a relational concept. These are among the major claims to be reexamined in this chapter. In this examination we do not presume to launch and exhaustive philosophical argument. We shall be satisfied to: (1) make clear the foundational theses upon which our rhetorical epistemology is based and (2) indicate the substance and direction of arguments in favor of our views.

THE INDEPENDENCE OF REALITY

One of the principal contentions of this book has been that reality exists independently of beliefs, attitudes, and values: that is, independently of subjective constructions by human beings. The existence of a reality separate from our human efforts to create or destroy it is the linchpin upon which turns the whole system of rhetorical epistemology we have developed. What case can be made for the independent existence of reality? We cannot *prove* reality's independence. Such a demonstration appears beyond the reach of analysis at this time. We can, however, undertake to convince readers that such an ontology is preferable to certain alternative ontologies, especially the alternative of subjectivism. To this end we offer the following arguments.

THE NAIVE ARGUMENT

One rationale for accepting the existence of an independent reality is what we shall term the *naive argument*. Briefly put, the contention is that humans *act* in their daily lives as though there were an independent reality. We treat the multifarious phenomena with which we are confronted as though they enjoy independent status. In and of itself, the fact that we act as if there were an independent world has little merit as a philosophical argument, but the power of the claim lies in what it would mean conceptually if individuals did *not* embrace such a view concerning an independent world.

It is hard to imagine what our world would be like if reality were not taken as independent. In the realm of human values, for example, we would never treat what appear to be other human beings in a manner that considered them as deserving equal ethical or moral status. We would have no basis for resolving disagreements among individuals, nations, or cultures. In day-to-day affairs, we would have no reason to take account of physical manifestations such as approaching storms, the onset of disease, or the change of a stoplight at a busy intersection. Neither would we respond seriously to nonphysical phenomena such as great ideas, warnings, commands, or advice. Yet it is clear that we do operate on the assumption that such phenomena have an autonomous status. For the most part, the things with which we are confronted in everyday experiences appear to have and are treated as though they have *objective* existence.

The question that arises, given all of this, is one that apologists for subjectivism consistently fail to ask: If the world is in fact subjectively constituted, why is the result of that systematic construction a world that appears to be an objective world? The heart of the argument may be more clearly seen if we rephrase that question: Why is it that the world we are phenomenally confronted with seems so different from what we would expect a subjective world to be like? Or again: How can one account for the disappointment we frequently experience upon matching our subjec-

116

tive expectations with a given experience? If human beings were capable of subjectively constituting their worlds, the features of the world they would *choose* would surely be more in keeping with their hopes, dreams, and aspirations. In short, if we are capable of subjectively creating our world, one would anticipate that the created world would contain more of what we find pleasing and less of what seems irksome. 1

The point we wish to press as a crucial one is that the context that enables us to conceptualize *both* what an objective and a subjective world would be like is a framework that exists by virtue of the notion of objectivity. It is only by assuming the existence of independent realities that one can even hope to render understandable the notions of subjective and objective. If the world were indeed subjectively created, if there were no independent reality, it would be impossible to conceive of a world different from the one subjectively constituted. Moreover, one ought to be able to assume that the individual who constructs the world would have a priori knowledge of such a world's construction. However, no such "self-knowledge" occurs.

From this conceptual analysis another dimension of the naive argument emerges. The very claim that there is no independent reality presupposes objectivity. Such a claim is offered as an objective truth, one transcending individuals. Any such claim guarantees the existence of an objective truth that stands apart from those humans who constitute their worlds. If the claim is true, it must be a claim *about* the subjective creation, and the claim is, therefore, an objective claim. If the claim is false, then clearly an objective world is preserved. Both conceptually and logically, the doctrine of subjectivism makes sense only if the world is objective in character. 2 The subjectivist, then, is in a position analogous to that of Epictetus, who confidently said to a chiding logician, "Prove to me that I need to know anything about logic." The logician replied, "How are you going to recognize it as a good proof?"

In sum, we take it that the way we conduct ourselves during the course of our everyday lives provides a persuasive argument for an objective world. Additionally, the way we use ordinary language and the way we argue (even the way subjectivists argue) reinforce our confidence in objectivity.

THE EVOLUTIONARY ARGUMENT

A second argument for the existence of an independent reality we shall call the *evolutionary argument*. In the past century we have come to place confidence in the thesis that human existence is part of an evolutionary process that had its beginnings in prehistory. In the sense in which we are using the term *evolutionary,* even those who subscribe to divine creationism contend that in the beginning there was *something* that preceded human existence. Thus, whether one is an evolutionist in the Darwinian sense or a creationist, some prehuman entities frame the emergence of the human part of one's cosmology.

To dismiss the thesis that reality exists independently of human experience requires abandonment of any sort of evolutionary explanation of the universe, whether Darwinian, creationist, or otherwise. To dismiss the possibility of an independent reality is to dismiss the implications of most of the modern sciences of archaeology, anthropology, geology, astronomy, zoology, and even linguistics. 3 Not even the most thoroughgoing subjectivist is likely to reject this body of knowledge to preserve the view that reality is subjectively constituted. Yet such a consequence does arise if one endorses the subjectivist view that all reality is a construction of humankind. No reality can then be said to have existed prior to the existence of humans. Likewise, no reality could be admitted to exist if all humankind were suddenly to perish. Not only would human institutions cease to exist upon the demise of all human entities, so too would the moon, the sun, the planets, the stars, the galaxies, and all else.

Like the naive argument with which we began, the evolutionary argument suggests that our accepted stock of knowledge relevant to a world existing independent of our attitudes, beliefs, and values is veridical.

THE ARGUMENT FROM LOGICAL CONSISTENCY

A third rationale supportive of the independent reality thesis may be labeled an argument from *logical consistency.* If it is the case that individuals subjectively create reality, it should follow that for each individual there will be a separate reality. If, however, we grant that there are two or more individuals in the world, there would be no guarantee that either of any two individually constructed realities will be coextensive. In fact, it is more likely that each subjectively created reality will be vastly different from others if all that exists is uniquely the product of each subject.

If we grant that what appear to be other human beings do create their own realities subjectively, then we have no reason to believe that any one individual worldview will be *logically* consistent with any other. This implies a world where logical system upon logical system, each a product of the subjective constitution of each individual knower, exist simultaneously and without any overarching logic or principle. The door is then open for inconsistent worldviews (a consequence which in itself is acceptable), and

118

for a plethora of mutually exclusive "truths," a consequence that would render a universe populated by two or more subjects chaotic, contradictory, and without the slightest possibility of coherence. Whether one is a subjectivist or an objectivist in one's theoretical musings about the world, and regardless of how cynical one is with respect to such problems as human relationships, human communication, or intercultural understanding, it is doubtful that anyone would seriously claim that *logical* chaos is descriptive of the world we confront in our everyday experiences. Instances of incoherence and even chaos exist, but these characteristics are neither systematically nor even typically constitutive of the world.

There appear to be two ways of looking at this conclusion. One could argue that the relative stability of world processes, human institutions, and relationships arises from an actual stability of events, objects and processes in the world existing externally to the perceiving subject. This is what we contend. However, another alternative has been proposed. This is the thesis that has been labeled *intersubjectivity,* a term not to be confused with our concept of "intersubjective validation." According to this view, there is some limited amount of agreement among and between individuals because humankind *communicates.* Put another way, linguistic interaction among and between people is held to result in intersubjective agreement through the mediating process of *discourse.*4 The argument that intersubjectivity is achieved in this way is tantamount to saying that individuals join together to create reality.

It is difficult to see how this thesis of intersubjective agreement can successfully extricate one from the unsatisfactory implications of subjectivism. This is because intersubjectivity must inevitably collapse into pure subjectivity. Trigg has put the point concisely:

> Both relativism as applied to societies [intersubjectivity] and subjectivism as applied to individuals are alike in what they deny, and this is presumably why the two are sometimes not distinguished. Neither allows for the logical possibility that the beliefs of an individual in the one case, or of a society in the other, can be judged by measuring them against anything external to the beliefs. The conception of something being the case apart from either a community or an individual thinking it is, is ruled out by both. Man [sic] effectively decides what is to count as true and what is to count as false. Truth is in the mind of the thinker, according to the subjectivists, or arises from the collective agreement of a society, according to the relativists.5

Intersubjectivity and subjectivity are based on a common ontological assumption: the denial of an external world that can be a standard against which to measure our epistemological claims. We contend that intersub-

119

jectivity must eventually repair to subjectivity. To the degree that one claims that "reality is meaning, yet meaning is something created and discovered in communication," that there is "no one standard against which to compare experience, . . ." and that "meaning is of first importance in human affairs, and in a real sense, *reality is meaning,*"6 there is little reason to believe there are even other "selves" who act in the capacity of interlocuters.

The heavy emphasis on the construction of reality through meaning must eventually entail solipsism, the doctrine that an individual thinker is the only thinker. This is because a rhetor, in order to *share* meanings *intersubjectively,* must first *create* meaning *subjectively*; otherwise, if meaning were found "out in the world" there would be no reason to ground an epistemology in "intersubjectivity" in the first place. As a consequence, there is philosophically no rationale for claiming the existence of anything or anyone beyond the subject that is not a product of subjective experience. With reality grounded in meaning, it is just as likely that the world is the result of *intra*personal communication within *a* mind (subjectivity), as that the world is the product of *inter*personal communication among several minds (intersubjectivity). As Trigg concludes:

> Everyone in a society may unthinkingly accept the same beliefs, and this is particularly liable to happen in an unsophisticated society immune from outside influences. If, however, they begin to consider consciously what to believe, they cannot all look at each other simultaneously to see what the majority thinks. It must therefore be assumed that individual judgments about what is true precede questions about what most people think. Each individual must have some prior conception of what it is for something to be true, which is totally independent of what others happen to think. A relativistic view of truth [intersubjectivity] appears to collapse at this point. 7

For these reasons an intersubjectivist ontology, like a subjectivist ontology, fails to account for the logical consistency of the phenomena of experience, which the argument from logical consistency does explain. For the same reasons, an intersubjectivist ontology suffers from the same problems as a subjectivist ontology with respect to the naive argument and the evolutionary argument.

THE ANTHROPOLOGICAL ARGUMENT

A fourth reason for preferring an objectivist ontology is what we shall call an *anthropological* argument. To set forth this argument, we can begin by granting the intersubjectivist's worldview. Let us assume that there

120

are groups of people (whom we shall label "cultures") who intersubjectively agree on the way the world is, and let us further suppose that this agreement then translates into the way the world really is. We are presuming that these hypothetical cultures create their worlds out of language.

If this situation actually existed, we would expect that different cultures would have radically different worldviews. Many worldviews would be so different that some of them would be entirely incommensurate with others. Yet experience tells us that this is not the case. In fact, not only is it possible for one culture to come to understand the *language* of another, it is possible for one culture to come to an understanding of the customs, habits, and internal workings of other cultures. What is surprising is the relative ease with which cross-cultural understanding can and does occur. Amid whatever uncertainties anthropologists confront, there exists a host of commonalities. For example, cultures may worship different gods, but their astronomy never has more than one sun. Cultures may have different sexual habits, but there are never more than two basic sexes identified by the culture. And even though Eskimos may have several dozen names for various varieties of snow, it is clear to the rest of us just what the Eskimo identifies as snow. It is not that there are different entities in the Eskimo's "subjectively" constructed world; the Eskimo has just made finer distinctions among the kinds of snowflakes, snowstorms, and the like. Had we an understanding of what it means to live in a world where snow is so important to survival and livelihood, we would doubtless make the same or similar distinctions ourselves.

Such examples do not indicate that Eskimos *create* several dozen types of snow with their language; they indicate that objectively obtaining conditions of the environment encourage Eskimos to make more linguistic distinctions than would be made in more moderate climates. The argument can be extended beyond contemporary cultures to those of ages past.

When archaeologists study Easter Island and the monoliths that stand there as the only remnants of some past culture, the immediate goal of researchers is to interpret the monuments *vis-à-vis* what they themselves know about the world. Hence, for example, the investigation becomes one of trying to explain the monuments on the basis of certain astronomical factors, or seeing that the ruins on Easter Island resemble those of Stonehenge, perhaps explaining both sets of monuments as parts of ancient astronomical observatories. If such an "educated hunch" can be defended, eventually the "secret" of Easter Island is unlocked and the positioning of the monoliths becomes explainable. Such intellection occurs, not because two cultures separated by eons of time and perhaps totally unrelated languages construct the same reality from discourse, but because reality itself intrudes to construct discourse. Our general point is that the way we speak or write—the way we communicate—is shaped predominantly by the objective world with which we are confronted. Were this not so, what reason could an intersubjectivist (or subjectivist) give to explain how two disparate cultures could possibly interact and translate one another's languages? Without some standard ontological state of affairs standing outside the language community, *and itself determining to a large extent the final form of any language,* the sciences of anthropology, linguistics, and etymology could not succeed as they have. While some theorists have focused upon cultural and individual *differences* in support of subjectivity, we believe the far greater amount of *sameness,* including the linguistic agreement, lends greater support to the objectivist view.

THE ARGUMENT FROM PERSUASIVE DISCOURSE

A fifth reason in support of the existence of independent reality is an argument from *persuasive discourse.* The thesis is that the objectivity of much of reality is implied by the manner in which humans employ language, especially persuasion.

As part of our preceding argument, we attempted to reduce intersubjectivity to subjectivity and hence to solipsism. It appears that in order for an intersubjectivist to defend his or her position successfully, the existence of independent and autonomous thinking beings must be preserved. Yet implicit in independence and autonomy is the recognition that some entities within the universe, namely, sentient human beings, have an *objective* existence. After all, it is the process of individual rhetors engaging in the activity of communication that is said to render intersubjectivity plausible in the first place. Persons persuade *other* persons, and it is held that through such discursive activity "reality is constructed." But a question immediately suggests itself: What are the grounds on which an intersubjectivist can advance the objective existence of sentient language users while contending that the apparent existence of external reality can only be explained by the linguistic creations of these same language users?

It is much more parsimonious to believe that individual human beings have an objective existence independent of one another and that they also are ensconced in a world that enjoys a similarly independent status. It appears much more consistent and elegant to maintain the naive position

122

with which we began our discussion, readmitting into our ontological worldview such familiar objects as audiences composed of individual, objectively existing, human beings who apprehend and discourse about other items in an objective world: the sun, the moon, the stars, and all else. The upshot is that such rhetorical concepts as speaker, audience, persuasion, and opinion change—notions we all treat as given—refer to objective phenomena and represent concepts that, when employed by anyone, signal the existence of an independent reality.

If the difficulties of resisting the theory of objective reality are as debilitating as we have just contended, it is reasonable to ask how the theories of subjectivity and intersubjectivity come to exist. We suggest it is because of a basic dilemma with which theorists are confronted. We are all met by a world where it is often difficult to penetrate to the heart of matters whose truth or falsity interests us. Innumerable questions, both "physical" and "nonphysical," have yet to be answered. Such questions range from those about the existence of an elementary particle in physics to those about the moral "rightness" or "wrongness" of individual and collective behaviors. Faced with disagreement over the ultimate resolution of such questions, some theorists take the tack of asserting that there simply are *no* answers to such questions—answers of an ultimately true or false/right or wrong variety. To account for phenomena that seem to defy assessment, these theorists contend that the phenomena themselves are subjectively created and that *in principle* they are opaque to the kinds of answers sought under the presuppositions of objectivity. Unwilling to embrace an attitude that admits the fruitlessness of endeavors to resolve the most difficult issues with which we are confronted, some theorists have pursued the intersubjectivist "solution" on the grounds that if we create our reality through language, we must have some control over what appears on the surface to be uncontrollable.

We suggest, however, that rejection of the objectivist worldview is at best premature. Rejection ignores the fact that much of the "objective" world does make sense, does cohere, is tractable, and can be spoken of, managed, and penetrated by discourse. The avenue that is most inviting, even if not demonstrably the way to truth, is to admit that there is some level of opacity in the world, but not such a level as warrants a retreat from objectivity.

The task with which the objectivist is confronted—the task from which the subjectivist recoils—is to account for the *level* of disagreement and opacity that does obtain while preserving objectivity. It is this task to which we now turn.

123

RELATIONALITY AS THE FOUNDATION OF REALITY

To preserve objectivist epistemology and dispose of the problems mentioned in the preceding pages, we need to say more about the character of reality than is said or implied by the general claim that reality exists largely independent of human beings. To accomplish this and to explain more fully the ontological grounds upon which objectivity can be defended, we advance a theory termed "relationality."

In Chapters 4 and 5 we posited that meaning, the interface between communication and knowledge, is relational, functioning to "embody" the relationships among rhetor, tacit audience, and extralinguistic phenomena. In addition, we argued that rhetorical discourse functions to make relations conspicuous to selves. Underlying both of these contentions is the ontological claim that reality is essentially relational in character. The remainder of this section is devoted to an explanation of the grounding of that view.

THE BASIC TENETS OF RELATIONALITY

In one form or another, a theory of relationality has served as the basis for a number of philosophical epistemologies, including those of Blanshard, Russell, Mead, Biser, and Ushenko. One of the most systematic treatments of relational theory is the cornerstone of the perspectivist view we presented in Chapter 5. It was offered by E. B. McGilvary, and we now return to his exposition. 8

To suggest that the world is essentially relational in character is to suggest that it is composed of numerous particulars, each a member of a context of particulars, and each particular deriving whatever nature it has from that context. As a result, each particular exhibits various characters or aspects which emerge wholly as a function of the relations in which the particular stands to other members of its context. A version of this theory holds that entities in the universe are what they are solely because of the relationships in which they stand to other entities. McGilvary provides a number of examples that adumbrate the relational nature of the world:

> The tables and chairs and trees and mountains we see have different seen shapes and sizes according to the distances and directions in which they stand to us. Until some nagging dialectician raises the question it never occurs to us that these different shapes and sizes of any particular are incompatible with its particularity. In fact one of the means whereby we identify a particular is the set of relations in which it stands to other particulars, as well as the characters it has in these varying relations. 9

McGilvary defends commonsense perception on the basis of a relational analysis. Pressed by those skeptical of an objective reality, citing an example such as the illusion that a "straight" stick "appears" bent when placed in a glass of water, the perspectivist would simply retort, What would you *expect?* Of course the stick appears bent. Given that it is immersed in water, there arises a different set of *relations* between the perceiver and what is perceived; there is no surprise in the fact that the stick appears bent. What would be most surprising is if the stick were immersed in water and did *not* appear bent. In other words, relational theory suggests that the characteristics of entities in the universe will differ according to the relationships in which the entity stands to other members of its context of particulars.

To understand more fully these basic tenets of relational theory, consider the contrary of the proposition that what is is what it is because of its relationship to all else. A contrary assertion would be: Something can exist wholly independent of everything or anything else, which is to launch the claim that a one-item universe is possible, wherein the "one item" dwells alone and not in relation to anything else. It is impossible to imagine what such an item would be like. In the experience of everyday life we are aware of such items as tables, chairs, cats, dogs, the sun and moon, and myriad others. These items of experience have characters that appear more or less permanent because they are apprehended from stable points of view in space and time. For example, a tree may exhibit the characteristics green or brown, tall or short, rough-barked or smooth-barked, alive, dead, dormant, healthy, or diseased, *depending upon the constituent relationships between and among its several parts and the context of particulars in which it, as a whole, stands* (its relationships to the things around it). When viewed by perceivers from the same or similar perspectives, the constituents of objects of experience, and hence the objects themselves, appear in a stable fashion. As a result, what makes the green, healthy oak tree a green, healthy oak tree and not a frog or some other green object, nor a building or some other tall object, nor a maple or some other rough-barked object is the presence of some characteristics and the absence of others, standing in specific relationships to one another. That is, distinctiveness and distinguishability arise from certain characteristics "arranged" in a certain way with respect to one another.

Newton's law of gravitation captures a complex set of relationships between "objects" with particular characteristics such as mass, distance from one another, and velocity. In this way, the objects of reality emerge from a set of relationships. Theories of nuclear physics are likewise comprehensible because the features that characterize what they are about—features such as atomic weight and valence—are discerned and understood in relationship to other features. These relationships are understood and comprehended *qua* relationships. As McGilvary notes:

> What is true of the particulars recognized by common sense is also true of scientific objects, such as electrons, protons, and neutrons. A lone electron, constituting all by itself a universe, could not have the opportunity of being an electron, since there would be no other electrons for it to repel or protons for it to attract. And a neutron could not be a neutron if there were no other particles to which it could be neutral. 10

In sum, what is is what it is solely because of its relationships to whatever else is. A one-item universe is, ontologically, impossible. We must add, however, that we are advancing relationality as an explanation of *how* entities come to possess the natures they have; we are *not* presenting relationality as a description of the individual characteristics or aspects that constitute the entities of the universe.

While readers may feel comfortable with the relational explanation of existence insofar as it applies to what we commonly call "physical" or "material" objects, there may be less satisfaction with such an account of "mental" or "non-material" concepts. In agreeing with McGilvary that "neither an international politician, nor an experimental scientist, nor a hod carrier, nor an abstract logician, could get his teeth into any sort of particular that was what it was all by itself," we explicitly extend the notion of relationality beyond the domain of tables and chairs, and protons and electrons, beyond what are traditionally labeled "physical" entities. 11 Our theory of relationality is equally applicable to nonphysical or nonempirical concepts. This is suggested by McGilvary when he notes in reference to neutrons that "neutrality, whether of particles or of nations, has meaning only in relation to what is going on in a larger world." 12 This seems clear enough as long as we are speaking at the level of metaphor. A clearer idea of what is encompassed by relationality may be gained if we consider a more specific nonempirical example. Consider the concept of *transitivity*, as exemplified in the following formula:

$$[(A > B) \cdot (B > C)] \supset A > C$$

This is a familiar relation. We know it to be the case that if A is greater than B and B is greater than C, then A is greater than C. Notice that this formula (it is unimportant whether we call it mathematical or logical or something else) expresses a truth about no specific objects of reality. It merely expresses a set of relationships, though a vitally important set of relationships, about any objects of reality that may, in fact, exist. This relationship is important because, like similarly specifiable relationships, it identifies certain features of the universe. Transitivity serves both an ontological *and* an epistemological function. It embodies both *what can be* and *what can be known.*

The same concept of relationality may be applied to those issues that have traditionally constituted the domain of rhetorical studies. Relationality is the single feature that gives distinctness and character to such notions as "peace," "honor," "justice," "aggressor," or "neutrality," or to notions that are collections of particulars, such as "Idi Amin's ruthlessness," the "benefits of quitting smoking," or "the wisdom of positioning cruise missiles in Europe." Relationality is all about us, as is communication, and we may therefore take it too much for granted, not noticing the implications of its presence. Yet a few moments' reflection will reveal that all-inclusive sense of the relational claim we are advancing: The knowable nature of all that is, physical and nonphysical, is a function of relationality.

The ontological and epistemological question that the theory of relationality proposes to answer is: How does the human knower confront what is known? Put in a different way, How do subjects come to be acquainted with objects? This problem has been a perennial one in the history of philosophy. For example, during the period from 1600 to 1725, epistemological concerns were preeminent in the writings of such philosophers as Bacon, Descartes, Locke, and Vico. One textbook describes these thinkers' contributions in a chapter titled "The Epistemologists."13 For these philosophers the haunting question was how a knowing, perceiving subject could apprehend a world that existed in some sense or other *apart from* that subject. It is this question that the theory of relationality can help to answer, but the answer involves us with another perennial philosophical issue: the nature of human consciousness. A relational analysis of consciousness opens the way to an understanding of how reality that stands independently of us can be apprehended and known, and of the importance of rhetoric in acquiring that knowledge.

CONSCIOUSNESS

One of the first theorists to treat the subject of consciousness at length was John Locke. Locke held that consciousness is one of the "internal operations" of the human mind. According to him, virtually all of those properties that make up cognition, such as reasoning, thinking, doubting, willing, and knowing, are products of consciousness. Additionally, Locke viewed consciousness as a uniquely internal or *intrapersonal* process,

127

wherein "the understanding turns inward upon itself, reflects on its own operations, and makes them the object of its own contemplation."14 Locke's approach to consciousness was adopted by the majority of Western philosophers, and variants of his theory were expressed in psychology, eventually espousing the view known as "introspection." Thus vestiges of Locke's conceptualization of consciousness can be seen in, for example, the 1899 reference work, *A Manual of Psychology,* which defines introspection as "to attend to the workings of one's own mind."15

Although philosophers such as Anthony Flew have suggested that the traditional Lockean formulation of consciousness ("introspectionist" theories) have been "widely discredited in contemporary philosophy," contemporary philosophical interest in the concept is as evident as in Locke's day. Thus Flew concedes that "there is considerable interest in the question of the relation of consciousness to mental states."16 Indeed, recent developments in cognitive psychology, artificial intelligence, neurophysiology, and the philosophy of mind have rekindled interest in the traditional questions surrounding the concept of consciousness. Perhaps it is enough to point out that in the years between 1950 and 1962 nearly a thousand scholarly papers from a wide variety of disciplines were published on the question "whether 'machines' can 'think.' "17

One of the most problematic issues that arises when any discussion of consciousness begins is: How is consciousness to be described? or What *is* consciousness? Sir William Hamilton underscored the difficulty of rendering a definition of the phenomenon:

> Consciousness cannot be defined: we may be ourselves fully aware what consciousness is, but we cannot without confusion convey to others a definition of what we ourselves clearly apprehend. The reason is plain: consciousness lies at the root of all knowledge.18

The elusive nature of consciousness is illustrated by Shaffer:

> Stare at something on this page, some word, for example, making yourself conscious of its form and character. Now try to notice what your *consciousness* of that word is. What do you get? Perhaps you will find that all you observe is the *word* on the paper and not the *consciousness* of the word on the paper. As G. E. Moore wrote (using a blue patch as his object of consciousness): "The moment we try to fix our attention upon consciousness and to see *what,* distinctly, it is, it seems to vanish: it seems as if we had before us a mere emptiness. When we try to introspect the sensation of blue, all we can see is the blue: the other element is as if it were diaphanous." This, I think, is the result that most of us would get when we try this experiment. Yet, of course, we know perfectly well we are conscious of the word on the page. What is this consciousness?19

We are more optimistic than Hamilton, for we believe useful things can be said about what consciousness *is*. The effort seems important to our project for, as Hamilton says tantalizingly, "consciousness lies at the root of all knowledge." We must recognize with Shaffer the elusive quality of the phenomenon, but we must agree with him that no matter how ephemeral consciousness is, we all realize that it is *something*.

From the general position we have taken concerning relationality, whatever else consciousness may be, if it exists it exists relationally. Happily, from our viewpoint, a number of philosophers have made considerable progress toward identifying consciousness as a relational phenomenon. We shall draw especially on the thinking of William James and McGilvary.

Though he was a proponent of the concept, "stream of consciousness," William James is often held to have been antagonistic to any *theory* of consciousness. In fact, between publication of *The Principles of Psychology* and *Essays in Radical Empiricism* his views shifted. The "stream" came to be conceived as a stream of "experience," rather than of "consciousness." He could therefore write in a 1912 essay, "Does 'Consciousness' Exist?" that "I believe that 'consciousness'. . . is the name of a nonentity, and has no right to a place among first principles."[20] He did not mean, however, to reject further analysis of the flow of "experience," once denominated "consciousness." James goes on to elaborate what is clearly a relational view of the phenomenon. When James wrote of a "nonentity" he meant "not an object"—"consciousness" was a name for something that did not exist as a specific entity or object; "experience" was the phenomenon of interest, as James now saw it. In the same essay, he continued:

> If we start with the supposition that there is only one primal stuff or material in the world, a stuff of which everything is composed, and if we call that stuff "pure experience," then knowing can easily be explained as a particular sort of relation towards one another into which portions of experience may enter.[21]

Russell made use of James' relational account of experience/consciousness, but both he and James eventually ran into problems, largely owing to the difficulties of reconciling a theory of relationality with an ontology that included "primal stuff" or "material."[22] For the present, we wish to proceed without these physicalist notions, closely following McGilvary's lead to see whether something useful can still be said about "consciousness" as a concept.

Despite the problems James, Russell, and Moore had in "locating" or "observing" consciousness, none could ignore the phenomenon of awareness to which the term normally refers. Neither could Flew, although he believed that philosophy had disposed of introspectionist analysis of consciousness. Indeed, like philosophy itself, ever since Plato consciousness has been a notion that seems successfully to have buried its undertakers in generation after generation. A reason probably is that there are things we can and do say with confidence about consciousness. One of these things is that when we are conscious, we are always conscious *of* something. Among the things we are conscious of are sights, sounds, tastes, smells, memories, fantasies, illusions, our own intentions, and so on.

There are, of course, times when we are deceived about any or all of these things. The tower we perceive from a distance as round, turns out on closer view to be square. The oasis in the desert may turn out to be a mirage. The self-assessment that our motive was "generosity" may be mistaken because we also believed our gift would pay dividends in the future. But even to be deceived is to be deceived *by something* in terms *of something else,* much as James said of knowing. Consciousness *is* always *of* something. If we examine closely how we explain what we are conscious of, a greater understanding of consciousness and its relationship to knowledge and communication can be achieved.

Such an examination was conducted by McGilvary. He began by noting that modern science has provided what may be termed the "inferential/representational view."[23]

> Scientific physiology leaves little room for reasonable doubt that no one ever sees or hears or remembers or thinks except in response or reaction to a stimulus. Such a stimulus may be external or internal, but stimulus there always is when any one is conscious. Calling a physiological reaction to a stimulus a "doing" or an "act" on the part of the reagent, one is tempted to say that seeing and hearing and thinking are "doings" or "acts" or "physiological functions" of the person who sees and hears and thinks.[24]

Not only does the inferential/representational view hold that consciousness is the product of some type of stimulus, a "doing" or "act," it more specifically contends that consciousness comes at the end of a long *chain* of stimuli. One source in functional neuroscience describes visual processing in the following terms:

> When thinking of vision it is natural to think first of the eye, where light is received by the organism. Important transformations of visual information occur in the eye, but they are only the beginning of a complex series of processing stages that carry visual information to the higher centers of the brain.[25]

Employing terms such as "receptors," "the transduction process," "bipolar and ganglion cells of the retina," "input," and "bridges of fibers," modern physiology traces the genealogy of particular instances of perception through the long and complex process ending in a perceptual experience—as an instance of consciousness. 26 Thus, when we are conscious of, say, the sun, the process is held to begin with the emission of stimuli (photons) from the surface of the sun that travel through space, taking some eight minutes to reach the earth, at which point they impinge upon the retina of the eye and begin a complex journey through the labyrinth which is the nervous system and eventually end up as the conscious perception of the sun.

It is this complex journey that prompts us to use the label, "inferential/representational," for it is clear on this account that what we perceive when we perceive the sun is perceived, *not directly,* but *inferentially.* We *infer* that there is a sun ninety-three million miles from earth on the basis of the *representation* of the "real" sun given us by the image that comes before our consciousness at the end of the chain of events beginning when the photons of the sun's light left its surface.

McGilvary agrees with the neurophysiologist who claims that "no one ever sees or hears or remembers or thinks except in response or reaction to a stimulus," but McGilvary rejects the inferential/representational conception. He does so because, as Russell noted, there are serious philosophical problems associated with the physiological explanation of perception:

> This theory has two parts. First there is the rejection of the view that perception gives direct knowledge of external objects; secondly, there is the assertion that it has external causes as to which something can be inferred from it. The first of these tends toward skepticism; the second tends in the opposite direction. The first appears as certain as anything in science can hope to be; the second, on the contrary, depends upon postulates which have little more than pragmatic justification. 27

The problem with the inferential/representational view is that if consciousness is reduced to consciousness of the last stage of human brain processes, as the neurophysiological evidence in itself suggests, what we are conscious of *is just that*—the last stages of human brain processes and not "real" objects of perception like the sun and moon and stars existing "out there" in space and time. This is the meaning of Russell's remark that physiological approaches to perception tend toward skepticism. Why? Because if this view is correct, then all we have evidence for is brain processes themselves, and brain processes are obviously not at all like what we take them to be representing. 28

To extricate ourselves from such a skeptical view ought to be our highest priority insofar as we are concerned with epistemological issues,

131

for it is difficult to construct any consistent or informative epistemological system in the absence of that most basic ingredient, namely, entities which may serve as objects of knowledge. One way to proceed would be to deny the physiological explanation of consciousness in favor of some view more compatible with the variety of realism—*direct* realism—that is required to provide the objects of knowledge and perception and to avoid the skepticism to which we are inextricably led by inferential/representational theories. 29 Yet we are in agreement with McGilvary that this is not a viable alternative. Science has shown clearly that the chain of events leading from the conscious event "outward" or "downward" to the stimuli causing consciousness is a prerequisite for perception. Additional evidence accumulates almost daily supporting the view that physiological activity in the brain is attendant to conscious experiences ranging from visual perception to willing, remembering, having and expressing emotions, and so on. 30

There is at least one alternative that may help avoid the problems that seem inherent in taking the physiological explanation of consciousness as the *whole* explanation. The alternative involves conceptualizing consciousness as being both a physiological act *and* a product of relationality. Again, McGilvary illustrates the possibilities of this view. If one operates solely under the physiological theory and if I am observing the star Sirius and if what I see is the actual Sirius as it exists in space as *a physical object,* then "my *action* in seeing, which occurs at the end of a long space-time chain of physical processes, must 'suddenly jump back to the starting point' over a spatial distance of more than eight light years and a temporal interval of more than the same number of years!" McGilvary claims this is "absurd." 31 The reason for the space/time differential is that modern astronomy asserts that light travels about 186,000 miles per second and, given the distance of the star Sirius, it takes a bit over eight years for this light to reach the earth.

But it is precisely this notion of "suddenly jumping back to the starting point" that relationality can account for. In reconsidering the position initially labeled "absurd," McGilvary illustrates with several examples.

> We are told that a disastrous fire "followed" the San Francisco earthquake of April 18, 1906. But that must be a mistake, for, if it were true, then the *action* of the fire must have suddenly jumped back to the somewhat earlier earthquake "like a stretched rope when it snaps." It should not take much discrimination to discover that the word "followed" here expresses not an action (or at least not an action alone) but a relation of temporal sequence, and it is this relation which (if you wish to use a striking metaphor) jumps back with all the suddenness that characterizes the occurrence of the sequent event. 32

132

Consider as well McGilvary's example of an individual "acting physiologically."

> "Mary's entrance into the room followed Jane's by a few minutes." Unless Mary was a paralytic wheeled in by a nurse, her entrance was a physiological act of hers; but Mary's *act* in following Jane's entrance did not "pass over" to Jane's act in her entrance. Mary's act concerned Jane's, not in the way of reaching it physically, but in the way of *ex post facto* making Jane's entrance a *term of a relation* in which that entrance did not stand at the time of its occurrence. Here the verb "followed" expresses not only a physiological act (which does not pass over to its "object") but also a relation that arises with the act and *does* reach its "object." 33

McGilvary's analysis helps us understand how the discoveries of modern physiological research can be reconciled with the commonsense view that the earth and heavens and all its attendant furnishings do not exit "in our heads" but rather exist as they appear to us, in an external world which we apprehend as we go about our daily lives:

> "See" names an occurrence analyzable, as I think, into a physiological process or act, *and* a relation of its own specific kind; and the grammatical object of the verb "see" does not name an object to which the *physiological act* physically passes over. It names a *term of this relation* whose other term is named by the grammatical subject of the verb. A relation of the same kind is found in occurrences that are named by the verbs "remember," "think," etc. In each of these cases there is also a physiological process or "act." This *act* does not "go over" to what is denoted by the grammatical object of the verb, but the *relation does* "go over" in the way in which any relation "goes over" from one term to another in relating the terms. 34

Consciousness (or James' "experience"), can be understood in relational terms, just as any existing "thing" can be understood in relational terms. This outcome of our investigation can also be taken as another confirmation of the fundamental tenet we have put forward: Whatever is, is what it is because of its relationship to all else. The all-encompassing nature of this ontological principle is easy to forget. In a sense, McGilvary occasionally departs from his own dictum, as when he bifurcates the "physical" notion of physiology from the relational character of consciousness. In any case, having shown the relevance of the principle to understanding the nature of consciousness, it remains to analyze the relational nature of consciousness. Still borrowing heavily from McGilvary, we would define consciousness relationally as: *A natural event that occurs when and only when an entity stands in a particular relationship to other entities within a context of particulars. Consciousness is itself a character or aspect of a*

133

specific kind and is always part of a corresponding asymmetrical relation also of a specific kind. 35

By "natural event" we mean an occurrence independent of individual attitudes, beliefs, and values. For example, our readers may have fully intended to examine our printed words and may choose at any time to stop reading, but once a particular set of relations has been brought to fruition, consciousness will occur or will cease to occur in the same way independent of what readers "wish." For instance, if an individual stands within a certain distance of this page, under certain conditions of lighting, having "normal" vision and certain "brain processes," and there is no intervening set of relations (such as a blank piece of paper or closed eyelids "obstructing" the view), consciousness of the words on this page will *necessarily* occur. As a "natural event," the occurrence of consciousness is often beyond the control of the person who is conscious.

Of course, it can be said fairly that a reader "brings" certain attitudes, beliefs, or values to his or her reading of this chapter and consequently will "read it" or "read *into* it" quite differently from another reader. Moreover, someone reading this chapter for the first time may come away with a different perception of what was intended than he or she would have after reading it several times. The explanation for such variables in reading is to be found in the difference between *consciousness of* an object (where "object" is understood as object of thought and not in physicalist terms) and certain other notions *additional to* consciousness, such as meaning, reflection, understanding, and comprehension.

By "entity" we mean a discrete collection of characters. It is important that the term "entity" not be thought of as referring to something "physical" or "mental," since what some have called "physical entities" and "nonphysical" or "mental" entities (such as love, justice, and goodness) are not *qualitatively* distinct within our theory of relationality. Thus, people, inanimate objects, and values are all entities, as we are using the term. Consciousness, then, is a purely relational concept, its "physical" attributes themselves having the characteristics they do as the result of relationality. Consciousness refers to a condition arising out of the relationship in which a complex entity, a human being, stands to other entities. While some features of the perceived universe *appear* to display "linear," "chain-linked," or "physical" characteristics, and while some features *appear* to "go over" to their object in similar linear, chain-linked, physical—that is, in certain *causal* ways—consciousness is not explainable in these terms. Like the terms in a logical, spatial, temporal, or mathematical relation, consciousness does "go over" to the objects of consciousness.

Our phrase "context of particulars" denotes all those entities and the various relationships in which they stand to one another—relationships that affect or condition some other individual, specifiable entity. Thus, on this account, a complete rendering of the conscious state of an astronomer viewing the moons of Jupiter, or a mathematician grappling with a complex equation, or an ethicist struggling to determine a proper course of action, would entail a description of all the entities and relationships among entities that have a significant bearing on the conscious event. Included in this description would be not only those physiological data that inform our understanding of the human organism *qua* organism; the description would include as well a *relational analysis*. Such an analysis would begin in ways similar to McGilvary's explanation of the San Francisco earthquake or "Mary's entrance into the room." It would seek to discover the physiological explanation for how it is we are conscious *as an organism,* but also how it is we are conscious *of something.* Claims to the contrary notwithstanding, this second question is simply not answered—indeed, in principle it cannot be answered—on the basis of a physiological account alone. Only when the terms of a conscious relation have been made conspicuous can that which we are conscious *of* be explained in a way that permits us to avoid the skepticism thinkers like Russell have been concerned with.

A conscious relation, we said, is "asymmetrical." This means that when an entity "A" is conscious of some other entity "B," it does not follow that "B" is necessarily conscious of "A," nor that "B" is conscious of "A's" consciousness of "B." According to the relational theory we are using, human consciousness is an occurrence arising when a particular entity, such as a human being, comes to stand in a certain relationship to another entity or entities. These entities and the conscious subject comprise a complex, interrelated array of constituents, called a "complex of particulars." To be clear, it is because of the *particularity* or *uniqueness* of human relational organization that *human* subjects (and perhaps certain other higher organisms) can and do experience consciousness.36 Entities lacking the requisite relational organization, such as fence posts, rocks, tables and chairs, presumably are not and cannot be conscious. The human mind (as opposed to the physiological construct, the human brain) is the repository of relational understandings as well as the product of relational influences reposed and organized within it.

Having put into the foreground our premise that mind is a repository of relational understandings and a product of relational influences, we can begin to tie together four notions that occupied us earlier: (1) the notion of reality; (2) the notion of meaning; (3) the notion of consciousness; and (4) the notion of knowledge. Summarizing the interconnections among these four concepts will enable us to see how rhetoric is afforded epistemic significance; which is to say, how knowledge can be acquired through communication.

The idea that reality is grounded in relationality undergirds our entire argument. Moreover, we take all relations to be *internal* to the thing whose nature the relations determine. 37 If this interpretation of relationality is correct, it would be impossible to know everything about anything unless one knew all there was to know about every relationship in which an object of inquiry stood to everything else. We are not likely to attain that kind of knowledge, but our situation is still not bleak. We are rarely interested in knowing every relationship in which any object of knowledge stands in relation to all else. To illustrate, we are interested in the carcinogenic properties of nicotine but not in the substance's color or how it is affected by immersion in a 10 percent salt solution. We *can* try to sort out exploratively (1) the relata forming the universe of carcinogenic phenomena, (2) trace the epistemological lineage of claims about carcinogenesis, (3) subject alternative judgments to counterargument in order to (4) secure the judgments dialectically within (5) the specific perspective about which we inquire. By these processes we avoid the evaporative skepticism that an inferential/representational formulation presents, and we replace *inferences* about the external world as representing objects of reality with an epistemology that shows how we are *directly* aware of the objects of reality. We are aware of them because within the conscious subject, relationship to the object of consciousness "passes over" to the "object" of consciousness.

It is language that, through meaning, functions to make relations conspicuous to conscious selves. A conscious being is presented with a host of phenomena, such as the complex of particulars we perceive when we see a tree or think of a friend or intend to give to charity. To manage these complexes, to discriminate among them, we must have means of categorization. Such means are required for functions such as memory and for communicating with others of our species. Through meaning, language makes relations conspicuous to selves—our own selves and the selves of others. It is through language that a subject's relationship to an object of consciousness "passes over" to the "object." Thus, in such enterprises as argument, communication functions epistemologically to generate opinion, belief, true belief, rational belief, or knowledge. The ways in which use of language has the greatest potential for achieving epistemic status under these circumstances were detailed in Chapter 5.

136

We wish now to point out how the theories we have been outlining help avoid some of the epistemological problems referred to earlier. No philosophical problem area will better illustrate the advantages of our relational ontology than what has become known as "the problem of dualism."

THE PROBLEM OF DUALISM

The viability of a relational ontology and the advantage of grounding an epistemology on the relational view can be seen by examining one of the most perplexing ontological/epistemological problems confronting modern philosophy—one which is the subject of continuing controversy. Since Descartes' *Meditations* in 1641, philosophy in general and epistemology in particular have been plagued by the problem of dualism. 38 Simply put, if there are mental events that have their locus in minds and physical events that have their locus in physical space distinct from minds, it is difficult to account for the influence of one on the other. Yet it is equally difficult to argue that mental activities are independent of physical events or that all physical events occur independently of human thought.

The problem of dualism has traditionally posed theoretical roadblocks for subjectivists and objectivists alike. Consider, for example, how a theorist adhering to subjectivism or intersubjectivism might confront dualism. On the one hand, subjectivists can and have attempted to circumvent the dualist problem by questioning that part of dualism that argues for the independent existence of physical entities. Here, a *strict* subjectivist would contend that mental constructs, such as "meaning," are all that are required to explain the way the world is and the way it is created and managed through discourse. 39 However in adopting this solution, the strict subjectivist invites all of the nettlesome difficulties we have already discussed, including the problem of solipsism—the inability to account for or find a theoretical place for other minds. If the world is a mental construct, what appear to be other thinking beings may well be constructs of the thinker, not realities at all.

On the other hand, a subjectivist could avoid solipsism and other attendant difficulties by embracing dualism. There are those whom we may describe as *mitigated* subjectivists. They are theorists who explicitly separate mental and physical entities into distinct realms. According to this analysis, there exists a category of entities that we might describe as technical or scientific. Their reality is held to be independent of knowers. In addition, there is also a category of entities that are contingent: entities to which nothing in the physical world corresponds. These entities are created through discourse. 40 This position, which we are calling mitigated subjectivism, avoids most of the solipsistic charges lodged against strict subjectivists, but mitigated subjectivism still falls prey to the dualist enigma because it leaves the major quandary of dualism unanswered: How can one account for the influence of one realm (scientific or technical) on the other (contingent)? How is it that two so qualitatively distinct worlds coexist and interact?

The concept of dualism also generates problems for objectivists: At least two theoretical formulations attempt, implicitly or explicitly, to meet the problem of dualism. *Strict objectivists* include the early positivists in philosophy. These theorists contend that the only knowable entities and the only meaningful statements about reality are those that are empirically verifiable. 41 While avoiding the problem of dualism by their strict denial of nonempirical existents, they render it impossible to confer epistemic status on those ideas and beliefs that are the subjects of day-to-day discourse. Those who have taken issue with positivism have insisted that to dismiss all nonempirical matters as meaningless and unknowable permits one to escape dualism but is unacceptably counterintuitive. In the world of prudential conduct nonempirical issues *are* both meaningful and of crucial importance in managing our lives. To ignore them does not solve the philosophical problem in any practical way.

Mitigated objectivists argue for the existence of independent realities in both the empirical and contingent realms. 42 Terms such as "goodness," "justice," and the "rightness" and/or "wrongness" of an act are as "real" as the subjects treated within the domains of the physical sciences. This position avoids dualism by denying any bifurcation between the physical and nonphysical. However, in maintaining the independence of both contingent and scientific questions, mitigated objectivists leave themselves vulnerable to the complaint that contingent matters such as moral, religious, and political issues, if they are external to mind in the same way as are empirical ones, should be similarly verifiable. It is not, however, easy to show that "goodness" is truly good, beyond the possibility of falsification.

RELATIONALITY AND DUALISM

The theory of relationality and its epistemological counterpart, perspectivism, escape most of the difficulties presented by the problem of dualism. In the eyes of a relationalist, the mental/physical distinction and the problems of dualism that arise from it result from an unfortunate "category mistake." 43 By treating the constituents of the world as collections of characters that cohere relationally to form particulars within a context of particulars, and by treating consciousness as a phenomenon

138

that *itself* emerges when a human being stands in a particular relationship to other entities, a relationalist avoids bifurcating the world into "physical" and "mental" realms. To a relationalist that kind of bifurcation is an artificial and improper categorization of the objects of experience. In the relational view all objects of experience, including the objects of scientific inquiry and such characteristics as "good," "bad," "justice," and "virtue," are endowed with a similar ontological status. They all *exist* and are *entities* in the world of nature, deriving their separate natures according to the relationships in which they stand to their own characters and to the characters and complexes of characters exhibited by other entities.

To be sure, the concept "goodness" (a "nonphysical" notion) and Socrates (a "physical" concept) exhibit differences. It is tempting to say that such differences are at base ontological. For example, one may predicate goodness of Socrates but it is impermissible to predicate Socrates of goodness. Such factors suggest the ontological differences alluded to. We contend that such factors can be accounted for in other ways than to posit *fundamentally different ontological categories*. In the examples of goodness and Socrates, for instance, one might simply suggest that the inappropriateness of predicating both terms of each other is simply an instance of the commonly recognized fact that not all *relations* are symmetrical. Take the utterance, "Tanya sits to the right of Dannelle." Here the spatial relationship expressed by the phrase "to the right of" is nonsymmetrical—it cannot be predicated of Dannelle. What appears to be a basic ontological difference, then, is, from a relationalist view, merely characteristic of the single underlying ontological property of all that is, namely, relationality.

Escaping the perplexities that arise from dualism has special importance when one is conceptualizing rhetoric and its functions. The foundation of the dualist problem is the familiar and ubiquitous *subject/object distinction*,44 one that implies an *ontological* distinction between perceivers and things perceived. For centuries people have wittingly and unwittingly labored under the conceptual consequences of this implied dualism, and the problem has been exacerbated by the growth of science and ensuing conflicts between science and the arts. In rhetoric, the tendency has been further accentuated by elevating Aristotle's contingent/apodictic distinction to the status of an axiom. The general result has been to treat use of language as *either* objectively true or as speculative.

The theory of relationality, on the other hand, asserts that there is no ontological distinction among the entities populating the universe. Because everything that is is what it is by virtue of its relationship to whatever else is, the subject/object distinction is otiose. This assertion, however, is not inconsistent with our claim that reality is independent of human attitudes, beliefs, and values. In a relationalist's view such independence does obtain; it obtains in the sense that the objects of reality are collections of *relata* standing in an asymmetrical conscious relationship to human subjects who are also collections of relata. The ontological glue holding together all entities—whether abstract entities, empirical entities, or conscious entities—is *the relation*. For this reason we may still refer to perceiving entities and perceived entities without becoming ensnared in dualism, as long as we keep at the forefront of our ontological system the realization that the perception of entities is made possible *because of relationality*. Let us be clearer about the notion of the independence of reality. It is possible to regard collections of relata ("things" such as rocks, stars, trees, cats, humans, thoughts, volitions, and memories) as independent in the sense that they can be identified *qua* collectivities of relations. Such "objects" are what they are because of their unique relational organization. Occasionally sentient beings are *conscious* of these collectivities. But the existence of the collectivities themselves does not depend entirely, nor even in most cases significantly, on their being the objects of consciousness. The collectivities which are the stars and planets will remain virtually unchanged when not perceived by sentient beings. This is because they are what they are because of their relationships to humans, but they are what they are *predominantly* because of their relationship to *all* else that is. Is it plausible to suggest that the perception by even many astronomers of the extragalactic nebula in Andromeda contributes in a substantial way to the galactic nature of the nebula? And, should these astronomers disappear from the earth and cease to perceive the nebula, would such a relational change alter the nature of the Andromeda nebula in any significant way? The answer to both questions is surely, "No." This is so, not because human perception (the consciousness relation) plays *no* part in contributing to the nature of things; it is so because human perception plays only an infinitesimally minute role.

Several questions arise, however: What does it mean to enter a relationship? Is relationship objectively real or does it depend on a perspective, i.e., on a preexistent consciousness? Do entities have existence outside relationship? Can relationships be socially determined?

Technically, it is impossible to enter *anew* into a relationship in the sense of entering afresh into the vast relational complex that is the universe. The relational determiners which, for example, prescribed the occurrence of the massacre of Palestinian refugees in Lebanon, were as present in the world a thousand years ago as on September 16, 1982. The only sense in which entering into a relationship can be understood is the

140

sense in which conscious human beings *become aware* of the possibility and, in retrospect, the actuality of relationships. Relations are without exaggeration more than objectively real; they are the determiners of the specific items comprising reality. Hence, rather than being shaped by perspectives, relations form the bases *of* human perspectives. Finally, relationships (relations) *themselves* cannot be socially determined. Thus, although a skillful rhetor might convince an audience that the assassination of John F. Kennedy was the result of a conspiracy, only the existence of individuals other than Lee Harvey Oswald, standing *in fact* in a conspiratorial relation to the events of November 22, 1963, can make the tragedy the product of a conspiracy. At best, a rhetor can make us aware of a *possible or actual* relationship, one we were not conscious of prior to rhetoric. But a rhetor cannot, strictly speaking, "create" a world of both relations and relata in defiance of relations *actually* existing.

The doctrine of relationality illuminates the four ontological positions. With respect to *strict subjectivism*, relationality accounts for how individuals apprehend the world in distinct and frequently conflicting ways; the theory thereby retains a valuable portion of the strict subjectivist thesis. Because each individual stands in a unique perspective to the multiplicity of events and things in the world, individuals' accounts of the world are often distinctive. Yet although rhetors can view and talk about the world from different perspectives and although propagandists may argue for combinations of relations that do not occur and therefore are untrue, meaning is not wholly a product of individuals nor is reality entirely socially constructed. Thus, relationality as theory is less vulnerable to the charge of solipsism. In a world where everything is intimately related in strictly ontological terms, solipsistic estrangement is less likely to occur because all entities including the conscious minds of humans stand intimately interconnected. Mind does not create reality; rather, mind takes its natural place as a relational complex among all other entities in the universe. Should all sentient life on earth become extinct, the nature of every other thing in the universe would change but only infinitesimally. The fifth moon of Jupiter would not be, at any point in time, X miles from anyone. But the fifth moon of Jupiter would continue to exist in space and time. Moons, like most else in the solar system, are not created by consciousness or mind.

Relational theory echoes the mitigated subjectivist's belief that not all classes of items making up reality are the same. The differences stem from the fact that each and every entity within the world stands in a special and unique relationship to all else that is. Unlike the mitigated subjectivist's theory, however, relationality avoids the conclusion that classes of items are *ontologically* distinct, which is the source of the dualist enigma. For the relationalist, there is no division of the world into technical and social phenomena. In relational theory the most basic explanation possible for the nature of all phenomena is that such foundational relations as "difference" ground the objects of knowledge. Differentiations among classes of objects of knowledge may be useful for some purposes, but are not, for the relationalist, to be made on the basis that language (communication) "creates" some classes or "assesses" others. Relationality recognizes one advantage of the mitigated subjectivist thesis, namely, that the objects of reality exhibit significant differences, but it rejects the claim that such differences are a function of a *qualitative* mind/body type of distinction. Such a distinction is, on the relational view, both artificial and improper, since all objects of reality hold equal ontological status. In this way, the dualist enigma is avoided.

With *strict objectivism,* relational theory affirms that because reality is independent of us, it cannot be willed into existence nor wished away. The relationalist, however, rejects the strict objectivist's contention that the only knowable items of reality are those that are "empirical." Relationality holds that we are capable of knowing, and in fact do know, much about the nonempirical world of prudential affairs. Relational theory takes issue with any attempt to locate qualitative ontological differences among the items constituting reality. For this reason, terms such as "empirical" and "nonempirical" are at best euphemistic; they do not refer to a basic ontological distinction. The doctrine of an independent reality is applicable to *all* items in the world. One can, and frequently does, stand in a conscious relation to "nonempirical" as well as to "empirical" entities. Such a claim is less problematic, according to relationalists, if we keep our language and thought free of such empirical connotations as "test," "proved," and the like mistakenly imply. That task becomes more manageable when we remember that all phenomena are what they are because of their relationship to all else.

Finally, relationality offers an important extension of the *mitigated objectivist's* thesis. In fact, relationality has more in common with this school of thought than with any of the other three. To begin with, the relationalist would share the contention of the mitigated objectivists that all reality is independent of the knower and is, at least in principle, capable of being known. However, the relationalist posits this claim without introducing an empirical/nonempirical vocabulary. In this way, the relationalist both avoids the dualist enigma and addresses the complaint that nonempirical items of reality, if they are independent of us in the same way

142

as empirical items, should be similarly verifiable. For the relationalist, the problem of verifiability is a problem ensconced within a dualist vocabulary. The tendency to make distinctions between empirical and nonempirical objects, subjects and objects, and contingent and apodictic knowledge is the problem; that tendency misrepresents reality. These dichotomies become unnecessary if one approaches the notion of verifiability and the process of coming to know from the standpoint of consciousness as relational. In short, if we think of coming to know as a process beginning when a conscious human being becomes aware of a relation, it is just as easy to imagine how one could have awareness of so-called nonempirical objects as of empirical objects. That which permits knowledge or understanding is *the relation*.

Thus far, we have argued that the problem of dualism may be circumvented by a relational epistemology. It is now incumbent upon us to say with more precision what our central term, relationality (or the "relation") is. Let us begin by recalling what relationality is not: A relation is not an object of reality in the traditional empirical sense, nor is a relation an abstract, otherworldly, ideal phenomenon. What alternative is left?

The most fundamental tenet of the doctrine of relationality is that everything is what it is in virtue of its relationship to all else. Inherent in this doctrine is recognition that a relation encompasses more than the relata which stand as terms of any given, instantiated entity. For example, consider those familiar objects, pieces of chalk. On a relational analysis, each piece of chalk is what it is in virtue of the myriad relationships in which it stands to all else, relations that determine such individual properties of the chalk as frangibility, color, texture, shape, and size. Clearly, for the various pieces of chalk to remain individual pieces of chalk requires that the same relations obtain in a consistent, stable fashion with regard to each piece; that is, all the relations that are relevant to the chalk maintaining its identity as chalk. Whatever constitutes the collection of relations that determines that an entity is a piece of chalk must be identical across the range of objects that are, in fact, chalk. If we consider what we are prone to say about pieces of chalk, we shall notice that we say that all pieces of chalk have identical properties such as whiteness, cylindricality, and frangibility. This kind of assignment of general qualities is tantamount to claiming that *universals* are in essence the products of relations. And it is tantamount to contending that a theory of universals is a direct consequence, is implied by, our relationalist ontology and epistemology. It is important to emphasize that by "universal" we do not mean a transcendent, ethereal, otherworldly, Platonic Form, existing as a paradigm in which the objects of the world participate and on which their existence depends. Neither do we take a universal to be a conceptual, mind-dependent phenomenon. For us, universals are the products of identical relations.

We do not propose to enter into debate on the long-standing philosophical problem of universals. In communication studies as in other intellectual pursuits, the very mention of the term "universal" can be cause for immediate rejection of a theoretical proposal. This attitude stems from many causes, perhaps the foremost among which is the tendency to view indictments of Platonic universals (such as Aristotle's objections) as revealing fatal defects in *any* theory of universals. Such an out-of-hand dismissal is wholly unwarranted. Indeed, the question of universals is very much alive in contemporary philosophy, though modern-day formulations of theories of universals look little like their Platonic ancestors. The particular theory of universals implied by our doctrine of relationality is defended at length by Panayot Butchvarov in *Resemblance and Identity: an Examination of the Problem of Universals.* 45

Briefly, Butchvarov is concerned with accounting for the obvious fact that we recognize existence in the perceptual world of numerous characteristics (for instance, the *color* of common objects, their *number*, their *position*, and their aesthetic or moral *value*), as well as "things" themselves, which are said to "have" or to be "composed of" these various characteristics. Butchvarov refers to such recrudescent characteristics as "the recurrence of qualities."46 Traditionally, philosophers have accounted for the recurrence of qualities in several ways. *Nominalist theories,* which are perhaps most consistent with subjectivist or intersubjectivist theories of rhetorical epistemology, hold that the applicability of singular general terms, such as "yellow" to various yellow "things" is simply a function of the fact that "yellow" is a word that *does* apply to various yellow things. In other words, recurrent qualities exist because the same general term applies to a number of individual things. *Resemblance theories* contend that the recurrence of qualities, such as the "squareness" of two geometrical figures, is to be explained by the fact that the shape of one figure exactly resembles the shape of the other.

Both the nominalist and resemblance theories are critiqued by Butchvarov. He contends that only a third theory, the *identity theory,* can adequately explain the phenomena of recurrent qualities. The identity theory claims that instances of the same quality possessed by several individual things are *literally* "one and the *same.*"47 "Whiteness" that is a quality of a piece of chalk taken from a new box of chalk is identical to the whiteness of all the pieces of chalk taken from the same box.

Butchvarov is careful to point out that to commit oneself to the identity theory of universals is not to endorse a theory of otherworldly, Platonic Forms. It is proper to describe universals as both qualitatively and quantitatively distinct from instantiated "things" (that is, things existing as products of relationality), and it is proper to say of universals that they are non-spatiotemporal in nature, but universals do not reside in some "other" world. As Butchvarov puts it:

> The denial of the existence of universal qualities in space and time must not be interpreted as lending support to the view that such qualities are not really the qualities of individual things in the spatiotemporal world, that they are literally separate from their instances, that since they have neither unique nor multiple locations in the spatiotemporal world they are "somewhere else." 48

The relationship between recurrent qualities (which we shall now call "universals" in the sense referred to by identity theory) and relations illuminates further the question of what a relation is. We suggest that relations are *the progenitors of universals.* To define relations in this way, by function, may seem unsatisfying, even appearing to beg the question. Yet the charge of question begging is unjustified. In locating relations as the source of universals, we arrive at the most fundamental ontological constituent of all that is. To require more than has been posited in the definition of relations as the progenitors of universals is unreasonable.

Two analogies will illustrate our point. If one is questioned as to what the definition of "leukocyte" is, one might retort that a leukocyte is a white blood cell, an overabundance of which is associated with leukemia. Such a response might be rejected on the basis that what was asked was not what the entity resulted in, but, for example, how it worked. This response would be fully warranted, because a specialist in diseases of the blood could better respond to the initial question by describing the parts of the leukocyte, the functions of the various parts, and how these functions sometimes result in something going terribly wrong with a patient's blood system. However, this type of answer cannot be given, and happily so, in response to queries about relationality. The relation, if our analysis is correct, is not divisible into working parts, cannot in principle be described in detail, and can *only* be analyzed in terms of its products or functions.

A second example illustrates this latter set of claims. For some time in nuclear physics scientists have been searching for the elementary particle that forms the most basic constituent of atoms. Although this search continues, it is clear that when and if such a particle is discovered, one could not ask—and indeed one criterion of a truly elementary particle is that one

145

should not be able to ask—questions about the particle's complex nature. Such a particle, in terms of nuclear physics, *has no complex nature*—it is the ultimate simple. Even now, as we move closer to the goal of uncovering elementary particles, scientists describe such particles increasingly in terms of their function or effects, not in terms of their structures or internal workings.

The same is true of the relation. In answer to the question, What is a relation?, one can only—and ought only—to reply: "The relation is the most fundamental ontological ingredient of all that is." In response to the question, How does the relation "work"?, one can only—and ought only—to reply: "The relation works by generating universals." Finally, in response to the question, How do you know there are such things as relations?, one might respond, "Without them, an adequate explanation of the world as it appears to us—including such furnishings as many pieces of chalk possessing identical properties—is not possible." This last assertion is bound up intrinsically with the doctrine of the identity theory of universals which is treated at length in a separate literature.

Admittedly, the contention that the identity theory of universals is implied by the doctrine of relationality, and that relations may be defined functionally as producers of universals, follows only if one accepts the initial postulates of the relational ontology/epistemology. However, readers should remember that the goal of our investigation is to provide a systematic and coherent discussion of rhetorical epistemology and its broad ontological foundations. Having arrived at the definition of relations as the progenitors of universals is to have uncovered the last major component of that discussion. Although the elementary and foundational character of relations precludes us from saying more by way of intrinsic definition, a better understanding of relationality can be gleaned by considering some examples of epistemic judgments that arise in day to day discourse. Our purposes are to make conspicuous the relational character of all rhetorical/epistemic judgments and to underscore the superfluousness of introducing subject/object distinctions when analyzing rhetorical/epistemic judgments.

Consider:
(1) $4 + 5,000,000 = 5,000,004$
(2)   Jan followed her older, taller sister, Mary, into the room.
(3)   At a temperature of $-459.69°$ Fahrenheit (absolute zero), there is an absence of molecular movement, i.e., an absence of heat.
(4)   Richard Nixon was a bad president.

146

Working with such traditional habits as separating mental from physical phenomena, maintaining a distinction between contingent and apodictic questions, and bifurcating internal and external matters, one could label statement (1) "mathematical," statement (2) "general descriptive," statement (3) "scientific" or "empirical," and statement (4) "contingent." Each statement would be taken as different in kind, perhaps involving a unique type of epistemological judgment. Using a relationalist ontology and the perspectivist epistemology to which it gives rise, all four statements will be seen as describing various constituents of the world as collections of characters that cohere relationally and that, under this analysis, are *not* qualitatively distinct. Although a relationalist would certainly hold that the objects comprising the subject matter of each of the four statements are independent of the utterer's attitudes, beliefs, and values, there is no reason to introduce a subject/object vocabulary that implies the objects in some of the statements are spatially external and, in other cases, spatially internal to mind.

"Four added to five million equals five million and four," involves a relationship of equality. Like other statements in pure mathematics, it is a clear example of the notion of relationality. The entities referred to in the statement are of the same, hence equal, status. But even the most fervent empiricist will have difficulty explaining the "truth" of such a statement in purely empirical terms. The reason is that the statement treats only nonempirical concepts. It does not deal with quantities of apples or trees or tables or chairs; it deals with the *concepts* "four," "five million," "equality," and "five million and four." Further, few of us have trouble operating with the two larger numbers in this equation, though probably none of us has ever experienced such quantities of anything. If we consider similar and more complex examples in mathematics, we will again see statements that assert relations and concepts that have no instantiation in the so-called "empirical world" or, if they are so instantiated, they are relations and concepts that have never been and are unlikely ever to be experienced by human beings *except in a nonempirical sense.* This nonempirical sense is precisely that sense in which individuals come to stand in particular relationships to concepts so as to become conscious of them. To employ the language of the relationalist, an individual becomes conscious of a mathematical equation when he or she stands in a certain relationship to that equation. The equation itself expresses a relationship among its various concepts and their relationship to the conscious individual; the concepts it contains all stand in a context of particulars determined by all the interrelationships involved.

An interesting corollary of the relational analysis of mathematical statements arises if we consider the hypothetical case wherein all conscious entities suddenly perish from the universe. (One may define perish as "to come into a state of complete and perpetual relational dissolution, so that consciousness is not possible.") In that event, the mathematical relation expressed by our first example, and all other mathematical relations, would continue to exist, since their ontological status is independent of thinking and perceiving, that is, independent of *conscious* beings. Extended to other objects of knowledge, relationality affirms the commonsense notion that the stars and planets will continue to exist "in space" even though no one is left on earth to perceive their existence. This is because all the characters in the relational complex, save those comprising sentient earthlings, would continue to enter into relationships with each other.

Again, the consciousness relationship among sentient earthlings and the objects of their consciousness contributes to the ontological fabric of the universe. And this, of course, follows directly from the first tenet of relationality, that a thing is what it is in virtue of the relationships in which it stands to all else. Hence, *any* object in the universe is partly describable in terms of its relationship to any and all entities, including those who may at any time be perceiving such an object. The red light on the electronic typewriter on which these words are being typed is an object of perception and, hence, may in part be described *relationally* as "the light currently perceived by Hikins." Yet the typist's (relational) contribution to the nature of the light is, within the context of all the other relations that make the light what it is, surely miniscule. Likewise, the elimination of the consciousness relation does not mean a significant alteration of the object of consciousness, given the numerous other relations contributing to the object's nature.

Our second example was the statement "Jan followed her older, taller sister, Mary, into the room." This epistemic judgment comprises several easily identifiable relations: "older," "taller," and "followed." In addition, other relations are present in somewhat covert form, for example, "sister." The notion of a person being a sister is vacuous unless treated as a relatum in a world where at least two objects exist—both involved in the relation of "sisterhood." In addition, the terms "Jan" and "Mary" may be treated in a relational way as well. They are terms that distinguish particular complexes of characters from other complexes of characters. This is clear when one asks a question such as, "Who is Jan?" The response is likely to be "Jan is the red-haired, short girl who is Mary's sister." In this type of response, though one rarely thinks of it as such, a complex of characters re-

148

ferred to as Jan is being distinguished within the complex of characters around her. That larger complex included other complexes of particulars called "Mary" and "Paula" and "Theresa." In every case, the distinctions employed in this and similar statements are ultimately analyzable into distinctions of a relational variety.

In the hypothesis of absolute zero, a number of relations are also discernible. Most conspicuous is the relation of the temperature, $-459.69°$ Fahrenheit. Both the numerical interval, -459.69, and the scale on which it is based are obvious relational concepts. There is no requirement that one think in terms of "external" and "internal" (subject/object). All that is needed for an understanding of statement (3) or any other is recognition that the nature of any entity ("physical" or otherwise) is expressible and hence comprehensible wholly in relational terms. All that is required to account for any item of interest, for any epistemological judgment, is a consideration of the relations obtaining between the item of interest and the context of particulars in which it stands. Conspicuously absent in this ontology are such phrases as "internal to mind" and "external to mind." An account that is both complete and in accordance with our common-sense beliefs about the world of experience demands only the concepts of: (1) independent relata and (2) their relations. The account does not require positing either "objects," in the physicalist sense of the term, or reified "social realities" in the subjectivist sense.

Finally, let us consider the statement about Richard Nixon's presidency. A relational analysis of this epistemic judgment begins with the common-sense assumption that the statement is as meaningful and important as any of the others. The term, "bad," like its opposite, "good," is a characteristic that is part of the complex of particular characters constituting the concept "Richard Nixon's presidency." Topics and statements of this sort are those traditionally thought of as belonging to the domain of rhetorical discourse. We shall now focus on these traditionally rhetorical themes and explain additional implications which the relational ontology holds for rhetoric.

RELATIONALITY AND RHETORIC

We have said that a relationalist views all objects of experience as having equal ontological status. Morals, ethics, and questions of politics are as real as trees, houses, planets, and atoms. One might challenge this position on grounds that most objects such as trees, stars, planets, and atoms are readily observable and that the scientific questions they occasion are not subjects of disagreement. The argument might continue with the claim that once a scientific question has been identified, we simply find a way to *measure* or otherwise *observe* the phenomena in question. Once measurement or observation is completed, disagreement is resolved. On the other hand, it can be said, disagreements about what have been called "contingent questions" continue for centuries without resolution. How can a relationalist respond? Does not the feature of disagreement signal a demarcation between two realms of thought that are, ontologically, qualitatively distinct?

The relationalist account of disagreement begins with the observation that there exists, especially within the more complex and advanced branches of modern science, an equivalent level of disagreement. There is disagreement on issues that are as difficult to resolve by verification as any question of politics or ethics. Examples range from nuclear physics, where scientists are currently grappling with disagreements that seem almost insolvable, to contemporary astronomy, where the discovery of quasars is prompting a radical reevaluation of previous conceptions of the universe.

But let us examine the fundamental tenets of relationality to see if they offer a clue to the reason for and the solution of disagreements on matters of a "contingent" nature. A relationalist posits a world of relationships, wherein every entity, conscious or inanimate, stands in relationship to one another. It follows from this that each of us, as perceiving, conscious beings, will perceive the world of relationships and the relata which populate it in a different way. Moreover, as each of us confronts very complex collections of relata such as the one referred to by the phrase, "Richard Nixon's presidency," the complexity of such collections will have two effects: (1) the collections will offer the perceiving subject multifarious characters, each itself a relata of the relational complex; and (2) the collections' "appearance" may alter radically as perspective changes for a given perceiver or for different perceivers.

One could hardly have found a topic that generated more controversy than Nixon's presidency. Was Nixon a good president? Some have answered "yes" and some have said "no." Both responses cannot be true, for it is both logically and conceptually impossible to entertain both answers as *knowledge* at the same time and in the same way. How, then, can we account for the existence of actual rhetorical discourse that embraced contradictory answers to the question?

Strict and mitigated subjectivists would answer that such a question is meaningless, since there is no "truth" or "falsity"—at least in any absolute sense—and, hence, there is no answer to the question apart from socially constructed attitudes, beliefs, and values. The advocate of mitigated objectivism would contend that there is an answer to this question and that it must be true or false. A strict objectivist would contend that such a question is without meaning because of its "nonempirical" character. A relationalist, however, would take a somewhat different approach. He or she would say the answer to disagreement regarding Richard Nixon's presidency lies in understanding each arguer's *perspective* and in the fact that the claimants may be conscious of collections of characters or aspects, each of which is a relatum within the collection of particulars that constitute Nixon's presidency. Those collections make the presidency *appear* to be different because of the differing perspectives in which the arguers stand in relation to the totality of particulars. The apparently contradictory judgments are really not contradictory at all then, for they are judgments about different aspects of the same object. One arguer may frame the answer to the question as a result of a close attention to the foreign policy aspects of the Nixon years. This arguer could put emphasis on such events as normalizing relations with China, and negotiating arms limitation agreements. He or she could conclude, "Nixon was a good president." The other arguer could focus on the effects of Watergate and conclude, "Nixon was a bad president." The relationalist argues that we should ultimately try to reduce the scope of our interest in a relational complex so that we can all talk about the same thing. Then we should be able to marshal the context of particulars in which arguers stand to an object of disagreement so they can argue on the same "plane." When this is done, it is possible to employ a rhetoric consistent with the criteria of epistemic discourse delineated in Chapter 5, both arguers agreeing on what is in dispute and, perhaps, standing inside the other's perspective. At that point, agreement might become possible.

Of course, one can imagine instances where individuals engage in argument and are brought "into perspective" with the view of an interlocutor and are still unable to embrace, understand, or otherwise recognize that perspective. In this case, one could not claim that the rhetoric which surrounded the argumentative interchange was epistemologically productive. As we have asserted before, not all rhetoric is epistemic.

These last two statements require clarification in light of what we have said in this chapter regarding relationality. It might be supposed, for example, that disputes between two arguers will on occasion be insolvable. It is still possible that out of the rhetorical interchange, the argumentative process, some knowledge claims will be uncovered that were unknown prior to debate. Many situations occur in which *a* or *the* central issue is very complex and in which this larger issue remains opaque to our best efforts to resolve it. This frequently happens with questions about ethics, politics, morality, justice, and the like. Nonetheless, in the course of arguing about such matters we often come to new insights regarding subissues connected with the general problem. It also happens that during the course of argument about a primary issue, discussion uncovers vital information about a related or even wholly separate matter. The history of science is replete with examples of scientists setting out to explore one phenomenon and ending with discoveries unrelated to the original inquiry. We are suggesting that the same happens when rhetoric is used as argument. Plato's dialogues illustrate. Conclusions respecting the central question(s) of a dialogue are seldom reached by the interlocutors, but during the course of argument numerous other discoveries and conclusions are arrived at.

We cannot, therefore, say that argument that results in little progress on the main issue is for that reason alone an instance of epistemologically unproductive rhetoric. It is possible, of course, that nothing will come of an argumentative encounter, but this can be established only after a full canvass of all major and minor points of controversy or doubt. Given the inherent interconnectedness of reality and language that strives to embody the relations that reality comprises, we ought to expect that verbal inquiry addressed to answering question "A" will often result in answering questions "B" and "C."

It is also clear that the best rhetoric—rhetoric conforming to the criteria set forth in Chapter 5—can fail to yield closure on an issue. When this occurs it may be owing to our not having isolated all relevant subissues or to our not having refined our vocabulary to the point where we are able to embody the appropriate relations that must be linguistically codified before we are able to make further progress. Given the complexity of issues humans find important and the historical baggage that linguistic concepts often carry with them, we should expect impasses on occasion. Still, the fact that language is not static should spur our optimism that rhetoric can eventually act in the function of a tool for discovery and social amelioration. As language and principles of argument are refined, progress toward understanding the relational world and toward resolving complex human issues can be expected.

An example of the promise of epistemic rhetoric as a means of enhancing human understanding may serve to clarify our position. Consider the racist who holds a severe prejudice against blacks, based in part on the premise that blacks are somehow mentally inferior to whites. Such an individual might labor under this misconception purely out of ignorance, that is, ignorance in that no credible studies support the notion that blacks are inherently less intelligent than whites. In an argumentative confrontation, a psychologist might enlighten the racist that such is not the case. In fact, the psychologist might produce a host of research to show just the opposite. If the evidence were overwhelming, the racist *might* be convinced that the former attitude toward black intelligence was in error. Yet the person might continue to hold racist views based on other considerations—that is, based on other perspectives. Or, regardless of the preponderance of the evidence against black inferiority, the racist might be unable to reconcile a new perspective with consequences for changed personal behavior or interpersonal relations with a peer group. In this case the racist might continue to espouse racist views even though the rationale for those views had been undermined. Impasse would have been reached, at least for the time being.

If the racist were to abandon prejudice as a result of being made aware of another perspective through argumentative encounter, we would have clear evidence of the value of a rhetoric grounded in perspectivist epistemology—one having its roots in a relational ontology. Even if the racist persists in prejudice, relationally grounded perspectivist rhetoric is useful for analyzing the situation. First, applying the theory allows us to determine whether in fact an impasse has been reached.49 Relationally grounded perspectivist rhetoric may allow us to see whether the disputants are arguing on the same level and are talking about the same aspect(s) of the problem. If they are not, there are no genuine grounds for disagreement. A relationally grounded account of the discourse can reveal when imprecision on the parts of interlocutors is the reason for controversy; they can then be helped to redefine or sharpen salient issues. Where this is done, continued discussion and possible agreement are facilitated by eliminating what at first appeared to be an impasse.

Second, relationally grounded rhetorical theory allows one to move among various perspectives on a given issue. Thus, even though our racist might be correct in the claim that large numbers of blacks live in ghetto communities, turning discussion to how these communities came into existence, covering such topics as economic segregation, denial of economic opportunities, and the failure of white-dominated city councils to provide essential services, might offer a number of different perspectives concerning the reasons for ghetto communities. By identifying perspectives not initially considered, the racist's attitude toward blacks may become subject to amendment.

Finally, even if additional perspectives are not identified in an argumentative exchange and even if the isolation of particular issues does not result in continued argumentative progress, by identifying precisely where an impasse is occurring we have an indication of why argument has stagnated. Accordingly, a relational analysis of discourse can tell us about ourselves

153

and others as arguers. It can underscore those moments when our emotions, preferences, values, dogmas, and prejudices have interceded to inhibit attainment of one or more of the criteria of epistemologically productive rhetoric.

This recognition offers opportunity to reduce the potential for nondiscursive forms of conflict. By admitting, for example, that both we and our potential adversaries have reached a point of impasse based on the values and myths which each uniquely holds, we can avoid charges of disingenuousness, deceit, frivolity, and truculence. Thus, while we may have to terminate rhetorical efforts because of an impasse, we can at least *understand* why negotiations have broken down. By agreeing, if only about the source of disagreement, we may be able to avoid the varieties of inflammatory charges that are the progenitors of and become rationales for nondiscursive conflict.

A relationally based perspectivist epistemology can remind us that because we each stand in unique perspective to all else, we may on occasion be simply unable to find solutions to grave problems. But this rhetorical epistemology ought also to remind us that pursuit of epistemologically productive ideas can and ought to be the regulative ideal of rhetorical interaction. Even when we cannot solve problems, it is possible through rhetoric to refine intermediate judgments and to discontinue argumentative controversy with knowledge that, having applied perspectivism as a means of understanding, we have done all that we can to achieve harmony. More than this, our ontology assures us that resolution of the most nettlesome problems is possible. We may be confident, then, that at some future time discussion can be restarted and fresh perspectives pursued.

Perspectivism based on a relational ontology offers opportunity and implies responsibility for continued efforts to solve differences by peaceful, discursive means. The theory asserts that, at least in principle, every person can realize the perspective of any other, and that once the relevant perspectives are understood, persons engaged in controversy can engage constructively. The rhetorical epistemology implies, further, that an invitation to additional rhetorical discourse needs always to be held open— even after agreement is reached. To those who might say we have now become naively idealistic we reply that (1) possibilities of epistemic rhetoric *do* exist, and (2) evidence can be drawn from history of philosophy, history of diplomacy, and the records of interpersonal reconciliation to show that new knowledge *can* be generated and disagreements minimized or even eliminated by continuous rhetorical exchange.

154

CERTAINTY

With the concepts of relationality and perspectivism before us, we need next to deal with *how* one can become certain that he or she has attained knowledge on an issue. In a universe of sometimes shifting relationships, overarching certainty about the most encompassing relationships can probably be only an aspiration or ideal for fallible humans. And a perspectivist epistemology carries implications that some conceivable perspectives on a given matter may be unknown at any given time, especially if highly complex relationships are involved. This is to say that fallible humans are unlikely to attain certainty about the most complex of problems, but it is not to define certainty as either pointless as a goal or unattainable in *all* cases. When we initially defined knowledge as persistently justified true belief, we set the ultimate, human standard for certainty at the fullest humanly possible level of confidence in beliefs. The tests for human certainty were therein implied.

The truth criterion for knowledge will be satisfied when one's statements about the world of relations accurately embody those relations and the context of particulars to which they give rise. Exclusionary statements, as those of propaganda, cannot be true because aspects of relevant relations and contexts are left out. *Inclusiveness* thus becomes one test by which to determine the degree of certainty one can have in a conclusion. The belief criterion simply says there can be no certainty where there is not clear belief. And the justification criterion implied that there is a point at which one can have sufficient evidence to guarantee that knowledge has been attained with the fullest humanly possible certainty. It is this last criterion that holds the key to ability to claim with certainty that we have knowledge.

If perspectival inclusiveness can be guaranteed for a statement about a set of relations and if we believe, how can we be sure persistent justification exists for the belief? On some matters it appears that we cannot be certain of our justifications, at least *now*. There are many areas of human inquiry where the matters under scrutiny are so complex that the issues are virtually impenetrable, given present understanding and methods of investigation. There, certainty cannot be attained at present and may not be attainable in the near future. But relationality as an ontology and perspectivism as an epistemology imply that *pursuit* of fuller justifications, hence greater degrees of certainty, is by no means fruitless. Breakthroughs to the knowledge we seek can and do occur in every domain of human endeavor. On any given subject, at a given time, we may have to content ourselves with pursuing persistently justified true belief, knowing that certainty will elude us at least for the time being. Rhetoric as the art of describing reality through language is our major means of carrying on that pursuit; knowledge is its ultimate product, and certainty is its goal. 50

About many matters no one who reads this book is likely ever to hold knowledge with certainty, but we should not lose sight of the fact that we *do* possess propositions that we can proclaim as truths and that attained that status through just the rhetorical processes we have focused on. We say with the fullest confidence humans can have: "The earth is roughly round"; "There is irony in the Socratic dialogues"; "Water is requisite to life." We are all confident that these and a host of other propositions will never be found false. Although we cannot say with certainty what precise level of justification *any* proposition must have, we are confident that in such cases the requisite level *has* been reached, and the propositions stand as *knowledge*. 51 Nor should we miss the fact that in each of these cases and many others, the status of knowledge was generated through perspectivally describing reality through language; that is, belief, persistent justification, and truth of the propositions were evolved *rhetorically*.

CONCLUSION

In its functions of accounting for disagreement and of pointing the way to solution of disagreements, our relational ontology reveals important implications for rhetorical epistemology. As rhetors, we stand in our own particular, unique relationship to the universe, whether we use rhetoric in formal oratory or in day-to-day discourse. Embracing relational theory allows us to retain useful and meaningful conceptions of "truth" or "knowledge"; it thus preserves the most important feature of objectivism. Moreover, by relieving rhetorical epistemology of the burden of dualism, relationality permits introduction of a richly endowed theory of knowledge capable of extending rhetorical knowing across the entire spectrum of what there is to know, from matters previously labeled scientific to those frequently called contingent.

Relationality makes clear the contribution of those who have argued for the existence of socially constructed realities. Such realities express the perspectives that different individuals and groups entertain on various phenomena. However, for the relationalist, they do not represent the termini of inquiry. Rather, such realities come to be viewed as more or less complete expositions of *a* perhaps limited perspective. These constructions may be invaluable in contributing to a fuller understanding of whatever phenomena are under investigation; but for a relationalist, a thorough understanding of a particular phenomenon can occur only when all *relevant* perspectives have been discovered, evaluated, and juxtaposed to form a comprehensive view of the object of inquiry and all the characters or aspects it exhibits within the context of particulars in which it stands. It is only through an active seeking out of perspectives that that goal can be approached.

NOTES

1. Of course, it could be argued that, in the subjectivist's account, not all of reality is created subjectively. Such a reply would entail a retreat from subjectivism, however, since it would admit that at least some portions of reality have their origins external to the creating subject. In such a case, some form of objectivism would be preserved.

2. This argument appears in slightly different form in C. Jack Orr, "How Shall We Say: 'Reality is Socially Constructed Through Communication'?" *Central States Speech Journal*, 29 (1978), 263–74, and Earl Croasmun and Richard A. Cherwitz, "Beyond Rhetorical Relativism," *Quarterly Journal of Speech,* 68 (1982), 1–16.

3. One is tempted to argue that to embrace subjectivism is, on this analysis, to endorse skepticism as a consequence.

4. The classic statement of this position in the communication literature is Barry Brummett's "Some Implications of 'Process' or 'Intersubjectivity': Postmodern Rhetoric," *Philosophy and Rhetoric,* 9 (1976), 21–51. Brummett's more recent defense of the intersubjectivist position appears in his "On to Rhetorical Relativism," *Quarterly Journal of Speech,* 68 (1982), 425–37. Sympathetic treatment of Brummett's position is found in, among others, Robert L. Scott, "On Viewing Rhetoric as Epistemic," *Central States Speech Journal,* 18 (1967), 9–17, and his "On Viewing Rhetoric as Epistemic: Ten Years Later," *Central States Speech Journal,* 27 (1976), 258–66.

5. Roger Trigg, *Reason and Commitment* (Cambridge: Cambridge University Press, 1977), pp. 3–4.

6. Brummett, "Some Implications," 28–30.

7. Trigg, p. 5.

8. The philosophical theory of perspectivism and the notion of relationality upon which it is based appear in Evander Bradley McGilvary, *Toward a Perspective Realism,* Albert G. Ramsperger, ed. (LaSalle, Ill.: The Open Court Publishing Co., 1956). The discussion of perspectivism and relationality and their relevance to rhetorical epistemology that appears in this chapter has its roots in McGilvary's work. While some departures from McGilvary's philosophical positions are evident in this chapter, our indebtedness to his analysis is apparent. Anticipating McGilvary's theory of relationality was the late nineteenth-century philosopher, F. H. Bradley. See his *Appearance and Reality,* 2nd ed., (Oxford: Oxford University Press, 1897).

9. McGilvary, p. 18.

10. McGilvary, p. 18.

11. The distinction between "physical" and "mental" or "spiritual" entities is one that has served little useful purpose and that, in fact, cannot be sustained. Again, the reader is cautioned against taking the term "entity," which we use frequently, to imply either physical or nonphysical existents.

12. McGilvary, p. 18.

13. James L. Golden, Goodwin Berquist, and William Coleman, *The Rhetoric of Western Thought* (Dubuque, Iowa: Kendall/Hunt Publishing Co., 1978).

14. An excellent and accessible discussion of consciousness is provided in *The Encyclopedia of Philosophy*, Paul Edwards, ed. (New York: Macmillan Publishing Co., and The Free Press, 1962), Vol. 1, p. 191.

15. *The Encyclopedia of Philosophy*, Vol. 2, p. 192.

16. Anthony Flew, *A Dictionary of Philosophy* (New York: St. Martin's Press, 1979), p. 69.

17. See Alan Ross Anderson, ed., *Minds and Machines* (Englewood Cliffs, N.J.: Prentice-Hall, 1964), p. 11.

18. Sir William Hamilton, *Lectures on Metaphysics and Logic,* Henry L. Mansel and John Veitch, eds. (Boston: Gould and Lincoln, 1859), Vol. 1, p. 191.

19. Jerome A. Shaffer, *Philosophy of Mind* (Englewood Cliffs, N.J.: Prentice-Hall, 1968), p. 9.

20. William James, *Essays in Radical Empiricism* (New York: Longmans, Green and Co., 1912), p. 2.

21. James, p. 4.

22. Any effort to draw an absolute ontological distinction between "mental" and "material" things creates an inextricable philosophical quandry, the problem of dualism. Positing a primal "stuff" or "material" contributes to the problem, though designed to eliminate it.

23. The label "inferential/representational" is our own. An inferential/representational view is one that holds that the objects of reality are never presented directly to us but are *inferred* by our cognitive facilities, operating on what are held to be the *representations* of reality which the organs of perception acquire.

24. McGilvary, p. 42.

25. Michael S. Gazzaniga, *Functional Neuroscience* (New York: Harper and Row, 1979), p. 123.

26. Ibid., pp. 125, 129, 143.

27. Bertrand Russell, *The Analysis of Matter* (New York: Dover Publications, 1954), p. 197.

28. See Shaffer, pp. 44–50.

29. The point that inferential/representational theories of perception do, in fact, entail skepticism is made by Stuart Katz and Gordon Frost, "The Origins of Knowledge in Two Theories of Brain: The Cognitive Paradox Revealed," *Behaviorism,* 7 (1979), 35–44.

30. See, for example, J. Jerison, "Paleoneurology and the Evolution of Mind," *Scientific American,* 234 (1976), 90–101, and W. T. Powers, "Quantitative Analysis of Purposive Systems: Some Spadework at the Foundations of Scientific Psychology," *Psychological Review,* 85 (1978), 417–35.

31. McGilvary, pp. 44–45.

32. McGilvary, p. 45.

33. McGilvary, p. 46.

34. McGilvary, p. 46.

35. This formulation of consciousness is similar to McGilvary's, which he frames in postulate form. See McGilvary, p. 47.

36. The phrase "relational organization" may seem redundant. We retain the redundancy to emphasize the point that the organization we have in mind is part and parcel of the doctrine of relationality.

37. To suggest that all relations are *internal* to a particular entity is to argue that the nature of that entity is determined by *all* the relationships in which it stands to *all* other existing things. This position has been defended by, among others, Brand Blanshard, *The Nature of Thought* (New York: The Macmillan Company, 1939), Vol. II, p. 452.

38. René Descartes, *Discourse on Method and Meditations on First Philosophy*, Laurence J. Lafleur, trans. (Indianapolis: Bobbs-Merrill, 1960).

39. This position is represented by Brummett in "Some Implications." See also, Scott, "On Viewing Rhetoric as Epistemic" and "On Viewing Rhetoric as Epistemic: Ten Years Later."

40. Representative of this view is Thomas B. Farrell, "Knowledge, Consensus, and Rhetorical Theory," *Quarterly Journal of Speech*, 62 (1976), 1–14, and "Social Knowledge II," *Quarterly Journal of Speech*, 64 (1978), 329–44.

41. Strict objectivism is characteristic of a number of rhetoricians, including François Fénelon, *Dialogues on Eloquence*. The position also finds sympathetic treatment among moderns, for example, Richard Weaver, *Language Is Sermonic* (Baton Rouge: Louisiana State University Press, 1970).

42. C. Jack Orr can be categorized as a mitigated objectivist. See his "How Shall We Say."

43. The notion of "category mistake" is treated by Gilbert Ryle, *The Concept of Mind* (London: Hutchinson's University Library, 1949).

44. In our view there obtains a basic, foundational, ontological unity in all that is. This ontological unity, we argue, is a product of the *relations* that have been the central focus of this chapter. As a result of seeing ontological foundations in terms of relations, and since relations determine the characters of both subjects and objects, the subject/object distinction and its attendant problems is removed.

45. See Panayot Butchvarov, *Resemblance and Identity: An Examination of the Problem of Universals* (Bloomington: Indiana University Press, 1966).

46. Ibid., p. 3.

47. Ibid., p. 4. Emphasis added.

48. Ibid., pp. 194–95.

49. One can imagine a dispute in which the weight of evidence is about even, or where the knowledge claims arrived at tend to support two opposing propositions. Given our theory, one can only continue the dialogue in such cases. If the question is specific and unitary, some answer *must* exist. Where precisely contrary knowledge claims exist (e.g., "the moon has mountains on the far side" and "the moon does not have mountains on the far side"), we must assume that eventually the *knowledge* we *can* have concerning the knowledge claims will be reconciling. Or, we may need to see whether what we take to be a unitary and specific question is not really a complex one. In the latter case, we can immediately make further progress by taking the relational analysis to further levels of discrimination, separating out the various additional questions to be grappled with.

50. One could argue that, because the universe is composed of a vast system of relations, the recognition that one has arrived at "truth" will be a function of comparing linguistic statements about reality. One would expect a kind of relational coherence to obtain if, in fact, truth has been discovered. Relational inconsistency would be indicative of error.

51. An important part of the justification criterion of knowledge must be the weight of evidence indicating relational coherence.

PROBLEMS AND PROMISES OF
RHETORICAL EPISTEMOLOGY

In the time it took us to write this book, the events we mentioned in Chapter 1 underwent considerable historical transformation. The Arab-Israeli conflict continued, but the face of that conflict changed. Yasir Arafat became a virtual refugee, and the Palestine Liberation Organization was scattered about the Arab world following Israel's siege of Beirut. The Iran-Iraq war went through numerous battles with neither side making much progress toward subjugating its enemy. In the Falklands, a British garrison of several thousand was left to stand guard over the few hundred sheep farmers whose islands had been the object of unsuccessful Argentinian invasion.

The author who had quit smoking when Chapter 1 was first written has long since resumed the habit, but the other author maintains a tobacco-free lifestyle. Our colleagues' personal lives, as well as our own, continued to rise to the peaks and descend to the valleys of ever-changing human existence.

In theoretical physics, the search for the elementary particle continued. The debate between evolutionists and creationists continued, and astrology maintained its mystical grasp on thousands.

In the realm of human rights, the National Organization for Women and the National Association for the Advancement of Colored People, while outspoken in their determination to see Ronald Reagan defeated at the polls in 1984, were unable to prevent a landslide victory for the incumbent President.

Radio astronomers continued to listen for the first signals from extraterrestrial intelligence, and the Voyager spacecraft left the solar system, heading for deep space with its gold plaque inscribed with messages for any extraterrestrial beings who might intercept the probe.

In short, the successes and failures of human life continued to accumulate as we wrote. These successes and failures were in several ways attributable to *communication* as well as to the stock of human *knowledge* represented by and transmitted through communicative processes. By the time this book is in print, there will have been additional permutations of the aforementioned events, still attributable to interplay between communication and knowledge.

We have written of what we call a rhetorical epistemology. We do not pretend that all human problems will be solved through reliance on what we have labeled "epistemologically productive rhetoric," but we do hope to have shown that such discourse was central to generation of that which we now count as knowledge. We contend further that by understanding the inextricable relationship between communicative processes and the stock of human knowledge, we acquire tools by which to attenuate much confusion, conflict, misunderstanding, and human error.

We have argued for a number of theses that touch on the way things are and also on prospects for productive human relationships. We have argued that claims have varying degrees of reliability and that elevating casual, everyday claims to the status of *knowledge* produces confusion and error. We have set forth criteria that claims to knowledge ought to meet if those claims are to be treated as true and justified. Among the many social implications of those propositions is an implied caution against treating slogans, myths, received opinions, and the like as true. On our terms, to do so is not simply to be careless, illogical, or morally inept; it is to ignore what it is to *know* something. In the dispute concerning who is the rightful sovereign over the Falkland Islands, a socially constructed "truth" was encapsulated in the slogan "My country right or wrong" and was invoked by *both* sides. The slogan hid the subtle fact that the cause for which so many Argentines and British gave their lives was treated as knowledge: "We shall attain the victory because we are *right!*" was frequently heard as assurance from both sides. The claim was certainly false "knowledge" for the Argentines.

The general lesson about the dangers of elevating casual claims to the status of knowledge is more important. Each of the geopolitical conflicts mentioned in Chapter 1 can be linked to what the nations or parties tacitly agreed upon as knowledge. Because "knowledge" was treated as *knowledge,* it was never or seldom subjected to argumentative criticism. However flawed, the "knowledge" was taken as true, without examination. We have tried to emphasize the importance of constantly testing, in the marketplace of ideas, whatever propositions are to be taken as foundations of action. It is especially ironic, therefore, that when nations wage war they rarely ask themselves about the soundness of the premises on which their conflicts rest, while they subject to closest scrutiny such issues as manpower, resources, costs, and geographical location. Yet the premises of conflicts may be as complex as the question of when one nation has a right to intervene in the affairs of another or whether or when one's private wishes ought to stand paramount over the wishes of one's partner. What emerges from the epistemological analysis presented in this book is that, in general, attitudes, beliefs, and values of groups or individuals are too seldom questioned for veridicality. Our analysis shows that clear distinctions among *mere belief, rational belief, true belief,* and *knowledge* are necessary. Given human fallibility and limited means of inquiry, maintaining these distinctions is unlikely to solve all human conundrums or meliorate all human conflicts, but the distinctions point the way toward rational resolution of problems by resort to *knowledge* rather than ideas of lesser standing.

We defined rhetoric as description of reality through language. A most important observation deriving from this definition is that all rhetoric *purports* to describe how the world is, in fact. Rhetorical discourse may or may not accurately and inclusively display the interrelations of phenomena in their contexts. As we pointed out in Chapter 4, language always embodies relationships presumed to exist between and among entities in the world. However, descriptions allegedly describing reality can be sweepingly generalized, contain half-truths, or baldly misrepresent what attention to relationality of phenomena in the world and attention to possible perspectives on the world would reveal as true. One sees these possibilities and tendencies repeatedly in marital disputes, advertising, geopolitics, and in a host of other settings. For example, much official discourse of the Israeli government in the early 1980s portrayed the Palestine Liberation Organization as bent upon eradication of the Jewish state. Likewise, PLO propaganda cast Israelis in the role of tramplers on God-given Arab rights. The intention implicit in both bodies of rhetoric was to paint for target populations a highly selective picture of the world and to do so for the specific purpose of eliciting certain ranges of behavior. It is easily demonstrated, however, that both bodies of rhetoric went beyond accurate, justified description of reality. The language chosen overstated and oversimplified the facts and issues in dispute. Further, overstatement and oversimplification functioned to raise the emotive levels of the target populations, rendering them unable to recognize reality even when accurately depicted. Not only is such rhetoric not epistemologically productive, it is rhetoric that obstructs epistemologically productive inquiry through discourse. There is no dearth of such rhetoric, privately and publicly used. The position for which we have been arguing in this book is that no one *needs* to be victimized by it; pursuit of justified true belief is possible, and the methods of that pursuit are explicable and intelligible.

This leads to a third lesson issuing from our inquiry. It is that when and if discourse is employed in the service of discovering *knowledge,* it must be used systematically and in accordance with clear and defensible criteria of acceptability. We have described five properties of epistemologically productive, truth-seeking rhetoric: its differentiative, associative, preservative, evaluative, and perspectival features and functions. We have shown that if any of these properties does not exist in discourse, that discourse cannot be epistemologically productive. The discourse is epistemologically defective and cannot contribute to discovery of *knowledge*. These five properties can serve as inventional measures for anyone concerned about the epistemological fruitfulness of his or her discourse. From the standpoint of consumers of rhetoric, canvassing what is heard or read for the presence of these five properties constitutes a test for probity in what is presented. Once more, by such tests, epistemologically productive rhetoric can be distinguished from less productive forms, and rhetors and recipients can approximate or even attain certainty in their knowledge.

Fourth, our discussion of ontological issues bearing on the epistemology of rhetoric revealed some of the dangers of conceiving of the world as the mere construct of language. Not only is this conception too limited to be true, but relativistic attitudes that flow from it can have deleterious consequences in everyday affairs. Treating complex issues as simply the products of language communities, each with the right to conduct its affairs as it chooses since whatever "reality" the community agrees on *is* real, renders conflicts conceptually unresolvable. Witness the Iranian hostage crisis. Some said Iran and the United States could not negotiate understandingly because of their radically different cultures and languages. Yet the Israeli-Egyptian accords worked out at Camp David cast doubt on such generalizations about intercultural roadblocks to understanding. And the very fact that the Iranian crisis ended with the safe release of the hostages assures us that some measure of intercultural communication was successful.

Our contention has been that roadblocks occur to prevent amicable solutions to problems as consequences of parties' unwillingness or inability to risk self in argument, to engage in correction, to allow equal initiative and control, and to subscribe to the criteria for epistemic rhetoric. These are *procedural* protections against terminating private or public negotiations and inquiry too soon, and they fulfill the moral imperative that communicative engagement implies—collaboration. At personal or geopolitical levels, failure to persevere in epistemic pursuit of justified true belief is failure to exercise full human potentiality. Succumbing to the notion that individuals, groups, societies, and cultures are right whenever they can garner support for their attitudes and beliefs renders advancement of human understanding and knowledge all but impossible.

Fifth, we have stressed the importance of multi-perspectival viewpoints in rhetorical engagements with self or others. Most fundamental human problems, we said, force consideration of data and ideas of great complexity. We illustrated with the multifaceted array of subissues associated with the problem of racism. Our entire book has been an attempt to com-

164

prehend and command the complexes of ideas associated with the problem of how we come to *know* anything. A student seeking to comprehend the biological complexities that constitute a frog confronts this necessity to adopt a number of relevant perspectives: anatomical, evolutionary, chemical, embryological, and more. In all pursuit of *knowledge,* pursuit of all relevant perspectives is essential to epistemic judgment.

The principle applies to so mundane a matter as whether or not to read a book. The book may appear drab; its subject may seem formidable; its author may be unheralded. These, however, are only *some* of the book's complex of relevant characteristics. The totality of its characteristics includes also its potential relevance to the prospective reader's ultimate aspirations, the author's purpose in writing, and whatever obligations for knowing the book's subject have been imposed on the prospective reader. Accurate appraisal of the wisdom of reading the book entails canvass of all such relevant perspectives on the prospective act.

The importance of multi-perspectival viewpoints has implications for all who act as rhetors, auditors, or readers. We have tried to make clear that epistemologically productive rhetorical discourse must attempt to embody the broadest range of perspectives relevant to the circumstances that justify rhetorical engagement. For rhetors, this principle is an inventional guideline and a presentational guideline. For auditor or reader, it is an evaluative guideline, a critical test of epistemological worth. Awareness and use of a perspectivist epistemology in creation or consumption of discourse is essential in anyone's determination of whether difference and disagreement really exist concerning whatever is discussed. As we have seen, apparent disagreement is often caused by failure of one or both parties to delineate germane perspectives.

The above are some of the advantages and promises of adopting the principles of rhetorical epistemology, as we have presented them. One must grant, however, that even the strictest adherence to these principles will not guarantee that pressing issues will always be resolved. We have implied that a perspectivist rhetorical epistemology can solve most problems. This presupposes meticulous and exhaustive inquiry. But humans are fallible, impatient, and often busy. As is true when one employs complex mathematical formulas, a perspectivist's task in calculation is a difficult one. Because human problems are often more complicated than even many mathematical proofs, the requisite expertise and commitment are often beyond the capability of many. Even when needed commitment and expertise do exist, resolution of a particular problem may still remain beyond one's grasp. It could be, for example, that not enough energy has been expended by others or too little time has elapsed to allow all relevant perspectives to come into view. For example, both factors block present understanding of birth defects. As we indicated in our discussion of the preservative function of rhetoric, issues may require extensive deliberation before we can be made aware of all relevant perspectives. This does not, however, minimize the need for relational, perspectival rhetoric; it argues for vigorous exercise of such rhetoric to preserve the problem, keep it in focus, and thereby maintain the prospect for ultimate resolution.

Progress in the solution of human problems is often slow, as the problems of civil rights, poverty, and law attest. But even when knowledge as justified true belief is unattainable, there is still value in striving for knowledge in accordance with the method presented in this book. In our judgement the most important implication of all that we have said is that *the process of striving for knowledge systematically is more important than the attainment of knowledge itself.* It is not always the case that lack of knowledge is due to human failure. The resources for coming to know may simply not be available. However, it is the *manner* in which humans attempt to acquire knowledge that attests to their rationality. Even to err is not invariably failure of rationality. We may believe our epistemic judgements conform to the criteria of knowledge but err somewhere in well intentioned, informed exploration. It is rational recognition of this possibility that dictates continued risking of self, avoiding shutting the door to additional inquiry. Conferring the status of knowledge on our beliefs does not, given the limitations of human capacities, relieve us of the obligation to sustain and renew the rhetorically epistemological activities of *differentiating, associating, preserving, evaluating, and placing in perspective.*

We have been dealing with what are largely personal implications of the philosophy of rhetoric presented in this book. We wish now to turn to the applicability of perspectivist rhetorical epistemology to professional disciplines. Insofar as such fields as political science, philosophy, the social and physical sciences, and even theology employ discourse as an integral part of research and exposition or persuasion, what has been said in this book has bearing on the work done by professionals in these fields. At minimum, the *discovery* function of discourse that conforms to our description of epistemologically productive rhetoric operates in all of these fields—if the work of the field is done as well as it can be done. For instance, although individual scientific disciplines employ their own unique methods, equipment, and theories, all scientific disciplines share a common feature. Indeed, they share this feature with all disciplines, scientific or otherwise. That feature is what we might term *the discourse of inquiry.*

Regardless of what discipline we consider, a vital feature of the discipline will be communication among and between experts. In even the most "nondiscursive" fields such as mathematics, the textbooks, the theoretical treatises, and the journals carry large quantities of linguistic interaction. Anyone who attends a conference or seminar on one of the "nondiscursive" subjects will also see that the role played by language is fundamental to advancing the "state of the art" in that field. The vital function of linguistic interaction among theorists can be discerned by attending carefully to the *form* of the interactions, as well as to their content. Mathematicians, biologists, astronomers, logicians, paleontologists, and all other scholars must make some effort to function as rhetorical critics. They must monitor their own discourse and the discourse of their colleagues. Only so can they judge how nearly the discourse of inquiry resembles the ideals of perspectival, rhetorical epistemology. We think this statement is almost self-evident, but a profitable line of investigation for the future is critical/theoretical analysis of the communicative habits of particular academic disciplines, especially the scientific disciplines. Some work of this sort has already been done. 1

A related line of inquiry is investigation to determine the extent to which our tendency to separate scientific inquiry from other domains of inquiry is justified. We take it as undeniable that science is in large part an enterprise dependent on epistemologically productive discourse. To that extent science is subject to the same foibles and fallibilities that plague other areas of inquiry. From out point of view, scientific certainty, however ensconced in technical presentation, is as difficult to attain as is certainty in other domains. The history of science itself documents that what is taken as certain knowledge in one age gives way to new discoveries in subsequent ages. To guarantee that scientific, as well as other, knowledge remains cumulative, it is essential to remember that science, as enterprise, is significantly *rhetorical.* Scientific pronouncements are enhanced, though they are not fundamentally guaranteed, through an epistemologically productive discourse of inquiry.

A related problem is the usefulness of the traditional notions of "contingent" and "apodictic" realms of knowledge. We argued in Chapter 6 that this distinction may at best be euphemistic. It is beyond the scope of our project to provide a thorough philosophical exegesis of this important claim, but we believe we have cast sufficient doubt on the distinction to warrant further inquiry. The importance of this task lies in the implications of the distinction. Whether we shall eventually entertain a relativistic stance regarding those questions of the most basic importance to human

167

society, questions of politics, ethics, and so on, is but one such implication. A second implication is the nettlesome problem of dualism which seems attendant to the contingent/apodictic distinction.

The problems and promises engendered in rhetorical epistemology are best explored further by employing the discourse of inquiry on which we have focused. Such discursive inquiry is at the heart of productive scholarship. The case we have made is that our ability to learn and to advance that stock of human knowledge depends on our capacity to engage in a specific variety of discursive procedures and interactions, an enterprise that is epistemologically productive *because* it conforms to criteria that offer the greatest likelihood of knowledge acquisition. These criteria, we contend, define the essence of rationality. Moreover, this uniquely *rhetorical* formulation of human inquiry is at the core of what distinguishes the human species from all others. "Humanity" has been defined in various ways throughout the history of ideas. Some have held that humanity is defined by its rationality; others have contended that it is the quality of "symbol using" that sets us apart from other life forms. There is a grain of truth in these pronouncements, but we suggest that individuals become human when they abandon nondiscursive forms of conflict and "empty" or "self-serving" rhetoric in favor of discourse whose goal is the attainment of truth and whose method is faithful to the almost-lost sense of the Greeks' term "dialectic"—discourse conceived as the pursuit of serious inquiry. If we have achieved our goal in writing this book, we have made it apparent that communication and knowledge are inherently and fundamentally connected, and that in at least one important sense rhetoric can be and often is epistemic.

We have written a treatise on knowledge, developed from the perspective of communication studies. We think that what we have said makes a difference for those who are primarily interested in understanding literary, philosophical, and rhetorical issues related to communication. We think further that what we have said and implied has significance for general scholarship.

Will Durant was concerned that in the present age of closely focused research, specialists come to know more and more about less and less, while generalists seem to know less and less about more and more. This bifurcation of scholarly enterprise is easy to make, and it sounds good. The phrasing is catchy and tempts one to say it has a ring of truth. Our concern is not so much with the accuracy of Durant's assessment as with whether the scholarly divisions and narrowings Durant perceived may forecast the future of scholarly enterprise. Few would deny that the proliferation of alleged subdisciplines within virtually every field of scholarly inquiry has resulted in scholars' concentrating on ever narrower ranges of knowledge and issues.

The danger of such tendencies seems to us to be development of territories of study and knowledge in which experts contract an ever-worsening case of conceptual myopia. When a narrow area of interest can be explored with consistent methodologies that yield coherent conclusions, why look beyond the boundaries of the territory? One needs only to read a number of highly specialized journals of recent appearance to observe this kind of narrowing of questioning and of audiences addressed. Generalists confront comparable temptations. Need they delve into the intricacies of specialized studies, since they seek overarching theories and knowledge? If they do not take specializations into account, their general postulates cannot face tests at the level of specific knowledge. Both generalists and specialists compound the possibilities of error if they do not touch seriously each others' levels of concern and inquiry. Specialized knowledge does not become integrated into general theory and knowledge, and general knowledge and theory cannot be subjected to qualifying specifics. Either result stems from not testing the veracity of one's work against sources *external* to the methodologies one creates to serve a personal interest.

An implication of what we have said is that conceptual myopia can be forestalled if we recognize the inherently *systemic* nature of knowledge. We hope to have made clear that one cannot afford, epistemologically, to align oneself exclusively with either specialization or generalization. It is necessary to check specialized conclusions in reference to perspectives provided by larger collections of data and inferences, *and* to test conclusions from general inquiries against their applicability in relevant, special domains of scholarship. If one fails to take the first course it is all too easy to construct *internally* consistent worldviews that do not cohere with the larger stock of knowledge. If one fails to take the second course, there is no way to determine whether theory is an accurate representation of reality.

The perspectivist approach to rhetorical epistemology permits one to disarm, in some degree, the skepticism that stands behind Durant's assessment. One need not be *either* a specialist *or* a generalist in Durant's sense. One can understand the fundamental interconnectedness of the phenomena comprising the universe. One can understand that, as we have said, "everything that is, is what it is in virtue of its relationship to everything else." One can understand that because the phenomena of experience cohere in collections of relata, and stand in identifiable relationships with other relata, a thorough knowledge of any one domain can *potentially* illuminate any other related domain. To actualize this potentiality requires us to look frequently toward the other domains in order to guide our inquiry and validate our conclusions. This does not mean that in scholarship one must have personally located the persistently justified true beliefs of every domain of inquiry; it does mean that one needs to "look toward" the justified beliefs of domains related to one's own. To do otherwise is to condone competing perspectives on aspects of reality—perspectives that often yield contradictory conclusions unless reconciled by epistemologically constructive rhetoric.

Let us bring these generalizations to bear on examples drawn from specific disciplines we mentioned earlier. To do so will illustrate how the epistemological concerns of our inquiry can contribute to coherence in various branches of study.

An important comtemporary issue in literary criticism is how standards of criticism shall be framed. In evaluating literary work, what should be the critic's focus? Is the best analysis of a literary work primarily dependent on the text? the author's intent? or the audience's response? Such questions have given rise to a number of theoretical orientations in criticism, among them: New Criticism, Structuralism, Phenomenology, Psychoanalysis, and Deconstruction.[2] What we have written in this book does not directly address many of the technical issues that have produced these schools of thought, but what we have said does suggest an alternative to "buying into" any *one* of these approaches. The perspectival epistemology developed throughout these pages underscores the need to view approaches to literary analysis as not necessarily mutually exclusive, though some may be. Perspectivism implies that each critical approach *could* contribute importantly to understanding of some aspect or aspects of the critical object. In a perspective analysis, the meaning of a literary work, like the meaning of a linguistic term, would be seen as located in the myriad relationships in which the work stands, evokes, and engages. Within this view it would be presumed that only an incomplete, if not misleading, analysis could come from criticism done solely in reference to the author's intent *or* the audience's reaction *or* any other singular dimension. Insofar as a complete understanding of a literary work could be attained, it must come from reconciling conclusions from all possibly relevant perspectives. Given the limits on humans' time and energy, it is unlikely that any one critic could from original inquiry command the work from all relevant perspectives, but this fact simply reinforces another thesis of this book: pursuit of comprehensive, justified, true belief is best carried out collaboratively and dialectically.

A perennial topic of interest in philosophy is ethics. One of the issues of contemporary debate in ethics is whether or not standards of conduct exist objectively.[3] One of our important conclusions has been that existence of objective standards cannot and should not be discounted for the reasons typically offered. Instead, there is needed a critique of ethical positions more searching than the critique usually offered. Such a critique would be likely to expose a number of ethical standards and to provide critiques of each. Most importantly, there is need to address and try to reconcile the standards of conduct that *do* lie behind our ethical choices. Reconciliation would require exploration of alternative perspectives, as we noted in Chapter 6. In any case, judgments of ethical systems and standards *solely* in accordance with cultural or time-bound variables would be called into question. As we argued in Chapter 6, relativistic considerations are important to understanding human affairs, but, exclusively relied on, they lead inexorably to legitimization of varieties of ethical systems in which dogmatism is inherent. A perspectivist approach that admits the possibility of a reality standing independently of humans (including ethical and other dimensions) can avoid implicit endorsements of dogmatism.

In rhetorical studies, under such labels as communication, English, anthropology, and linguistics, attempts are made to understand discourse. Research focuses on many different rhetorical variables, among them the effects of discourse on audiences, the aesthetic dimensions of language, recurrent linguistic and rhetorical patterns, and symbolic dimensions of discourse. There are even those who investigate patterns of proof and argument using the descriptive formulations of such traditional systems as those of Aristotle, Cicero, Whately, and others. These and other approaches to the study of rhetoric have produced interesting results and have been vigorously pursued. While such studies have produced valuable theory and criticism, their foci upon messages, texts, perceptions, and effects have been at the expense of exploring the relationship between discourse and the reality it purports to describe.

As we have said, rhetoric is description of reality through language. To rhetorical critics we would issue a challenge. A focus of rhetorical criticism ought increasingly to be on the ability of rhetors to describe reality *faithfully* through language. We suggest increased attention to what we might term epistemological criticism, criticism that evaluates discourse, not by some set of internal standards, but as occurring within the context of an independent reality apart from discourse. This is not to say that other modes of criticism should be abandoned, or to discredit them in any way. The more traditional modes of criticism can assist an epistemological critic in his or her evaluation of human discourse. For example, when content analysis suggests that a president's talk contains such qualities as leadership, confidence, and the like, a further question suggests itself: Do those discursive patterns reflect a *reality* with dimensions of leadership and confidence, existing apart from the discourse? Rhetorical critics perceive Harry Truman as a confident, in-charge President with a sign on his desk reading, "The Buck Stops Here." But how would, how could, and how should such critics accommodate their critical observations and pronouncements to the reality that Harry Truman was also a pawn of Franklin Roosevelt's legacy and of his advisers until after the end of the Second World War? From the perspective of discourse analysis one Harry Truman emerges, but from a perspective focused on political initiative another Harry Truman appears. Whatever the evidence derived from examining discourse on its own terms, such epistemological considerations as we have developed are also germane and, we suggest, form significant parts of the general enterprise of rhetorical analysis.

The value of the rhetorical epistemology developed in these pages inheres in more than just the capacity of the theory to cohere as theory. The value of the theory extends beyond its capacity to account for routine communicative experiences. Part of the theory's value rests in its capacity to refine and broaden the "doing of scholarship." The theory of rhetorical epsitemology presented in this book is not beyond argument, but it offers more than a philosophical commentary on rhetoric of concern only to a specialized audience of scholars. We have argued that rhetoric *is* epistemic. If we are mistaken, a comprehensive counterargument will have to be made. If we are right, the principles and criteria of rhetorical epsitemology are relevant to the study and conduct of all modes of communicative activity, whether by laypersons or academicians.

NOTES

1. See, for example, Mario Finnocciaro, "Logic and Rhetoric in Lavossier's Sealed Note: Toward a Rhetoric of Science," *Philosophy and Rhetoric,* 10 (1977), 111–22; James A. Kelso, "Science and the Rhetoric of Reality," *Central States Speech Journal,* 31 (1980), 17–29; Michael A. Overington, "The Scientific Community as Audience: Toward a Rhetorical Analysis of Science," *Philosophy and Rhetoric,* 10, (1977), 143–63; Phillip C. Wander, "The Rhetoric of Science," *Western Journal of Speech Communication,* 40 (1976), 226–35; and Walter B. Weimer, "Science as a Rhetorical Transaction: Toward a Non-justificational Conception of Rhetoric," *Philosophy and Rhetoric,* 10, (1977), 1–29

2. See Steven Mailloux, *Interpretive Conventions: The Reader in the Study of American Fiction* (Ithaca: Cornell University Press, 1982).

3. For an introduction to some issues surrounding the debate between objectivists and subjectivists, see Roger Trigg, *Reason and Commitment* (Cambridge, Cambridge University Press, 1973).

RHETORIC AND EPISTEMOLOGY
BIBLIOGRAPHY

Mortimer Adler, *Dialectic* (New York: Harcourt, Brace & Co., 1927).

Allan Ross Anderson, ed., *Minds and Machines* (Englewood Ciffs, N.J.: Prentice-Hall, 1964).

David Annis, "A Note on Lehrer's Proof that Knowledge Entails Belief," *Analysis*, 29 (1968–69), 207–8.

Karl-Otto Apel, *Towards a Transformation of Philosophy* (Boston: Routledge and Kegan Paul, 1980).

Aristotle, *Rhetoric*.

David M. Armstrong, "Is Introspective Knowledge Incorrigible?" *Philosophical Review*, 72 (1963), 417–32.

_____, "Does Knowledge Entail Belief?" *Proceedings of the Aristotelian Society,*" 70 (1969–70), 21–36.

_____, *Belief, Truth and Knowledge* (London: Cambridge University Press, 1973).

Carroll C. Arnold and John Waite Bowers, eds., *Handbook of Rhetorical and Communication Theory* (Boston: Allyn and Bacon, 1984).

Saint Augustine, *Against the Academicians* (Milwaukee: Marquette University Press, 1942).

Bruce Aune, *Rationalism, Empiricism, and Pragmatism* (New York: Random House, 1967).

J. L. Austin, *How to Do Things with Words,* J. O. Urmson, ed. (Cambridge: Harvard University Press, 1962).

A. J. Ayer, *The Problem of Knowledge* (Baltimore: Penguin Books, 1956).

_____, *Logical Positivism* (Glencoe, Ill.: Free Press, 1959).

_____, *The Central Questions of Philosophy* (New York: Holt, Rinehart & Winston, 1973).

Cyril Bailey, *The Greek Atomists and Epicurus* (Oxford: The Clarendon Press, 1928).

F. G. Bailey, *The Tactical Uses of Passion: An Essay on Power, Reason, and Reality* (Ithaca: Cornell University Press, 1983).

Alexander Bain, *English Composition and Rhetoric* (London: Longmans Green, 1888).

Gregory Bateson, *Steps to an Ecology of Mind* (New York: Ballantine Books, 1972).

_____, *Mind and Nature: A Necessary Unity* (New York: Bantam Books, 1979).

Emmettee William Beauchamp, "The Kuhn-Popper Debate," dissertation, University of Texas at Austin, 1975.

Peter Berger and Thomas Luckmann, *The Social Construction of Reality* (Garden City: Doubleday, 1966).

Richard J. Bernstein, *Beyond Objectivism and Relativism: Science, Hermeneutics, and Praxis* (Philadelphia: University of Pennsylvania Press, 1984).

Vincent M. Bevilacqua, "Philosophical Influences in the Development of English Rhetorical Theory: 1748–1783," *Proceedings of the Leeds Philosophical and Literary Society, Literary and Historical Section*, Vol. IXX, Part IV.

Bibliography

Lloyd F. Bitzer, "Aristotle's Enthymeme Revisited," *Quarterly Journal of Speech,* 45 (1959), 399–408.

_____, "Rhetoric and Public Knowledge," in *Rhetoric, Philosophy, and Literature,* Don M. Burks, ed. (West Lafayette, Ind.: Purdue University Press, 1978), pp. 67–93.

_____, "The Rhetorical Situation," *Philosophy and Rhetoric,* 1 (1968) pp. 1–14.

_____, "Functional Communication: A Situational Perspective," in *Rhetoric in Transition: Studies in the Nature and Uses of Rhetoric,* Eugene White, ed. (University Park: Pennsylvania State University Press, 1980), pp. 21–38.

Brand Blanshard, *The Nature of Thought* (New York: The Macmillan Company, 1940), 2 Vols.

H. Gene Blocker, "Back to Reality," *Metaphilosophy,* 5 (1974), 232–41.

Wayne C. Booth, *Modern Dogma and the Rhetoric of Assent* (Chicago: University of Chicago Press, 1974).

Francis Herbert Bradley, *Appearance and Reality,* 2nd ed., (Oxford: The Clarendon Press, 1897).

Alan Brinton, "William James and the Epistemic View of Rhetoric," *Quarterly Journal of Speech,* 68 (1982), 158–69.

_____, "Situation in the Theory of Rhetoric," *Philosophy and Rhetoric,* 14 (1981), 234–48.

Wayne Brockriede, "Constructs, Experience, and Argument," *Quarterly Journal of Speech,* 71 (1985), 151–163.

May Brodbeck, ed., *Readings in the Philosophy of the Social Sciences* (New York: Macmillan Publishing Co., 1968).

Jacob Bronowski, *Science and Human Values,* rev. ed. (New York: Harper & Row, 1965).

Oscar L. Brownstein, "Plato's *Phaedrus*: Dialectic as the Genuine Art of Speaking," *Quarterly Journal of Speech,* 51 (1965), 392–98.

Barry Brummett, "Intersubjectivity or Critical Rationalism?" Unpublished manuscript, Purdue University, 1980.

_____, "Some Implications of 'Process' or 'Intersubjectivity': Postmodern Rhetoric," *Philosophy and Rhetoric,* 9 (1976), 21–51.

_____, "Three Meanings of Epistemic Rhetoric," Paper presented at the 1979 Speech Communication Association Seminar on "Discursive Reality: Promises and Products of the 'Social Knowledge' Paradigm in Rhetorical and Communication Theory Research."

_____, "A Defense of Ethical Relativism as Rhetorically Grounded," *Western Journal of Speech Communication,* 45 (1981), 286–98.

_____, "On to Rhetorical Relativism," *Quarterly Journal of Speech,* 68 (1982), 425–37.

_____, "Consensus Criticism," *Southern Speech Communication Journal,* 49 (1984), 111–24.

Michael S. Bruner, "Argument from a Pragmatic Perspective," *Journal of the American Forensic Association,* 20 (1983), 90–97.

Robert C. Buck and Robert S. Cohen, eds., *Boston Studies in the Philosophy of Science,* Vol. 7 (Dordrect: D. Reidel Publishing Co., 1971).

Kenneth Burke, *Language as Symbolic Action* (Berkeley: University of California Press, 1966).

_____, *A Rhetoric of Motives* (Berkeley: University of California Press, 1950).

Panayot Butchvarov, *Being qua Being* (Bloomington: Indiana University Press, 1979).

_____, *The Concept of Knowledge* (Evanston, Ill.: Northwestern University Press, 1970).

Donald T. Campbell, "Natural Selection as an Epistemological Model," in *A Handbook of Method in Cultural Anthropology*, Raoul Naroll & Donald Cohen, eds. (Garden City, N.Y.: The Natural History Press, 1970), pp. 51–85.

George Campbell, *The Philosophy of Rhetoric*, Lloyd F. Bitzer, ed. (Carbondale: Southern Illinois University Press, 1963).

Paul N. Campbell, "Poetic-Rhetorical, Philosophical, and Scientific Discourse," *Philosophy and Rhetoric*, 6 (1973) 1–29.

_____, "The Personae of Scientific Discourse," *Quarterly Journal of Speech*, 61 (1975), 391–405.

Walter M. Carleton, "Theory Transformation in Communication: The Case of Henry Johnstone," *Quarterly Journal of Speech*, 61 (1975), 76–88.

_____, "On Rhetoric as a 'Way of Knowing:' An Inquiry into Epistemological Dimensions of a 'New Rhetoric,' "dissertation, Pennyslvania State University, 1975.

_____, "What Is Rhetorical Knowledge? A Reply to Farrell—And More," *Quarterly Journal of Speech*, 64 (1978), 313–28.

Richard A. Cherwitz, "Rhetoric as a 'Way of Knowing:' An Attenuation of the Epistemological Claims of the 'New Rhetoric,' " *Southern Speech Communication Journal*, 42 (1977), 207–19.

_____, ed., "Rhetoric and Epistemology," *Central States Speech Journal*, 32 (1981), 133–205.

_____, "The Contributory Effect of Rhetorical Discourse: A Study of Language-In-Use," *Quarterly Journal of Speech*, 66 (1980), 33–50.

Richard A. Cherwitz and James W. Hikins, "John Stuart Mills' *On Liberty:* Implications for the Epistemology of the New Rhetoric," *Quarterly Journal of Speech*, 65 (1979), 12–24.

_____, "Toward a Rhetorical Epistemology," *Southern Speech Communication Journal*, 47 (1982), 135–62.

_____, "John Stuart Mill's Doctrine of Assurance as a Rhetorical Epistemology," in *Explorations in Rhetoric: Studies in Honor of Douglas Ehninger*, Ray E. McKerrow, ed. (Glenview, Ill.: Scott, Foresman & Co., 1981), pp. 69–84.

_____, "Rhetorical Perspectivism," *Quarterly Journal of Speech*, 69 (1983), 249–66.

_____, "Meaning: The Interface Between Rhetoric and Epistemology," Paper presented at the 1983 Speech Communication Association Convention in Washington, D. C.

Roderick M. Chisholm, *Perceiving: A Philosophical Study* (Ithaca: Cornell University Press, 1957).

_____, *Theory of Knowledge* (Englewood Cliffs, N.J.: Prentice-Hall, 1977).

Alonzo Church, "The Need for Abstract Entities in Semantic Analysis," *Proceedings of the American Academy of Arts and Sciences*, 80 (1951), 100–12.

Herbert H. Clark and Eve V. Clark, *Psychology and Language* (New York: Harcourt Brace Jovanovich, 1977).

Bibliography

William Kingdom Clifford, "The Ethics of Belief," in H. R. Steeves and F. H. Ristine, eds., *Representative Essays in Modern Thought* (New York: American Book Co., 1913) pp. 46–72.

L. Jonathan Cohen, "Claims to Knowledge," *Proceedings of the Aristotelian Society,* spp. vol. 36 (1962), 33–50.

Scott Consigny, "Rhetoric and Its Situations," *Philosophy and Rhetoric,* 7 (1974), 175–86.

James W. Cornman, "Language and the Future of Metaphysics," in *The Future of Metaphysics,* Robert E. Wood, ed. (Chicago: Quadrangle Books, 1970).

J. Robert Cox, "Argument and the 'Definition of the Situation,' " *Central States Speech Journal,* 32 (1981), 197–205.

Richard E. Crable, "Rationality, Rhetoric, and Reason: On the Explanatory Power of Knowledge-as-Status." Paper presented at the 1979 Speech Communication Association Seminar on "Discursive Reality. . . ."

———, "Knowledge-as Status: On Argument and Epistemology," *Communication Monographs,* 49 (1982), 249–62.

Earl Croasmun and Richard A. Cherwitz, "Beyond Rhetorical Relativism," *Quarterly Journal of Speech,* 68 (1982), 1–16.

Donald P. Cushman, "Rhetoric in the Twentieth Century: An Insight from the Works of McKeon and Habermas." Paper presented at the 1979 Eastern Communication Association Convention in Philadelphia.

Donald P. Cushman and Lawrence Prelli, "Rhetoric and Epistemology from an Action Theory Perspective," *Central States Speech Journal,* 32 (1981), 273–78.

Donald P. Cushman and David Dietrich, "A Critical Reconstruction of Jurgen Habermas' Holistic Approach to Rhetoric as Social Philosophy," *Journal of the American Forensics Association,* 16 (1979), 128–37.

Donald P. Cushman and Phillip K. Tompkins, "A Theory of Rhetoric for Contemporary Society," *Philosophy and Rhetoric,* 13 (1980), 43–67.

Richard Daniels, "Craving Reality." Paper presented at the 1979 Speech Communication Association Seminar on "Discursive Reality. . . ."

Arthur C. Danto, *An Analytic Theory of Knowledge* (London: Cambridge University Press, 1968).

Donald K. Darnell and Wayne Brockriede, *Persons Communicating* (Englewood Cliffs, N.J.: Prentice-Hall, 1976).

René Descartes, *Discourse on Method and Meditations on First Philosophy,* Laurence J. Lafleur, trans. (Indianapolis, Bobbs-Merrill, 1960).

John Dewey, *Logic: The Theory of Inquiry* (New York: Henry Holt & Co., 1938).

———, *The Public and Its Problems* (New York: Henry Holt & Co., 1927).

Hugh C. Dick, ed., *Selected Writings of Francis Bacon* (New York: The Modern Library, 1955).

Otto Alvin Loeb Dieter, "Stasis," *Speech Monographs,* 17 (1950), 345–69.

Fred I. Dretske, *Knowledge and the Flow of Information* (Cambridge: MIT Press, 1981).

Douglas Ehninger, "Argument as Method: Its Nature, Its Limitations and Its Uses," *Speech Monographs,* 38 (1970), 101–10.

———, *Influence, Belief, and Argument: An Introduction to Responsible Persuasion* (Glenview, Ill.: Scott, Foresman and Company, 1974).

———, "On Systems of Rhetoric," *Philosophy and Rhetoric,* 1 (1968), 131–44.

_____, "Science, Philosophy—and Rhetoric: A Look Toward the Future," in *The Rhetoric of Western Thought,* James L. Golden, Goodwin F. Berquist William E. Coleman, eds. (Dubuque, Iowa: Kendall Hunt Publishing Co., 1978), pp. 323–31.

Jacques Ellul, *Propaganda: The Formation of Men's Attitudes,* Konrad Kellen, trans. (New York: Knopf, 1965).

Bjorn Eriksson, *Problems of an Empirical Sociology of Knowledge* (Stockholm: Uppsala, 1975).

Gareth Evans, "The Causal Theory of Names," *Aristotlian Society Supplementary Volume,* 47 (1973), 187–208.

Thomas B. Farrell, "Social Knowledge and Rhetorical Practice: A Progress Report." Paper presented at the 1979 Speech Communication Seminar on "Discursive Reality. . . ."

_____, "Knowledge, Consensus, and Rhetorical Theory," *Quarterly Journal of Speech,* 62 (1976), 1–14.

_____, "Social Knowledge II, *Quarterly Journal of Speech,* 64 (1978), 329–34.

Herbert Feigl, Wilfrid Sellars, and Keith Lehrer, eds., *New Readings in Philosophical Analysis* (New York: Appleton-Century-Crofts, 1972).

Mario Finnocciaro, "Logic and Rhetoric in Lavossier's Sealed Note: Toward a Rhetoric of Science," *Philosophy and Rhetoric,* 10 (1977), 111–22.

B. Aubry Fisher, *Perspectives on Human Communication* (New York: Macmillan, 1978).

Anthony Flew, ed., *David Hume on Human Nature and Understanding* (New York: Collier Books, 1962).

Anthony Flew, *A Dictionary of Philosophy* (New York: St. Martin's Press, 1979).

Gottlob Frege, *Philosophical Writings,* Peter Geach and Max Black, eds. (Oxford: Oxford University Press, 1952).

C. C. Fries, "Meaning and Linguistic Analysis," *Langauge,* 30 (1954), 57–68.

Michael S. Gazzaniga, *Functional Neuroscience* (New York: Harper and Row, 1979).

Peter Geach and Max Black, eds., *Philosophical Writings* (Oxford: Oxford University Press, 1952).

Edmund Gettier, Jr., "Is Justified True Belief Knowledge?" *Analysis,* 23 (1963), 121–23.

James J. Gibson, *Reasons for Realism: Selected Essays of James J. Gibson,* Edward Reed and Rebecca Jones, eds. (Hillsdale, N.J.: Lawrence Erlbaum Associates, 1982), pp. 374–84.

Carl Ginet, "What Must Be Added to Knowing to Obtain Knowing That One Knows," *Synthese,* 21 (1970), 163–86.

James L. Golden, Goodwin Berquist and William Coleman, *The Rhetoric of Western Thought* (Dubuque, Iowa: Kendall/Hunt, 1983).

Alvin Goldman, "A Causal Theory of Knowing," *Journal of Philosophy,* 64 (1967), 357–72.

Alvin W. Gouldner, "The Dark Side of the Dialectic: Toward a New Objectivity," *Sociological Inquiry,* 46 (1976), 3–15.

Ernesto Grassi, "Can Rhetoric Provide a New Basis for Philosophizing? The Humanist Tradition," *Philosophy and Rhetoric,* 11 (1978), 1–18.

_____, "Rhetoric and Philosophy," *Philosophy and Rhetoric,* 9 (1976), 200–16.

_____, *Rhetoric as Philosophy: The Humanist Tradition* (University Park: Pennsylvania State University Press, 1980).

Richard B. Gregg, "Rhetoric and Knowing: The Search for Perspective," *Central States Speech Journal,* 32 (1981), 133–44.

_____, *Symbolic Inducement and Knowing: A Study in the Foundations of Rhetoric* (Columbia: University of South Carolina Press, 1984).

Joseph Gusfield, "The Literary Rhetoric of Science: Comedy and Pathos in Drinking Driver Research," *American Sociological Review,* 41 (1976), 16–34.

Jurgen Habermas, *Legitimation Crisis* (Boston: Beacon Press, 1973).

_____, "Theories of Truth," Richard Grabau, trans. (unpublished manuscript).

Warren O. Hagstrom, *The Scientific Community* (New York: Basic Books, 1965).

Sir William Hamilton, *Lectures on Metaphysics and Logic,* Henry L. Mansel and John Veitch, eds. (Boston: Gould and Lincoln, 1859).

Gilbert Harman, "Knowledge, Reasons, and Causes," *Journal of Philosophy,* 67 (1970), 841–55.

Nancy L. Harper, "A Process Model of the Rhetorical Construction of Reality." Paper presented at the 1979 Speech Communication Association Seminar on "Discursive Reality. . . ."

John Hartland-Swann, *An Analysis of Knowing* (London: Allen and Unwin, 1958).

Herbert Heidelberger, "The Indispensability of Truth," *American Philosophical Quarterly,* 5 (1968), 212–17.

Carl G. Hempel, "Problems and Changes in the Empiricist Criterion of Meaning," *Revue Internationale de Philosophie,* 11 (1950), 41–63.

James W. Hikins, "The Epistemological Relevance of Intrapersonal Rhetoric," *Southern Speech Communication Journal,* 42 (1977), 220–27.

_____, "Plato's Rhetorical Theory: Old Perspectives on the Epistemology of the New Rhetoric," *Central States Speech Journal,* 32 (1981), 160–76.

Risto Hilpinen, "Knowing That One Knows and the Classical Definition of Knowledge," *Synthese,* 21 (1970), 109–32.

Jaakko Hintikka, *Knowledge and Belief* (Ithaca: Cornell University Press, 1962).

Lawrence A. Hosman, "Science as a Rhetorical Enterprise." Paper presented at the 1977 Central States Speech Association Convention in Southfield, Michigan.

John Hospers, *An Introduction to Philosophical Analysis* (Englewood Cliffs, N.J: Prentice-Hall, 1953).

Michael J. Hyde, "Acknowledging Rhetoric's Epistemic Function: A Hermeneutic Phenomenology." Paper presented at the 1979 Speech Communication Association Seminar on "Discursive Reality. . . ."

William James, *Essays in Radical Empiricism* (New York: Longmans, Green, and Co., 1912).

J. Jerison, "Paloeneurology and the Evolution of Mind," *Scientific American,* 234 (1976), 90–101.

Richard L. Johannesen, Rennard Strickland, and Ralph T. Eubanks, *Language Is Sermonic: Richard Weaver on the Nature of Rhetoric* (Baton Rouge: Louisiana State University Press, 1970).

Christopher Lyle Johnstone, "Ethics, Wisdom, and the Mission of Contemporary Rhetoric: The Realization of Human Being," *Central States Speech Journal,* 32 (1981), 177–88.

_____, "Dewey, Ethics, and Rhetoric: Toward a Contemporary Conception of Practical Wisdom," *Philosophy and Rhetoric*, 16 (1983), 185–207.

Henry W. Johnstone, Jr., *Validity and Rhetoric in Philosophical Argument* (University Park, Pa.: The Dialogue Press of Man and World, 1978).

_____, "Rationality and Rhetoric in Philosophy," *Quarterly Journal of Speech*, 59 (1973), 381–89.

_____, "Truth, Communication, and Rhetoric in Philosophy," *Revue Internationale de Philosophie*, 23 (1969), 405–6.

_____, Jr., "Truth, *Anagnorisis*, and Argument," *Philosophy and Rhetoric*, 16 (1983), 1–15.

Stuart Katz and Gordon Frost, "The Origins of Knowledge in Two Theories of Brain: The Cognitive Paradox Revealed," *Behaviorism*, 7 (1979), 35–44.

James A. Kelso, "Science and the Rhetoric of Reality," *Central States Speech Journal*, 31 (1980), 17–29.

George Kennedy, *Classical Rhetoric and Its Christian and Secular Traditions from Ancient to Modern Times* (Chapel Hill: University of North Carolina Press, 1980).

_____, *Quintilian* (New York: Twayne Publishers, 1969).

_____, *The Art of Persuasion in Greece* (Princeton: N.J.: Princeton University Press, 1963).

Charles W. Kneupper, "Rationality: A Constructivist/Interactionist View." Paper presented at the 1979 Speech Communication Association Seminar on "Discursive Reality. . . ."

_____, "Rhetoric, Argument and Social Reality: A Social Constructivist View," *Journal of the American Forensic Association*, 56 (1980), 159–72.

M. Kruger, "Sociology of Knowledge and Social Theory," *Berkeley Journal of Sociology*, 14 (1969), 152–63.

Thomas S. Kuhn, *The Structure of Scientific Revolutions* (Chicago: University of Chicago Press, 1970, 2nd ed.).

Imre Lakatos and Alan Musgrave, eds., *Criticism and the Growth of Knowledge* (Cambridge: The University Press, 1970).

Richard L. Lanigan, "Enthymeme: The Rhetorical Species of Aristotle's Syllogism," *Southern Speech Communication Journal*, 39 (1974), 207–22.

Michael C. Leff, "In Search of Adriadne's Thread: A Review of the Recent Literature on Rhetorical Theory," *Central States Speech Journal*, 29 (1978), 73–91.

Keith Lehrer, *Knowledge* (Oxford: Oxford University Press, 1978).

_____, "Knowledge, Truth, and Evidence," *Analysis*, 25 (1965), 168–75.

_____, "The Fourth Condition of Knowledge: A Defense," *Review of Metaphysics*, 24 (1970), 122–28.

_____, "Belief and Knowledge," *Philosophical Review*, 78 (1968), 491–99.

_____, "Believing That One Knows," *Synthese*, 21 (1970), 133–40.

Keith Lehrer and Thomas Paxton, Jr., "Knowledge: Undefeated Justified True Belief," *Journal of Philosophy*, 66 (1969), 225–37.

C. I. Lewis, *An Analysis of Knowledge and Valuation* (LaSalle, Ill.: Open Court, 1946).

John Locke, *Essay Concerning Human Understanding* (Oxford: Clarendon Press, 1975).

John Russell Lyne, "Rhetoric and Everyday Knowledge," *Central States Speech Journal*, 32 (1981), 145–52.

_____, "Discourse, Knowledge, and Social Process: Some Changing Equations," *Quarterly Journal of Speech,* 68 (1982), 201–26.

Bryan Magee, *Modern British Philosophy* (New York: St. Martin's Press, 1971).

Steven Mailloux, *Interpretive Conventions: The Reader in the Study of American Fiction* (Ithaca: Cornell University Press, 1982).

Joseph Margolis, "The Problem of Justified Belief," *Philosophical Studies,* 23 (1972), 405–9.

Evander Bradley McGilvary, *Toward a Perspective Realism,* Albert G. Ramsperger, ed. (LaSalle, Ill.: Open Court Publishing Co., 1956).

Michael McGuire, "The Ethics of Rhetoric: The Morality of Knowledge," *Southern Speech Communication Journal,* 45 (1980), 133–48.

Ralph M. McInerny, *A History of Western Philosophy,* Vol. 1 (Chicago: Henry Regnery Company, 1963).

Richard McKeon, "Discourse, Demonstration, Verification and Justification," *Logique et Analyse* II (1968), 35–92.

_____, "Introduction" to Marcus Tullius Cicero, *Brutus, On the Nature of the Gods, On Divination, On Duties* (Chicago: University of Chicago Press, 1950).

Robert K. Merton, *The Sociology of Science: Theoretical and Empirical Investigations* (Chicago: University of Chicago Press, 1973).

John Stuart Mill, *Autobiography and Other Writings,* Jack Stillinger, ed. (Boston: Houghton Mifflin, 1969).

C. David Mortenson, *Communication: The Study of Human Interaction* (New York: McGraw-Hill Book Company, 1972).

Charles S. Mudd, "The Enthymeme and Logical Validity," *Quarterly Journal of Speech,* 45 (1959), 409–14.

James J. Murphy, ed., *A Synoptic History of Classical Rhetoric* (New York: Random House, 1972).

Ray Nadeau, "Hermogenes' *On Stases:* A Translation with an Introduction and Notes," *Speech Monographs,* 31 (1964), 361–424.

_____, "Some Aristotelian and Stoic Influences on the Theory of Stases," *Speech Monographs,* 26 (1959), 248–54.

Maurice Natanson, "The Limits of Rhetoric," *Quarterly Journal of Speech,* 41 (1955), 133–39.

Maurice Natanson and Henry W. Johnstone, Jr., eds., *Philosophy, Rhetoric, and Argumentation* (University Park: Pennsylvania State University Press, 1965).

Douglas Odegard, *Knowledge and Skepticism* (Totowa, N.J.: Rowman and Littlefield, 1982).

C. K. Ogden and I. A. Richards, *The Meaning of Meaning* (New York: Harcourt, Brace and Co., 1938).

Daniel J. O'Keefe, "Logical Empiricism and the Study of Human Communication," *Speech Monographs,* 42 (1975), 169–83.

C. Jack Orr, "How Shall We Say: 'Reality Is Socially Constructed Through Communication'?" *Central States Speech Journal,* 29 (1978), 263–74.

Michael A. Overington, "The Scientific Community as Audience: Toward a Rhetorical Analysis of Science," *Philosophy and Rhetoric,* 10 (1977), 143–63.

Charles Pailthorp, "Knowledge as Justified True Belief," *Review of Metaphysics,* 23 (1969), 25–47.

George S. Pappas and Marshall Swain, eds., *Essays on Knowledge and Justification* (Ithaca: Cornell University Press, 1978).

Richard A. Parker, "Tu Quoque Arguments: A Rhetorical Perspective," *Journal of the American Forensic Association,* 20 (1984), 123–32.

John H. Patton, "Causation and Creativity in Rhetorical Situations: Distinctions and Implications," *Quarterly Journal of Speech,* 65 (1979), 36–55.

_____, "Rhetoric as Discursive Reality: Significant Omissions—Potential Syntheses." Paper presented at the 1979 Speech Communication Association Seminar on "Discursive Reality. . . ."

Charles Sanders Peirce, "The Fixation of Belief," *Popular Science Monthly,* 12 (1877); 1–15.

Ch. Perelman and L. Olbrechts-Tyteca, *The New Rhetoric: A Treatise on Argumentation,* trans. John Wilkinson and Purcell Weaver (Notre Dame: University of Notre Dame Press, 1969).

Plato, *Plato's Theory of Knowledge, The Theaetetus and the Sophist of Plato,* trans. with commentary by Francis M. Cornford (London: Routledge & Kegan Paul, 1960).

Plato, *The Collected Dialogues of Plato,* Edith Hamilton and Huntington Cairns, eds. (Princeton: Princeton University Press, 1961).

Eugene H. Peters, "Knowledge, Facts, and the Senses: A New Look at an Old Dialogue," *The Intercollegiate Review* (Spring, 1980), 87–93.

Michael Polanyi, *Personal Knowledge* (New York: Harper & Row, 1964).

_____, *Science, Faith and Society* (Chicago: University of Chicago Press, 1964).

_____, *The Tacit Dimension* (Garden City, N.Y.: Anchor Books, 1966).

Karl R. Popper, *Objective Knowledge: An Evolutionary Approach* (London: Oxford University Press, 1972).

_____, *Conjectures and Refutations: The Growth of Scientific Knowledge,* 2nd ed. (New York: Basic Books, 1965).

_____, "Truth, Rationality, and the Growth of Scientific Knowledge," in *Philosophical Problems of Science and Technology,* Alex C. Michalos, ed. (Boston: Allyn & Bacon, 1974).

W. T. Powers, "Quantitative Analysis of Purposive Systems: Some Spadework at the Foundations of Scientific Psychology," *Psychological Review,* 85 (1978), 417–35.

H. H. Price, "Our Evidence for the Existence of Other Minds," *Philosophy,* 13 (1938); reprinted in *Meaning and Knowledge,* Ernest Nagel and Richard Brandt, eds. (New York: Harcourt, Brace & World, 1965), pp. 617–34.

Anthony Quinton, "Knowledge and Belief," *The Encyclopedia of Philosophy* (New York: Macmillan Publishing Co., 1967), p. 345.

Colin Radford, "'Analysing' Know(s) That," *Philosophical Quarterly,* 20 (1970), 222–29.

_____, "Knowledge—By Examples," *Analysis,* 27 (1966), 1–11.

Michael Radner and Stephen Winokur, eds., *Minnesota Studies in the Philosophy of Science,* Vol. 4 (Minneapolis: University of Minnesota Press, 1970).

Celeste Condit Railsback, "Beyond Rhetorical Relativism: A Structural-Material Model of Truth and Objective Reality," *Quarterly Journal of Speech,* 69 (1983), 351–63.

Gunter W. Remmling, ed., *Toward a Sociology of Knowledge* (New York: Humanities Press, 1973).

Nicholas Rescher, *Cognitive Systematization* (Oxford: Basil Blackwell, 1979).
_____ *Dialectics: A Controversy Oriented Approach to Knowledge* (Albany: SUNY Press, 1977).
_____, *Methodological Pragmatism: A Systems-Theoretic Approach to the Theory of Knowledge* (New York: New York University Press, 1977).
I. A. Richards, *The Philosophy of Rhetoric,* (London: Oxford University Press, 1936).
Richard D. Rieke and Malcolm O. Sillars, *Argumentation and the Decision Making Process* (New York: John Wiley & Sons, 1975).
John M. Robertson, ed., *The Philosophical Writings of Francis Bacon* (London: George Routledge and Sons, 1905).
Richard Rorty, *Philosophy and the Mirror of Nature* (Princeton, N.J.: Princeton University Press, 1979).
_____, *Consequences of Pragmatism (Essays: 1972–1980)* (Minneapolis: University of Minnesota Press, 1982).
Michael Roth and Leon Galis, eds., *Knowing* (New York: Random House, 1970).
Bertrand Russell, *An Inquiry into Meaning and Truth* (New York: W. W. Norton & Company, Inc., 1940).
_____, "Knowledge by Acquaintance and Knowledge by Description," *Proceedings of the Aristotelian Society,* 11 (1910–11), 108–28.
_____, *Our Knowledge of the External World* (New York: New American Library, 1956).
_____, *The Analysis of Matter* (New York: Dover Publications, 1954).
_____, *The Problems of Philosophy* (Oxford: Oxford University Press, 1959), Ch. 13.
Gilbert Ryle, "Knowing How and Knowing That," *Proceedings of the Aristotelian Society,* 46 (1945–46), 1–16.
_____, *The Concept of Mind* (London: Hutchinson's University Library, 1949).
William P. Sandford and W. Hays Yeager, *Principles of Effective Speaking* (New York: T. Nelson and Sons, 1930).
Donald Scherer, "Incorrigibilist Dilemmas," *Southern Journal of Philosophy,* (Fall, 1973), 237–39.
Stephen P. Schwartz, ed., *Naming, Necessity, and Natural Kinds* (Ithaca: Cornell University Press, 1977).
Robert L. Scott, "On Viewing Rhetoric as Epistemic," *Central States Speech Journal,* 18 (1967), 9–17.
_____, "On Viewing Rhetoric as Epistemic: Ten Years Later," *Central States Speech Journal,* 27 (1976), 258–66.
_____, "Can a New Rhetoric Be Epistemic?" in *The Jensen Lectures: Contemporary Communication Studies,* John I. Sisco, ed. (Department of Communication: University of South Florida, 1983), pp. 1–23.
John R. Searle, *Expression and Meaning* (New York: Cambridge University Press, 1979).
_____, *Intentionality* (New York: Cambridge University Press, 1983).
_____, *Speech Acts: An Essay in the Philosophy of Language* (London: Cambridge University Press, 1969).
W. F. Sellars, *Science, Perception, and Reality* (London: Routledge, and Kegan Paul, 1963).
Jerome A. Shaffer, *Philosophy of Mind* (Englewood Cliffs, N.J.: Prentice-Hall, 1968).

182

A. P. Simonds, *Karl Mannheim's Sociology of Knowledge* (Oxford: Clarendon Press, 1978).

Herbert Simons, "Are Scientists Rhetors in Disguise? An Analysis of the Discursive Processes within Scientific Communities," in *Rhetoric in Transition: Studies in the Nature and Uses of Rhetoric,* E. E. White, ed. (University Park: Pennsylvania State University Press, 1980), pp. 115–31.

_____, "The Rhetoric of Science and the Science of Rhetoric," *Western Journal of Speech Communication,* 42 (1978), 37–43.

B. F. Skinner, *Verbal Behavior* (New York: Appleton-Century-Crofts, 1957).

Paul Snyder, "On Making Sense," in *Toward One Science: The Convergence of Traditions* (New York: St. Martin's Press, 1978), pp. 54–78.

Julius Stenzel, *Plato's Method of Dialectics,* trans. and ed. by D. J. Allan (Oxford: The Clarendon Press, 1940).

Ernest Sosa, "Two Conceptions of Knowledge," *Journal of Philosophy,* 67 (1970), 59–66.

Paul A. Soukup, S.J., "Rhetoric as Epistemic: A Classroom-Centered View," *Central States Speech Journal,* 32 (1981), 189–96.

John Stewart, "Concepts of Language and Meaning: A Comparative Study," *Quarterly Journal of Speech,* 58 (1972), 123–33.

A. Stroll, ed., *Epistemology: New Essays in the Theory of Knowledge* (New York: Harper & Row, 1967).

Frederick Suppe, ed., *The Structure of Scientific Theories* (Urbana: University of Illinois Press, 1974).

Marshall Swain, "Knowledge, Causality, and Justification," *Journal of Philosophy,* 69 (1972), 291–300.

R. Swartz, ed., *Perceiving, Sensing, and Knowing* (Garden City: Anchor, 1965).

Alfred Tarski, "The Semantic Concept of Truth," in *Readings in Philosophical Analysis,* Herbert Feigel & Wilfred Sellers, eds. (New York: Appleton-Century-Croft, 1949), pp. 52–84.

Irving Thalberg, "In Defense of Justified True Belief," *Journal of Philosophy,* 66 (1969), 795–802.

Phillip K. Tompkins, John H. Patton, Lloyd Bitzer, "The Forum," *Quarterly Journal of Speech,* 66 (1980), 85–95.

Phillip K. Tompkins, Richard E. Vatz, Lloyd Bitzer, "The Forum," *Quarterly Journal of Speech,* 67 (1981), 93–101.

Stephen Toulmin, Richard Rieke, and Allan Janik, *An Introduction to Reasoning* (New York: Macmillan Publishing Co., 1979).

Stephen Toulmin, *The Uses of Argument* (Cambridge: Cambridge University Press, 1958).

_____, *Human Understanding* (Princton, N.J.: Princeton University Press, 1977).

Roger Trigg, *Reason and Commitment* (Cambridge: Cambridge University Press, 1977).

Richard Vatz, "The Myth of the Rhetorical Situation," *Philosophy and Rhetoric,* 6 (1973), 154–61.

Phillip C. Wander, "The Rhetoric of Science," *Western Journal of Speech Communication,* 40 (1976), 226–35.

Barbara Warnick, "A Rhetorical Analysis of Episteme Shift: Darwin's *Origin of the Species,*" *Southern Speech Communication Journal,* 49 (1983), 26–42.

J. S. Watson, trans. or ed., *Cicero on Oratory and Orators* (Carbondale: Southern Illinois University Press, 1970).

Samuel D. Watson, Jr., "Polanyi's Epistemology of Good Reasons," in *Explorations in Rhetoric: Studies in Honor of Douglas Ehninger,* Ray E. McKerrow, ed. (Glenview, Ill.: Scott, Foresman, 1981), pp. 49–68.

Richard Weaver, *The Ethics of Rhetoric* (Chicago: Henry Regnery Co., 1953).

Walter Weimer, "Why All Knowing Is Rhetorical," *Journal of the American Forensic Association,* 20 (1983), 63–71.

_____, "Conventional Language Is No Substitute for a Theory of Rationality—A Reply to Parker—And More," *Journal of the American Forensic Association,* 20 (1984), 133–39.

Walter B. Weimer, "Science as a Rhetorical Transaction: Toward a Non-justificational Conception of Rhetoric," *Philosophy and Rhetoric,* 10 (1977), 1–29.

_____, "A Conceptual Framework for Cognitive Psychology: Motor Theories of the Mind," in *Perceiving, Acting and Knowing,* Robert Shaw and John Bradsford, eds. (Hillsdale, N.J.: Lawrence Erlbaum Associates, 1977), pp. 267–311.

_____, *Notes on the Methodology of Scientific Research* (Hillsdale, N.J.: Lawrence Erlbaum Associates, 1979).

Allen Wheelis, *The End of the Modern Age* (New York: Harper & Row, 1971).

Alan R. White, *The Nature of Knowledge* (Totowa, N.J.: Rowman and Littlefield, 1982).

Richard W. Wilkie, "Rhetoric and Knowledge among Some Contemporary Marx-Leninists," *Central States Speech Journal,* 32 (1981), 153–59.

James Winans, *Public Speaking: Principles and Practices* (New York: Century Company, 1917).

Ludwig Wittgenstein, *On Certainty* (New York: Harper & Row, 1969).

_____, *Philosophical Investigations* (New York: Macmillan, 1953).

Charles H. Woolbert, *The Fundamentals of Speech* (New York: Harper & Row, 1920).

A. D. Woozley, "Knowing and Not Knowing," *Proceedings of the Aristotelian Society,* 53 (1953), 151–72.

David Zarefsky, "Argument as Hypothesis-Testing." Paper presented at the 1976 Speech Communication Association Convention in San Francisco.

Herman Zanstra, *The Construction of Reality: Lectures on the Philosophy of Science, Theory of Knowledge and the Relation Between Body, Mind and Personality* (New York: Macmillan, 1962).

John M. Ziman, *Public Knowledge: An Essay Concerning the Social Dimension of Science* (London: Cambridge University Press, 1968).

Harold Zyskind, "Some Philosophical Strands in Popular Rhetoric," in *Perspectives in Education, Religion and the Arts,* Howard E. Kiefer and Milton K. Munitz, eds. (Albany: State University of New York Press, 1970).

NAME INDEX

Adler, Mortimer, 66–67, 70n
Alberic, 54
Allan, D. J., 113n
Alston, William P., 76, 89n, 90n
Amin, Idi, 127
Anderson, Alan Ross, 158n
Arafat, Yasir, 7
Aristotle, 4, 22, 50–52, 68n, 70n, 112n, 113n, 139, 144, 171
Arnold, Carroll C., x, 89n, 90n
St. Augustine, 32, 47n, 53
Aurelius, Marcus, 99
Austin, J. L., 76–77, 90n
Ayer, A. J., 21, 36, 45n, 46n, 47n

Bacon, Francis, 11, 16n, 56, 127
Bailey, Cyril, 47n
Bain, Alexander, 57, 69n
Berquist, Goodwin F., 68n, 158n
Bevilacqua, Vincent, 56, 69n
Biser, 124
Bitzer, Lloyd, 16, 30, 47n
Black, Max, 89n
Blanshard, Brand, 124, 159n
Booth, Wayne, 11, 17n
Bowers, John W., 89n, 90n
Bradley, Francis Herbert, 157n
Brockriede, Wayne, 114n
Brownstein, Oscar, 70n
Brummett, Barry, 17n, 90n, 113n, 157n, 159n
Bryant, Donald C., 58–59, 63, 69n
Burke, Kenneth, 11, 17n, 59, 83–85, 91n
Burks, Don, 47n
Butchvarov, Panayot, 21, 26, 45n, 47n, 48n, 89n, 111n, 144–45, 159n

Campbell, George, 16n, 56, 69n, 100–1
Carleton, Walter M., 17n, 111n
Carnap, Rudolf, 73
Cassiodorus, 54
Cherwitz, Richard A., ix, x, 17n, 35, 45n, 47n, 111n, 113n, 157n

Chisholm, Roderick, 21, 32, 36–37, 45n, 47n, 112n
Church, Alonzo, 73, 89n
Cicero, 4, 52–53, 68n, 171
Clark, Eve V., 89n
Clark, Herbert H., 89n
Clement, Donald A., 90n
Coleman, William E., 68n, 158
Comte, Auguste, 46n
Copi, Irving M., 112n
Cornford, Francis, 45n
Cornman, James W., 71, 89n
Croasmun, Earl, 17n, 45n, 157n
Cronkhite, Gary L., 89n, 90n

Descartes, Rene, 127, 137, 159n
Dewey, John, x, 36–37, 47n
Dick, Hugh C., 69n
Dieter, Otto Alvin Loeb, 113n
Durant, Will, 168–69

Edwards, Paul, 158n
Ehninger, Douglas, 11, 17n, 56, 59–60, 69n, 103, 112n, 113n
Ellul, Jacques, 114n
Eubanks, Ralph T., 69n

Farrell, Thomas B., 17n, 111n, 159n
Fenelon, Francois, 159n
Finnociaro, Mario, 172n
Fisher, B. Aubry, 89n, 114n
Flew, Anthony, 69n, 128–29, 158n
Frandsen, Kenneth D., 90n
Frege, Gottlob, 72–73, 89n
Fries, C. C., 90n
Frost, Gordon, ix, 158n

Galileo, 33
Geach, Peter T., 89n
Gettier, Edmund, 21, 28–29, 40, 45n, 47n, 101
Golden, James L., 68n, 158n

185

Name Index

Gorgias, 10, 16n
Gregg, Richard B., ix

Hall, Roland, 113n
Hamilton, Sir William, 128–29, 158n
Hikins, James W., ix, x, 17n, 114n, 148
Hume, David, 56–57

Ijsseling, Samuel, 55

James, William, 129–30, 158n
Janik, Allan, 32, 112n
Jerison, J., 158n
Jesus, 99
Johannesen, Richard, 69n
Johnstone, Henry W. Jr., 11, 17n, 32, 47n, 102, 112n, 113n
Jones, L. W., 68n

Katz, Stuart, ix, 158n
Kellen, Konrad, 108, 114n
Kelso, James A., 172n
Kennedy, George, 68n, 69n
Kennedy, John F., 141
Khomeini, Ayatollah, 7
Kuhn, Thomas S., 11, 17n

LaFleur, Lawrence J., 159n
Leher, Keith, 21, 45n, 47n
Leucippus, 47n
Lewis, C. I., 89n
Linsky, Leonard, 46n
Locke, John, 56, 89n, 127–28
Lucretius, 24, 25, 47n

Magee, Bryan, 76, 90n
Mailloux, Steven, 172n
Malinowski, B., 85
Mansel, Henry, 158n
McGilvary, Evander B., ix, 45n, 111n, 112n, 113n, 114n, 124–26, 130–33, 135, 157n, 158n, 159n
McInerny, Ralph M., 16n
McKeon, Richard, 68n
Mead, George Herbert, 124
Micken, Ralph A., 68n
Mill, John Stewart, 89n, 98–99, 101, 113n
Milton, John, 63
Moore, George Edward, 129

Mortenson, David, 65, 70n
Murphy, James J., 16n, 68n

Nadeau, Ray, 113n
Natanson, Maurice, 11, 17n, 104, 113n
Newton, Sir Isaac, 125
Nixon, Richard M., 22, 107–8, 146, 149–51

Ogden, C. K., 90n
O'Keefe, Daniel J., 90n
Olbrechts-Tyteca, L., 17n, 69n
Ong, Walter J., 69n
Orr, C. Jack, 17n, 157n, 159n
Overington, Michael, 172n
Oswald, Lee Harvey, 141

Pap, Arthur, 46n
Pappas, George S., 45n
Paxton, Thomas Jr., 45n
Perelman, Chaim, 4, 11, 17n, 60, 69n
Plato, 10, 11, 16n, 22, 42, 45n, 46n, 48n, 50, 68n, 70n, 89n, 95, 111n, 113n, 130, 152
Powers, W. T., 158n
Protagoras, 16n
Ptolemy, 34

Quintilian, 52–53
Quinton, Anthony, 21, 46n

Rabelais, 83
Railsback, Celeste C., 17n
Ramus, Petrus, 55–56
Ramsperger, Albert G., 111n, 157n
Reagan, Ronald, 161
Reid, Thomas, ix
Rescher, Nicholas, 47n
Richards, Ivor A., 11, 17n, 58, 69n, 71, 89n, 90n
Rieke, Richard, 32, 112n
Robertson, John, 16n
Roosevelt, Franklin D., 172
Rorty, Richard, 38–40, 47n, 48n
Russell, Bertrand, 32, 46n, 47n, 73, 124, 129, 131, 158n
Ryle, Gilbert, 159n

186

SUBJECT INDEX

Adherence. *See* Consensus; Intersubjectivity
Apodictic. *See* Truth
Argument
  and associative constituent of rhetoric,
    96–98, 109, 112n
  and contradiction, 150, 159n
  and evaluative constituent of rhetoric,
    102–5
  and impasse, 153
  and rationality, 32–33, 102
  and relationality, 149–54
  bilateral feature of, 102
  chains and clusters in, 96, 112n
  correction in, 103
  self risk and, 103–4, 110
  stasis in, 103, 107
  validity and soundness in, 97
Aspects. *See* Relationality

Being. *See* Consciousness; Ontology;
  Perception
Belief
  as a criterion of knowledge, 25–27
  mere belief, 31
  rational belief, 31–33
  true belief, 31–32
  varieties of, 31–35, 162
Brain. *See* Consciousness

Certainty, 9, 155–56
  analytical, 36–37
  and knowledge, 35–37
  and relationality, 155–57
  as dogmatic state, 35–36
  as rational judgment, 35–36
  in science, 167
Characters. *See* Relationality
Common sense
  and perception, 125
  Scottish school of, ix
Communicating
  and knowing, 7–15

Communication, 1. *See also* Rhetoric
  and rhetoric, 65
  as vehicle of transmission, 12, 110
  intrapersonal vs. interpersonal, 93–94,
    120, 113–14n
  knowledge and, 4, 7–15, 161
  nature of, 8
  need for a philosophical account of,
    4–5
Computer technology, 1–2
Consciousness, 93, 115, 127–37. *See also*
  Perception
  and illusion, 125
  and its relationship to being, 139–40, 148
  and the mind/body problem, 135, 142
  as emergent property, 138–39
  as intrapersonal process, 127–28
  as introspection, 128
  defined, 133–35
  inferential/representational view of;
    130–31, 158n
  neurological explanation of, 130–31
  of something, 130–35
  physiological explanation of, 131
  stream of, 129
Consensus, 11, 13. *See also*
  Intersubjectivity
  restraint of, 102
Content
  and form, 9, 110
Context. *See* Meaning
Context of particulars. *See* Relationality
Contingent. *See* Truth

Dialectic, 12, 13. *See also* Argument
  and rhetoric, 51–52, 93, 102, 104–5,
    113n
Direct realism, ix, 95. *See also* Reality
  and direct awareness, 94, 136
  reconsideration of, ix, 132
Disagreement. *See* Argument; Rhetorical
  perspectivism

188